BATMAN
THE BRAVE AND THE BOLD

Matt Wayne
J. Torres
writers

Andy Suriano
Phil Moy
Carlo Barberi
pencillers

Dan Davis
Phil Moy
Terry Beatty
inkers

Heroic Age
colorist

Randy Gentile
Steve Wands
Sal Cipriano
letterers

BATMAN created by Bob Kane

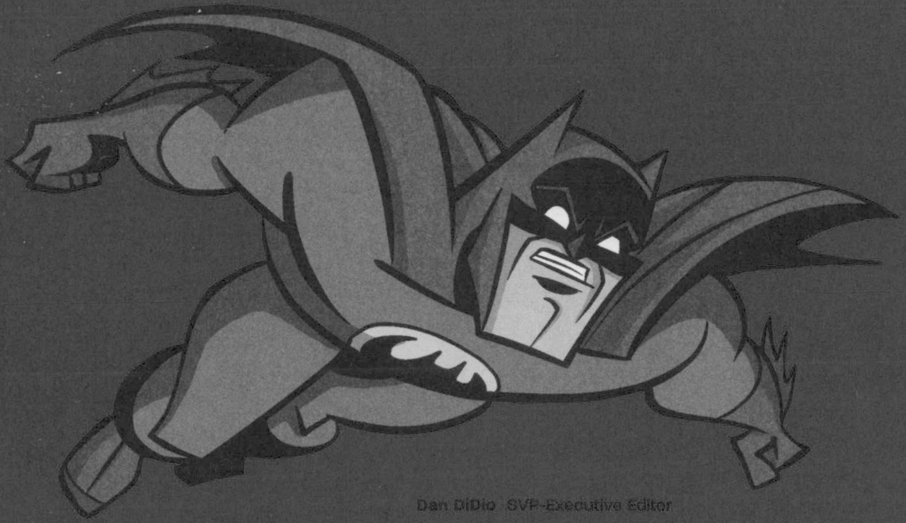

Dan DiDio SVP-Executive Editor
Rachel Gluckstern Michael Siglain Editors-original series
Harvey Richards Assistant Editor-original series
Georg Brewer VP-Design & DC Direct Creative
Bob Harras Group Editor-Collected Editions
Sean Mackiewicz Editor
Robbin Brosterman Design Director-Books

DC COMICS

Paul Levitz President & Publisher
Richard Bruning SVP-Creative Director
Patrick Caldon EVP-Finance & Operations
Amy Genkins SVP-Business & Legal Affairs
Jim Lee Editorial Director-WildStorm
Gregory Noveck SVP-Creative Affairs
Steve Rotterdam SVP-Sales & Marketing
Cheryl Rubin SVP-Brand Management

Cover by James Tucker with Hi-Fi

BATMAN: THE BRAVE AND THE BOLD

DC Comics, 1700 Broadway, New York, NY 10019
A Warner Bros. Entertainment Company
First Printing. Printed by World Color Press, Inc., St-Romuald, QC, Canada 12/16/09.
ISBN: 978-1-4012-2650-3

SUSTAINABLE FORESTRY INITIATIVE
Certified Fiber Sourcing

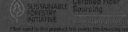

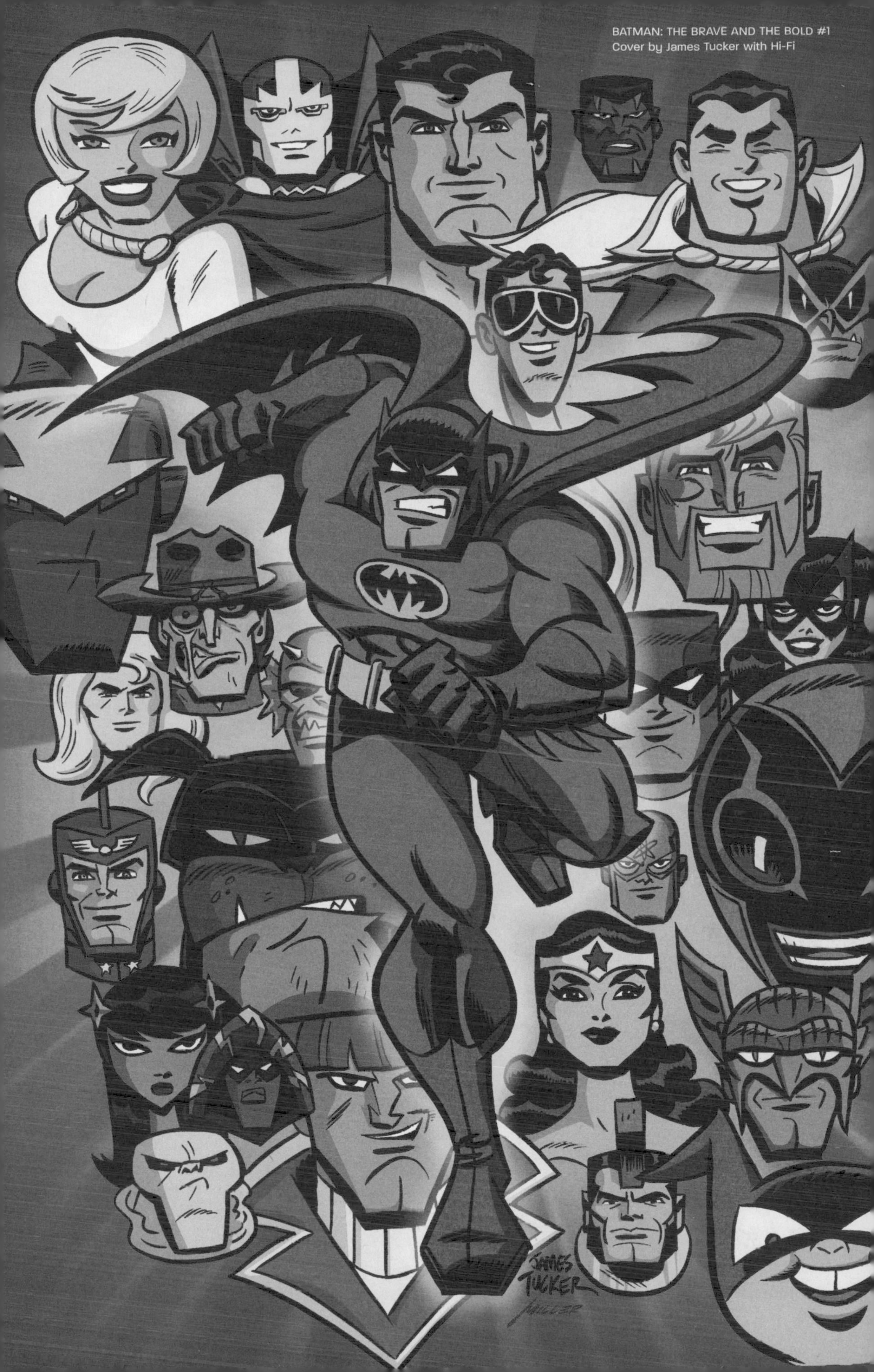
JAMES TUCKER

BATMAN: THE BRAVE AND THE BOLD #1
Cover by James Tucker with Hi-Fi

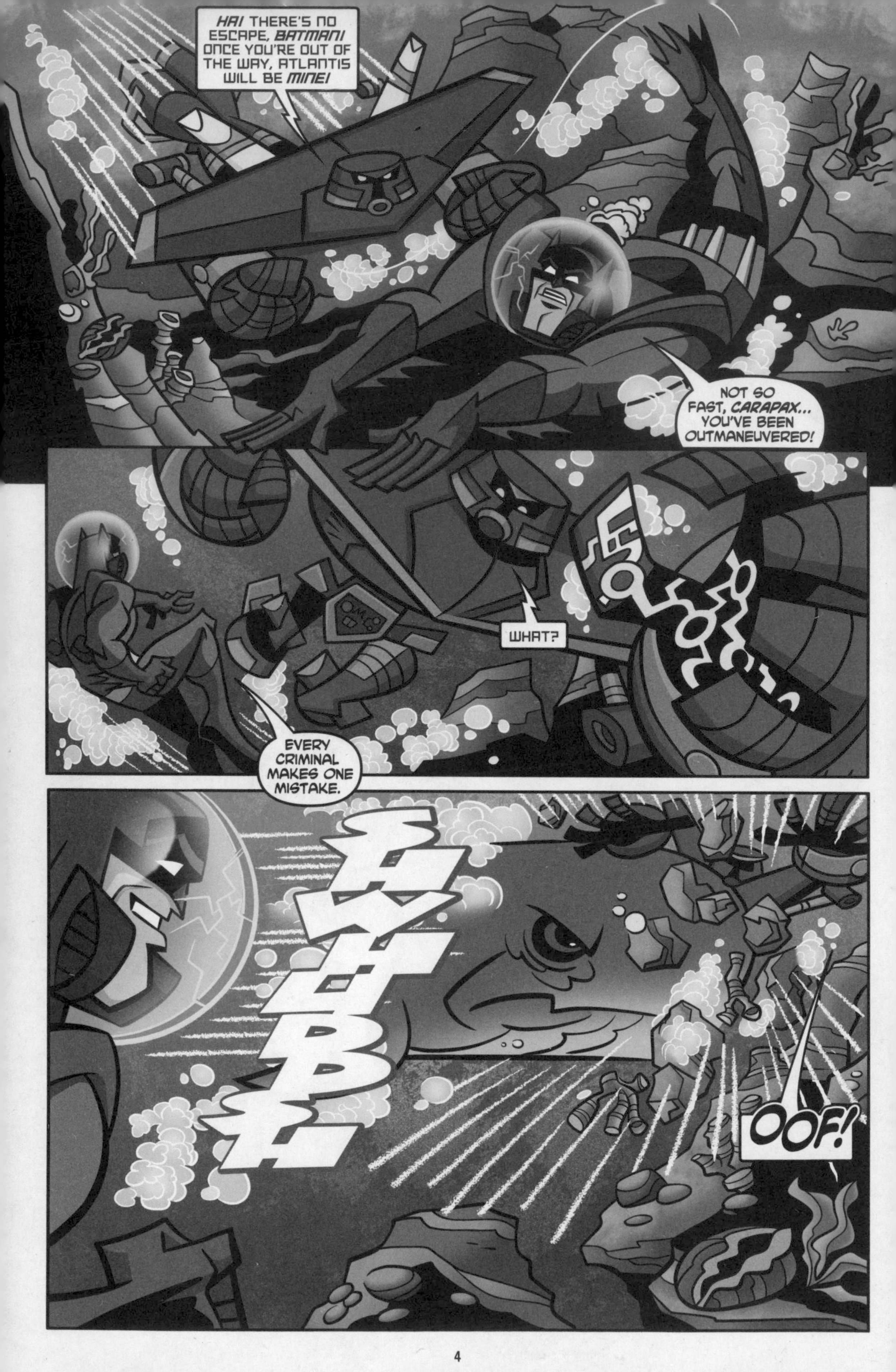
HA! THERE'S NO ESCAPE, BATMAN! ONCE YOU'RE OUT OF THE WAY, ATLANTIS WILL BE MINE!
NOT SO FAST, CARAPAX... YOU'VE BEEN OUTMANEUVERED!
WHAT?
EVERY CRIMINAL MAKES ONE MISTAKE.
SHHUBSH
OOF!

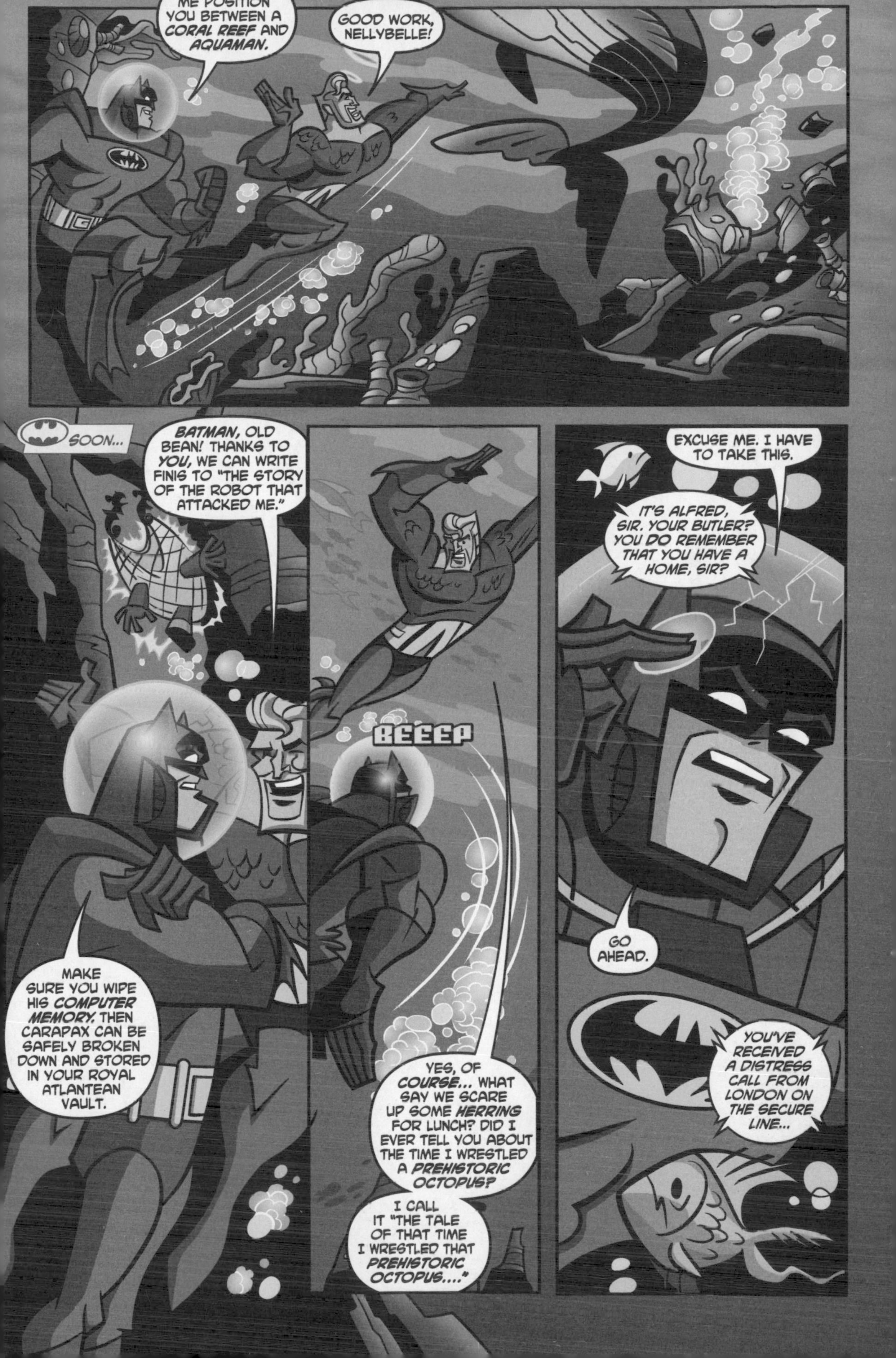
YOU LET ME POSITION YOU BETWEEN A CORAL REEF AND AQUAMAN.
GOOD WORK, NELLYBELLE!
SOON...
BATMAN, OLD BEAN! THANKS TO YOU, WE CAN WRITE FINIS TO "THE STORY OF THE ROBOT THAT ATTACKED ME."
MAKE SURE YOU WIPE HIS COMPUTER MEMORY. THEN CARAPAX CAN BE SAFELY BROKEN DOWN AND STORED IN YOUR ROYAL ATLANTEAN VAULT.
BEEEP
YES, OF COURSE... WHAT SAY WE SCARE UP SOME HERRING FOR LUNCH? DID I EVER TELL YOU ABOUT THE TIME I WRESTLED A PREHISTORIC OCTOPUS?
I CALL IT "THE TALE OF THAT TIME I WRESTLED THAT PREHISTORIC OCTOPUS...."
EXCUSE ME. I HAVE TO TAKE THIS.
IT'S ALFRED, SIR. YOUR BUTLER? YOU DO REMEMBER THAT YOU HAVE A HOME, SIR?
GO AHEAD.
YOU'VE RECEIVED A DISTRESS CALL FROM LONDON ON THE SECURE LINE...

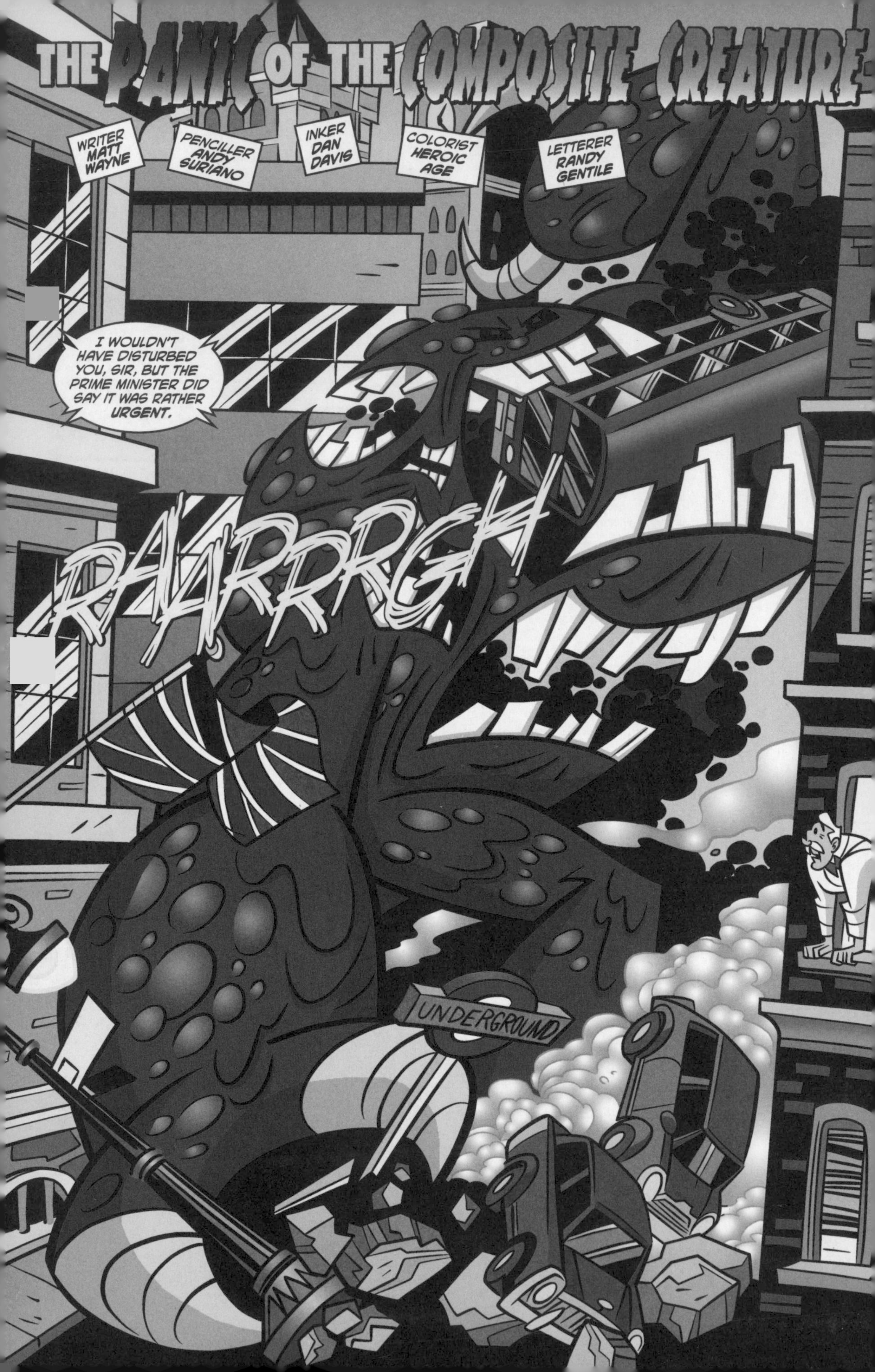
THE PANIC OF THE COMPOSITE CREATURE
WRITER MATT WAYNE
PENCILLER ANDY SURIANO
INKER DAN DAVIS
COLORIST HEROIC AGE
LETTERER RANDY GENTILE
I WOULDN'T HAVE DISTURBED YOU, SIR, BUT THE PRIME MINISTER DID SAY IT WAS RATHER URGENT.
RAAARRRGH
UNDERGROUND

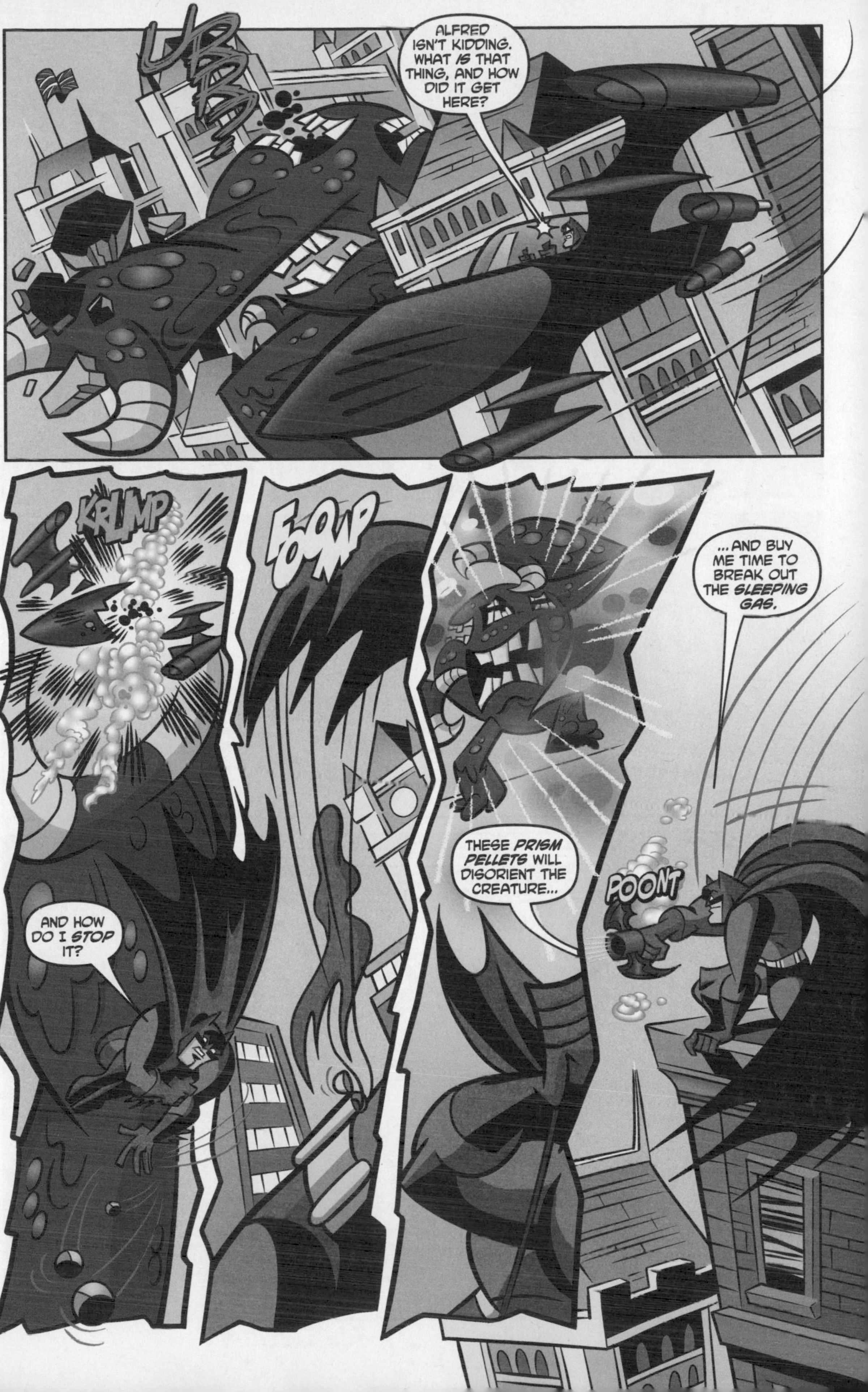

UBBB
ALFRED ISN'T KIDDING. WHAT IS THAT THING, AND HOW DID IT GET HERE?
KRUMP
AND HOW DO I STOP IT?
FOOMP
THESE PRISM PELLETS WILL DISORIENT THE CREATURE...
POONT
...AND BUY ME TIME TO BREAK OUT THE SLEEPING GAS.

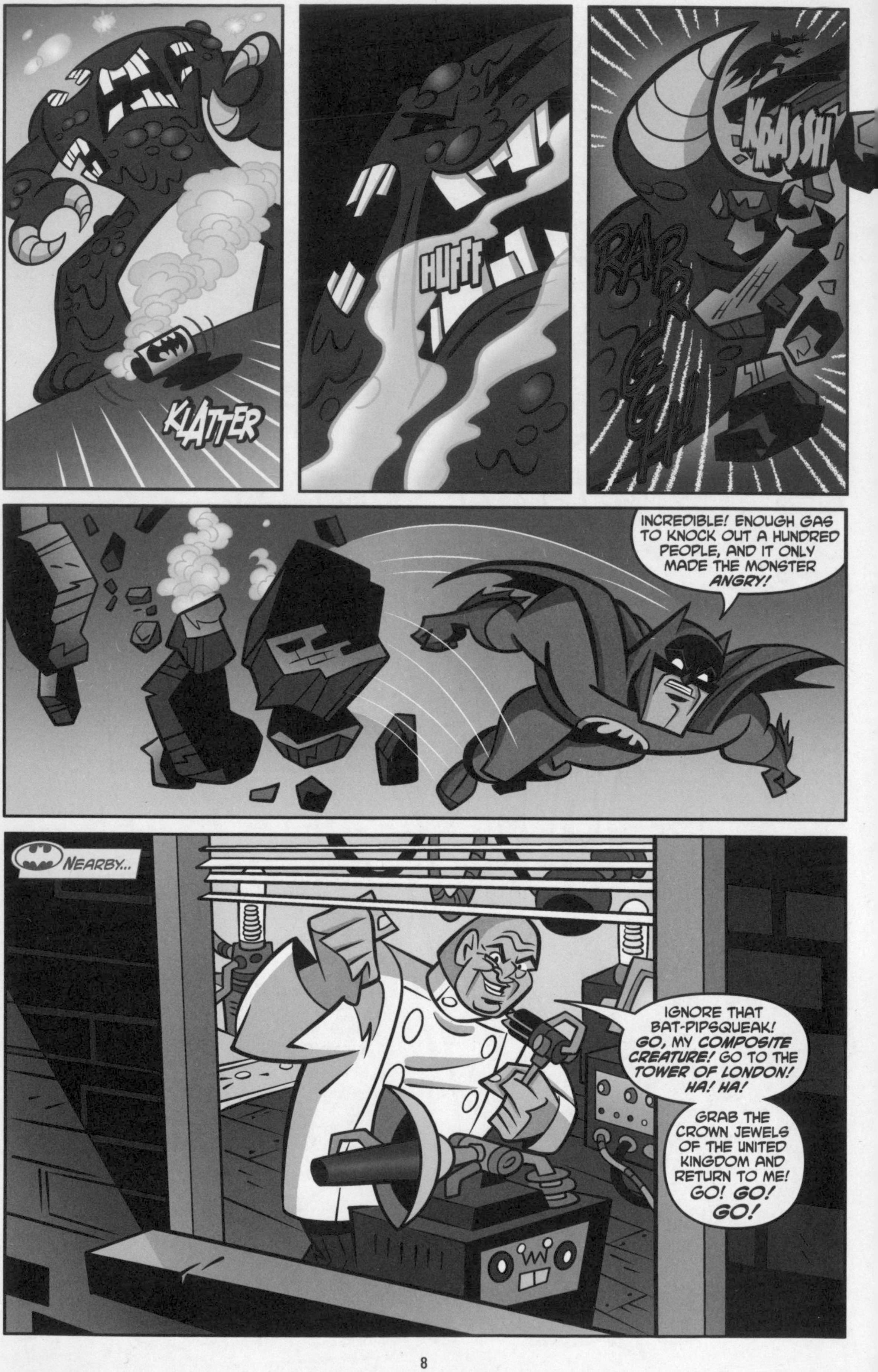
KLATTER
HUFFF
KRASSH
RARRGGGHH
INCREDIBLE! ENOUGH GAS TO KNOCK OUT A HUNDRED PEOPLE, AND IT ONLY MADE THE MONSTER ANGRY!
NEARBY...
IGNORE THAT BAT-PIPSQUEAK! GO, MY COMPOSITE CREATURE! GO TO THE TOWER OF LONDON! HA! HA!
GRAB THE CROWN JEWELS OF THE UNITED KINGDOM AND RETURN TO ME! GO! GO! GO!

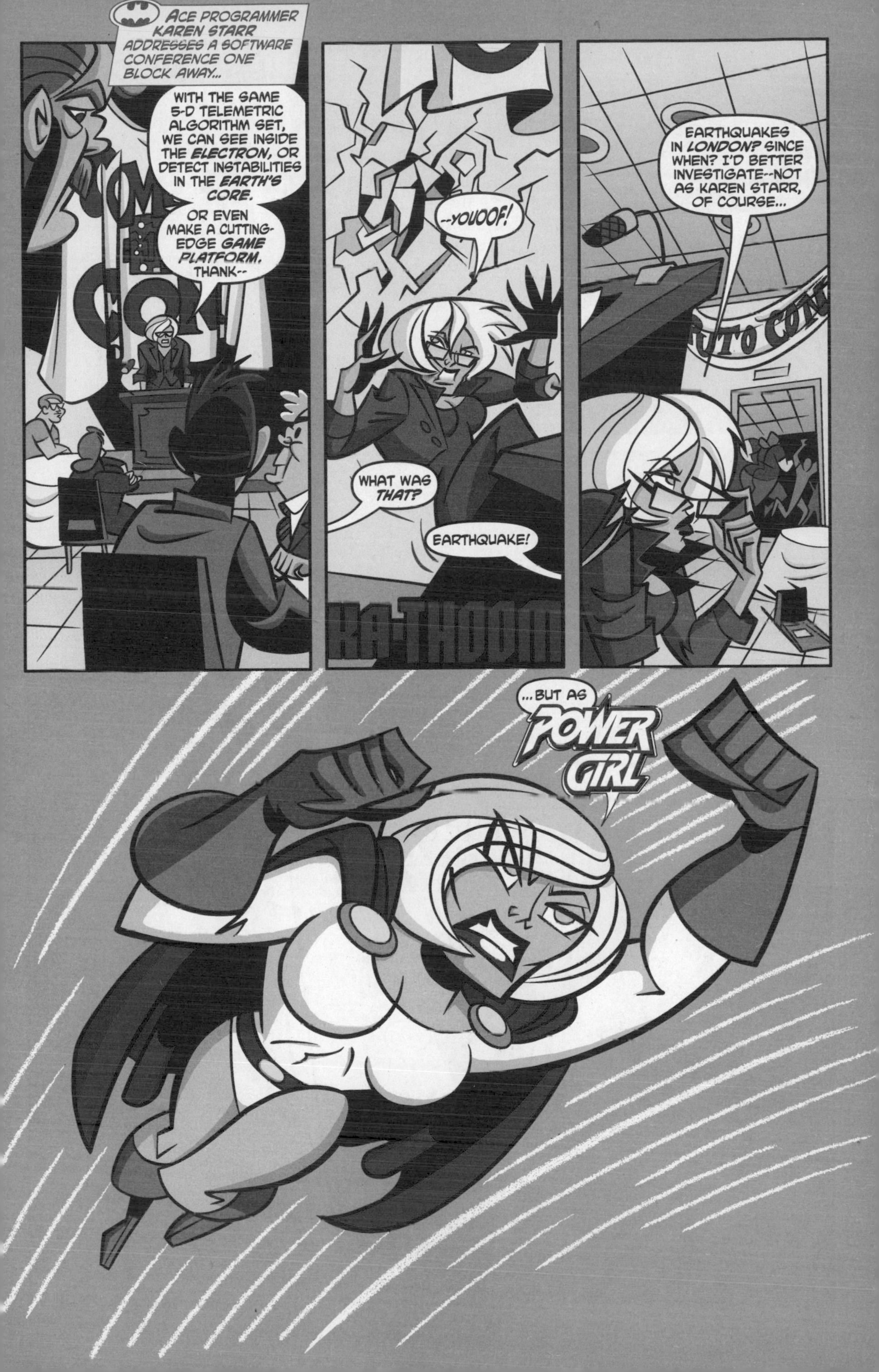
ACE PROGRAMMER KAREN STARR ADDRESSES A SOFTWARE CONFERENCE ONE BLOCK AWAY...
WITH THE SAME 5-D TELEMETRIC ALGORITHM SET, WE CAN SEE INSIDE THE *ELECTRON,* OR DETECT INSTABILITIES IN THE *EARTH'S CORE.*
OR EVEN MAKE A CUTTING-EDGE *GAME PLATFORM.* THANK--
--YOUOOF!
WHAT WAS *THAT?*
EARTHQUAKE!
KA-THOOM
EARTHQUAKES IN *LONDON?* SINCE WHEN? I'D BETTER INVESTIGATE--NOT AS KAREN STARR, OF COURSE...
...BUT AS POWER GIRL

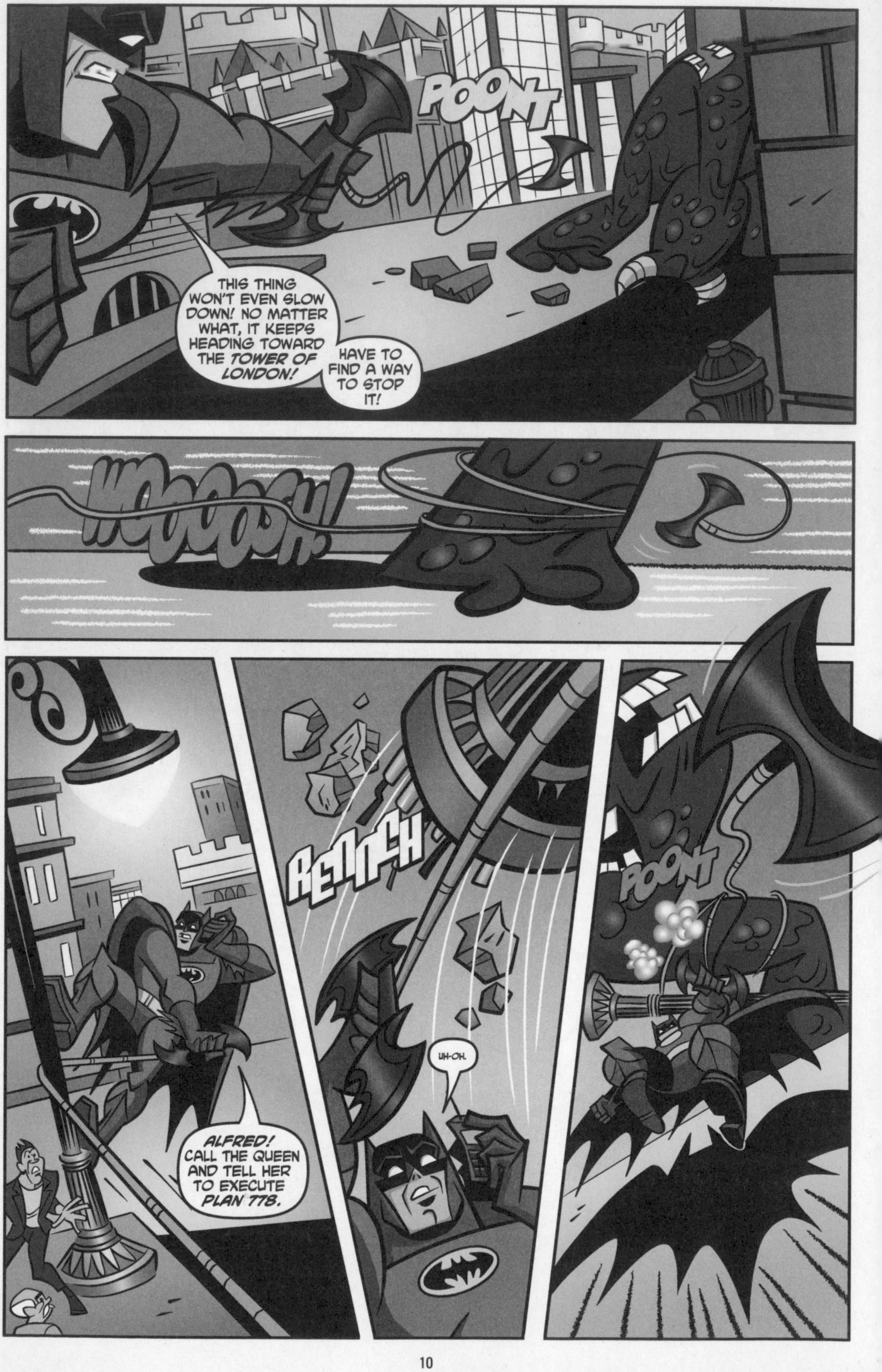
POOMT
THIS THING WON'T EVEN SLOW DOWN! NO MATTER WHAT, IT KEEPS HEADING TOWARD THE TOWER OF LONDON!
HAVE TO FIND A WAY TO STOP IT!
WOOOOSH!
ALFRED! CALL THE QUEEN AND TELL HER TO EXECUTE PLAN 778.
RENNCH
UH-OH.
POOMT

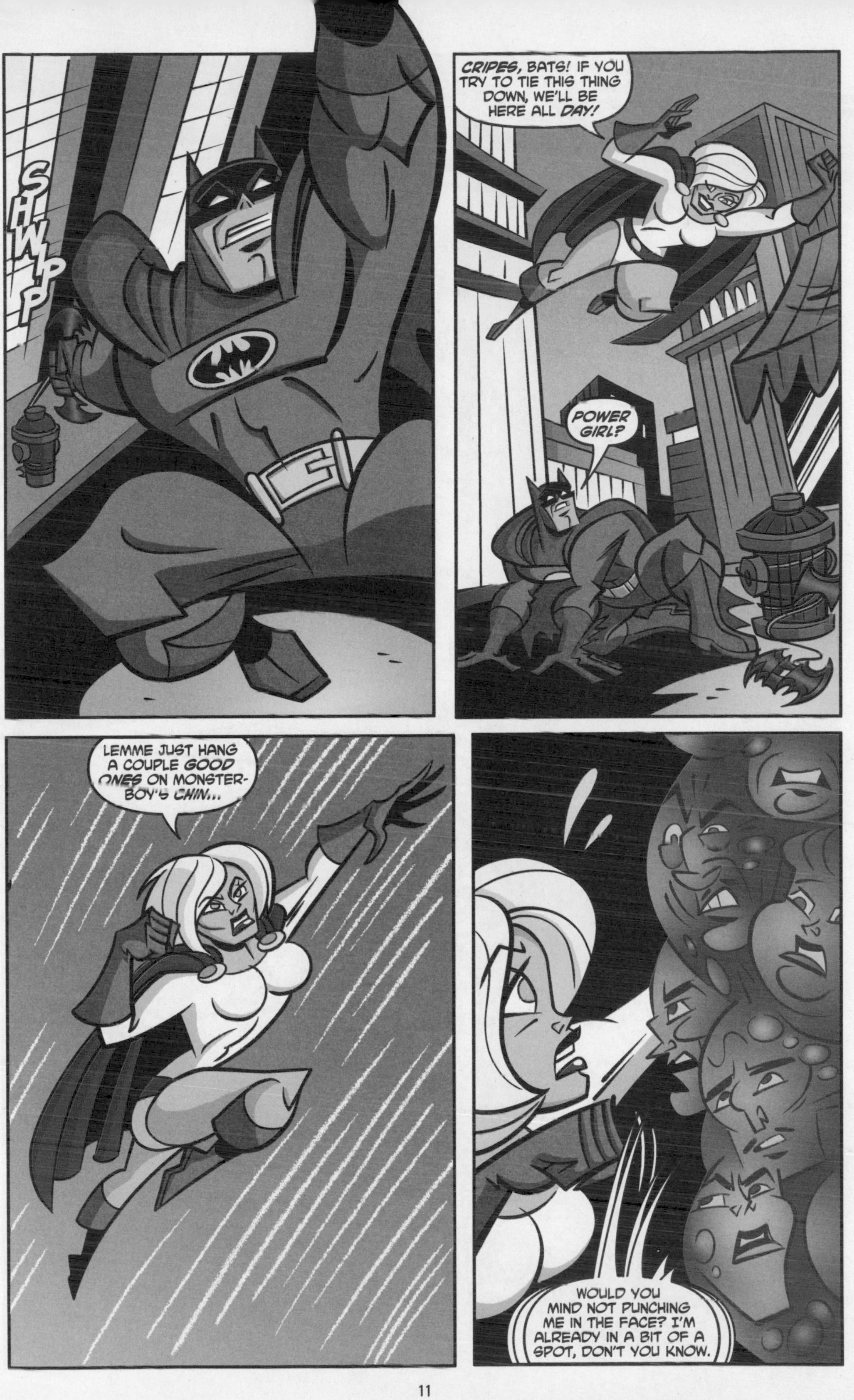
SHWIPP
CRIPES, BATS! IF YOU TRY TO TIE THIS THING DOWN, WE'LL BE HERE ALL DAY!
POWER GIRL?
LEMME JUST HANG A COUPLE GOOD ONES ON MONSTER-BOY'S CHIN...
WOULD YOU MIND NOT PUNCHING ME IN THE FACE? I'M ALREADY IN A BIT OF A SPOT, DON'T YOU KNOW.

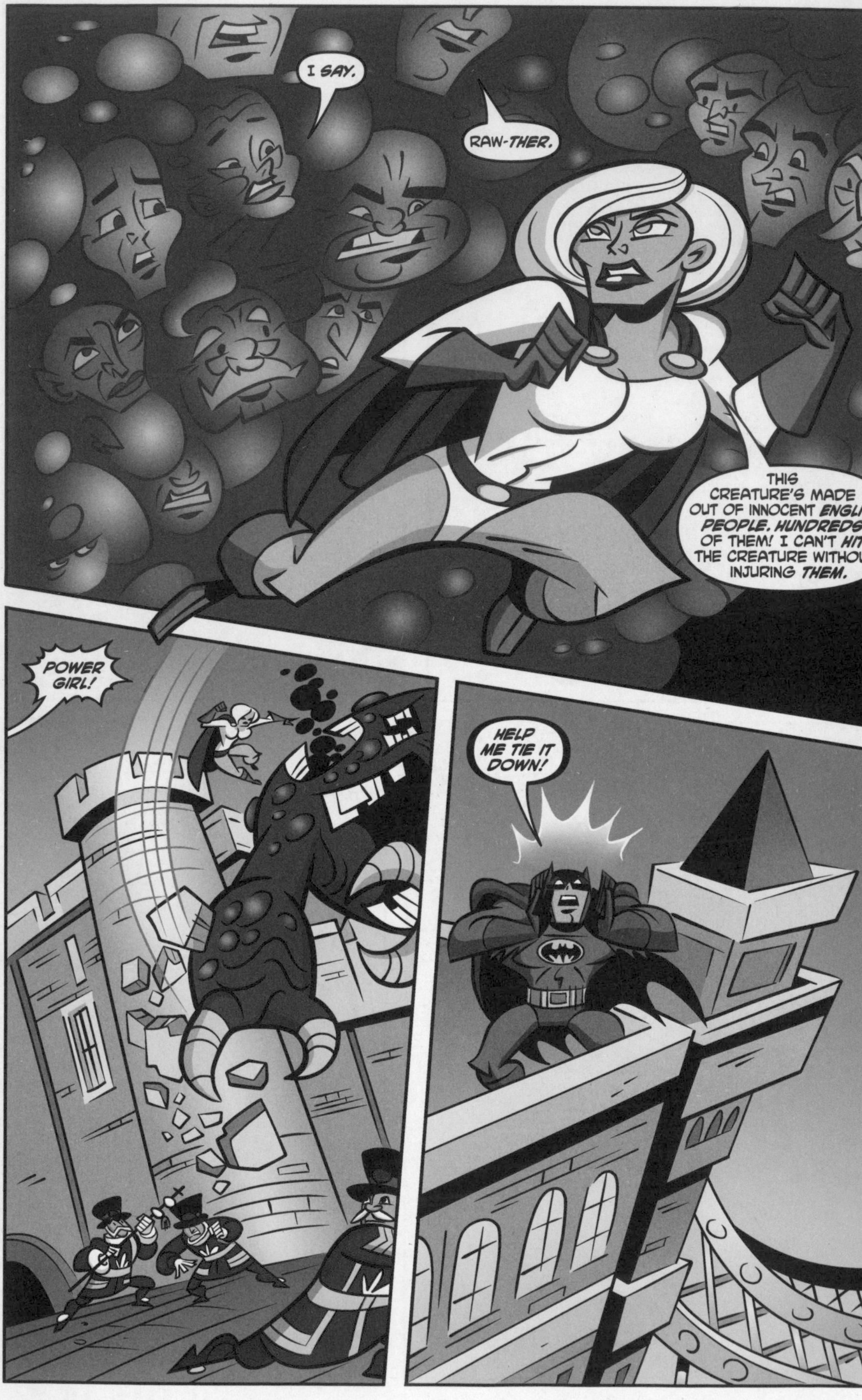
I SAY.
RAW-THER.
THIS CREATURE'S MADE OUT OF INNOCENT ENGLISH PEOPLE. HUNDREDS OF THEM! I CAN'T HIT THE CREATURE WITHOUT INJURING THEM.
POWER GIRL!
HELP ME TIE IT DOWN!

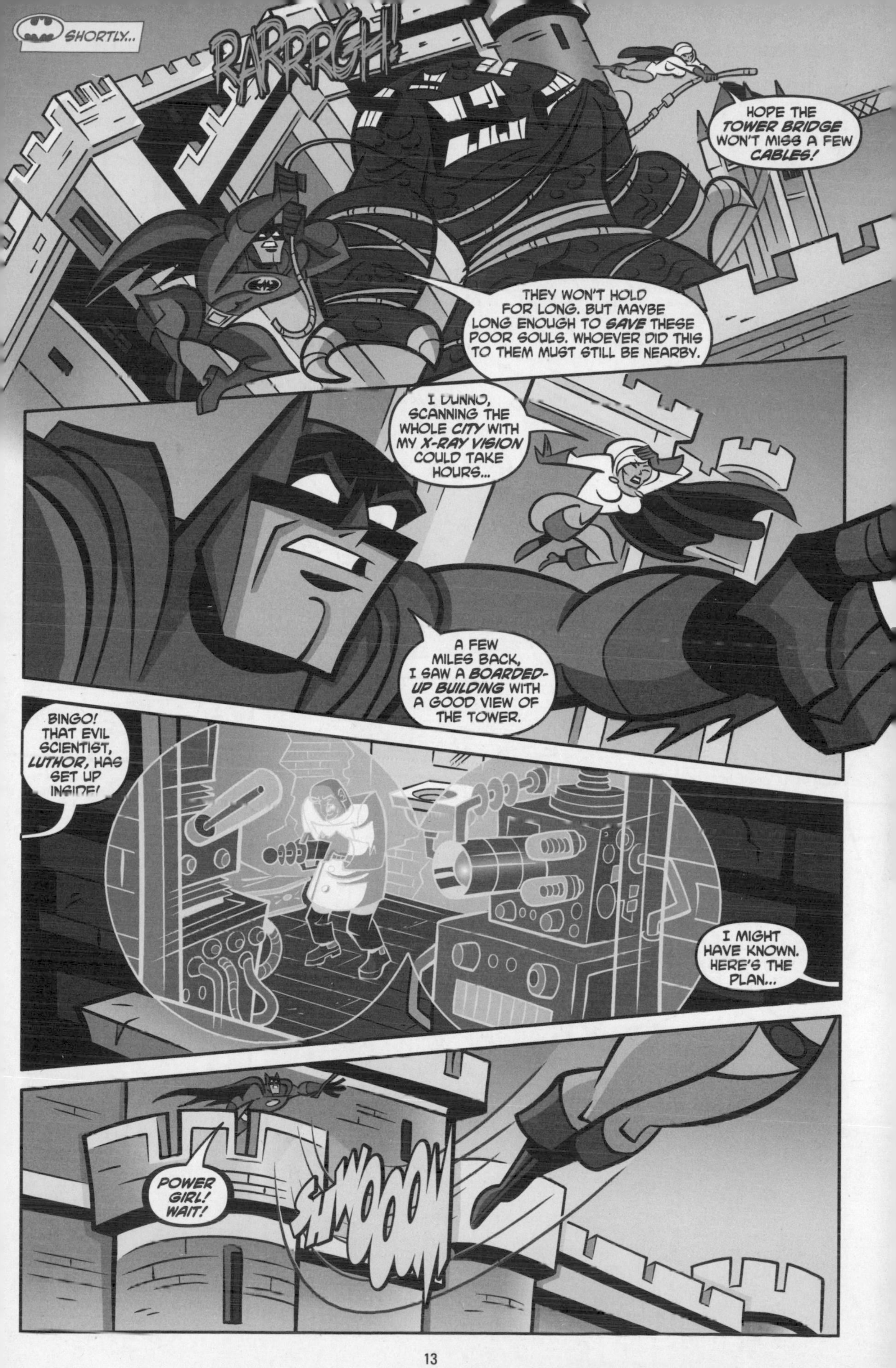
SHORTLY...
RARRRGH!
HOPE THE TOWER BRIDGE WON'T MISS A FEW CABLES!
THEY WON'T HOLD FOR LONG. BUT MAYBE LONG ENOUGH TO SAVE THESE POOR SOULS. WHOEVER DID THIS TO THEM MUST STILL BE NEARBY.
I DUNNO, SCANNING THE WHOLE CITY WITH MY X-RAY VISION COULD TAKE HOURS...
A FEW MILES BACK, I SAW A BOARDED-UP BUILDING WITH A GOOD VIEW OF THE TOWER.
BINGO! THAT EVIL SCIENTIST, LUTHOR, HAS SET UP INSIDE!
I MIGHT HAVE KNOWN. HERE'S THE PLAN...
POWER GIRL! WAIT!
SHWOOOM

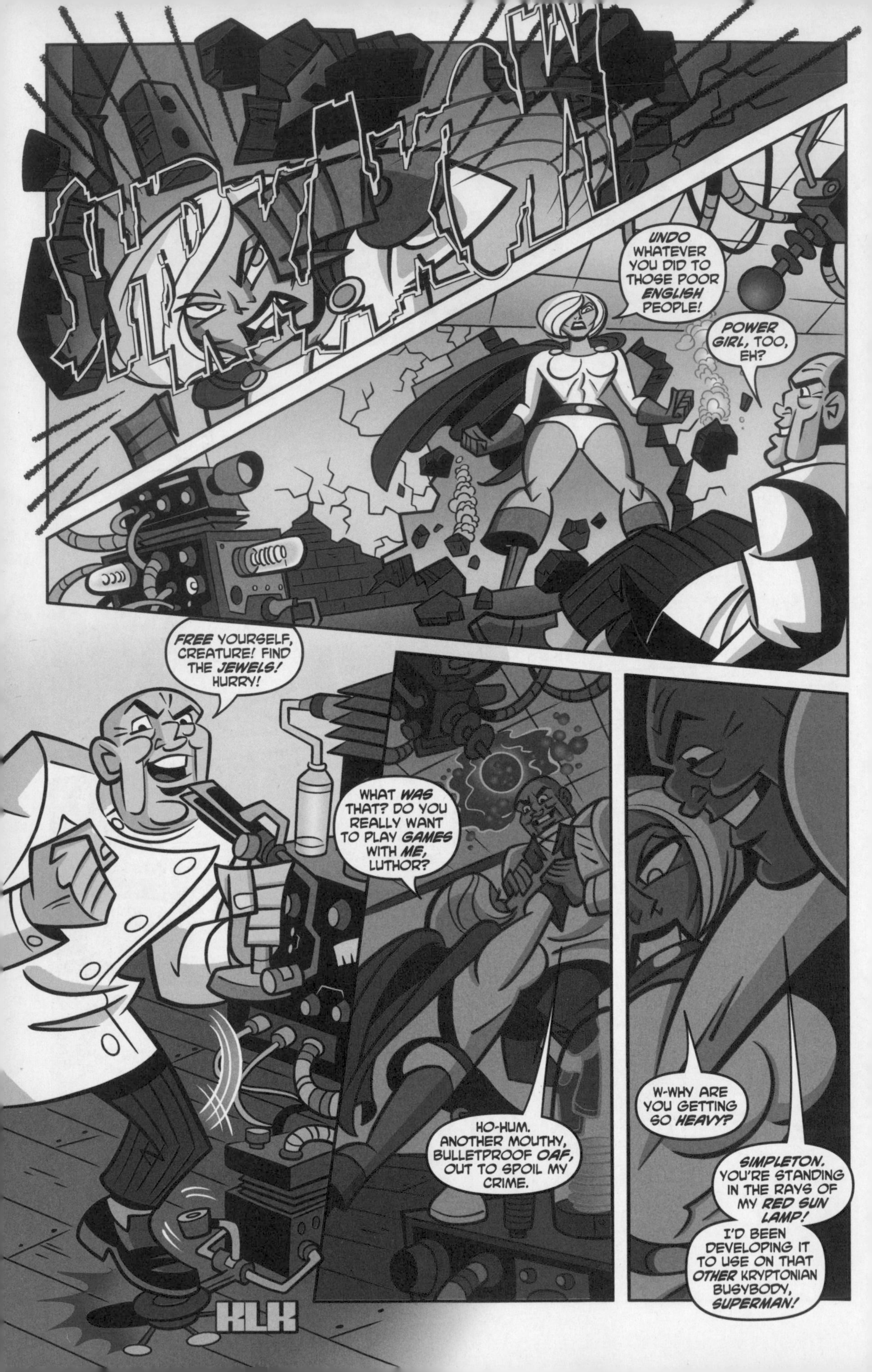
UNDO WHATEVER YOU DID TO THOSE POOR ENGLISH PEOPLE!
POWER GIRL, TOO, EH?
FREE YOURSELF, CREATURE! FIND THE JEWELS! HURRY!
KLK
WHAT WAS THAT? DO YOU REALLY WANT TO PLAY GAMES WITH ME, LUTHOR?
HO-HUM. ANOTHER MOUTHY, BULLETPROOF OAF, OUT TO SPOIL MY CRIME.
W-WHY ARE YOU GETTING SO HEAVY?
SIMPLETON. YOU'RE STANDING IN THE RAYS OF MY RED SUN LAMP!
I'D BEEN DEVELOPING IT TO USE ON THAT OTHER KRYPTONIAN BUSYBODY, SUPERMAN!

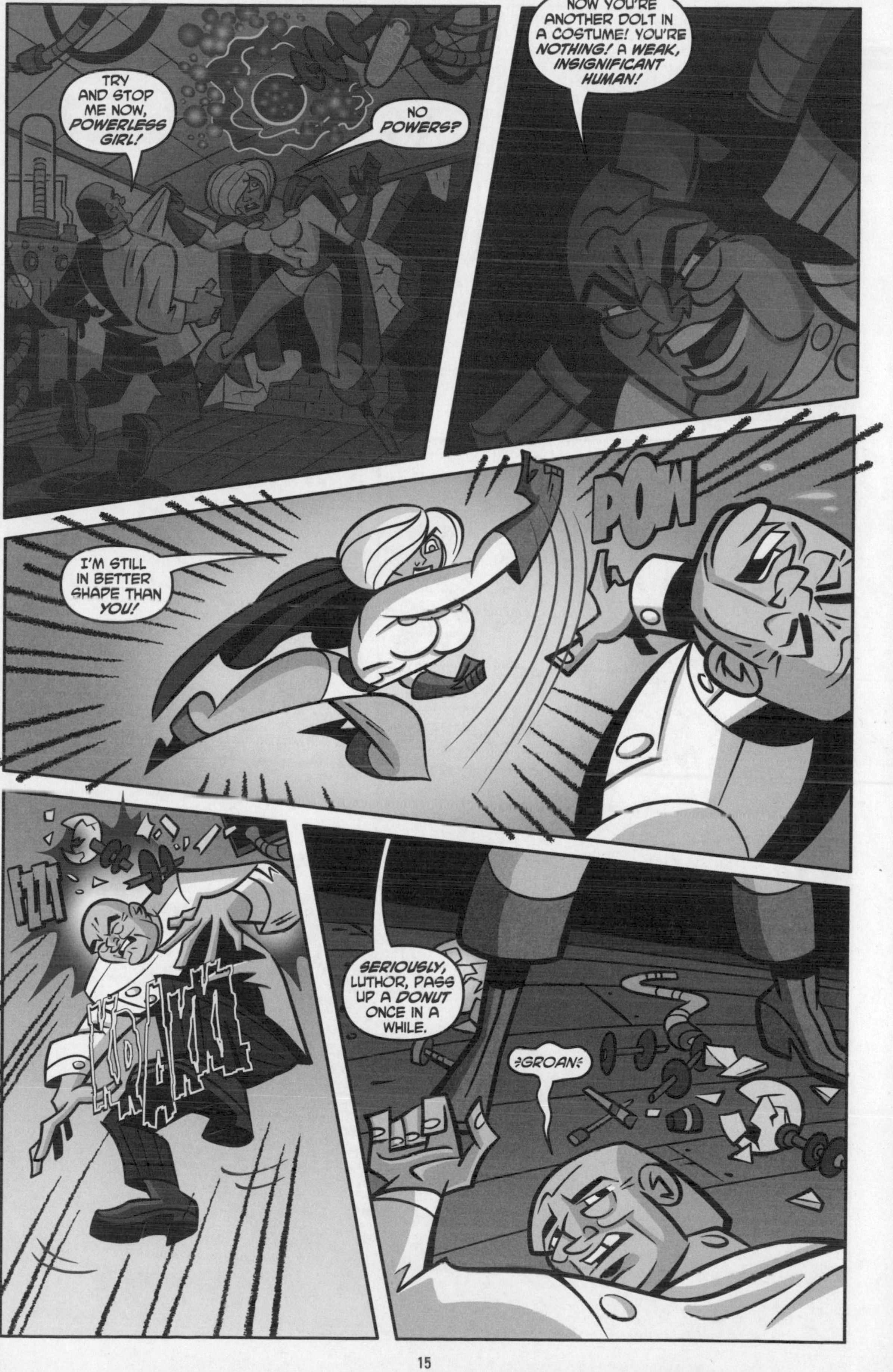
TRY AND STOP ME NOW, POWERLESS GIRL!
NO POWERS?
NOW YOU'RE ANOTHER DOLT IN A COSTUME! YOU'RE NOTHING! A WEAK, INSIGNIFICANT HUMAN!
POW
I'M STILL IN BETTER SHAPE THAN YOU!
FZZT
SERIOUSLY, LUTHOR, PASS UP A DONUT ONCE IN A WHILE.
GROAN

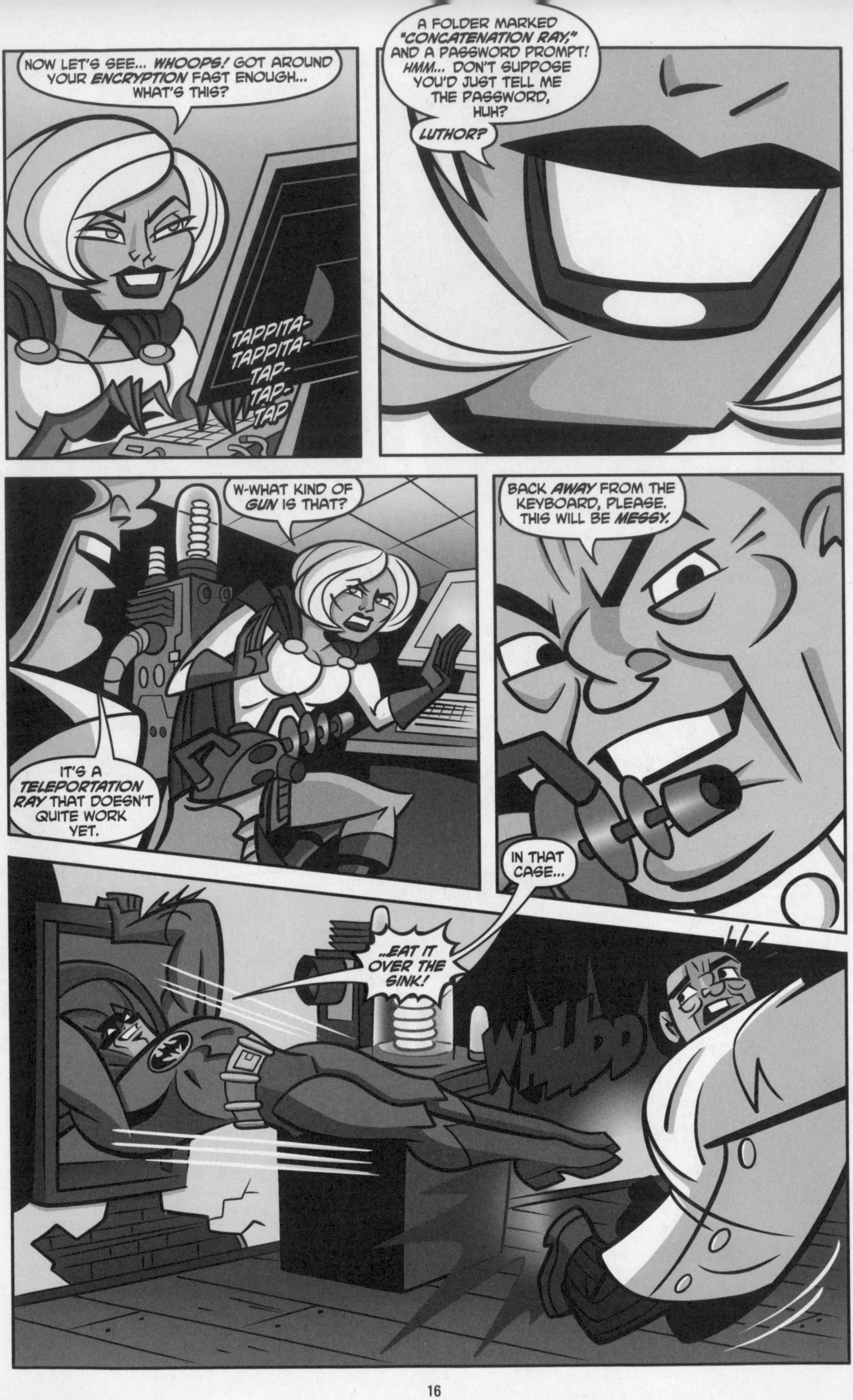
NOW LET'S SEE... WHOOPS! GOT AROUND YOUR ENCRYPTION FAST ENOUGH... WHAT'S THIS?
TAPPITA-TAPPITA-TAP-TAP-TAP
A FOLDER MARKED "CONCATENATION RAY," AND A PASSWORD PROMPT! HMM... DON'T SUPPOSE YOU'D JUST TELL ME THE PASSWORD, HUH?
LUTHOR?
W-WHAT KIND OF GUN IS THAT?
IT'S A TELEPORTATION RAY THAT DOESN'T QUITE WORK YET.
BACK AWAY FROM THE KEYBOARD, PLEASE. THIS WILL BE MESSY.
IN THAT CASE...
...EAT IT OVER THE SINK!
WHUDD

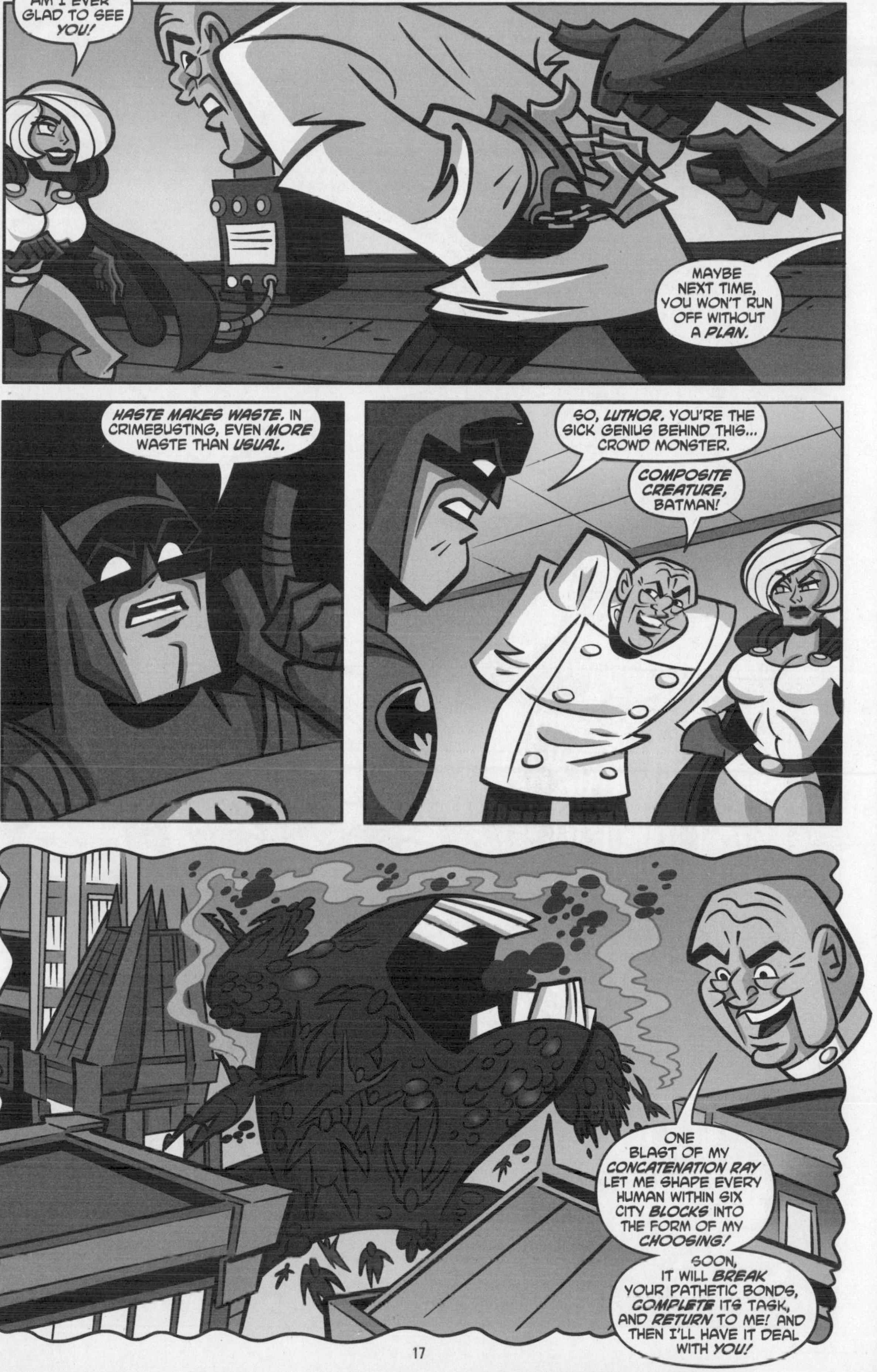
BATMAN, AM I EVER GLAD TO SEE YOU!
MAYBE NEXT TIME, YOU WON'T RUN OFF WITHOUT A PLAN.
HASTE MAKES WASTE. IN CRIMEBUSTING, EVEN MORE WASTE THAN USUAL.
SO, LUTHOR. YOU'RE THE SICK GENIUS BEHIND THIS... CROWD MONSTER.
COMPOSITE CREATURE, BATMAN!
ONE BLAST OF MY CONCATENATION RAY LET ME SHAPE EVERY HUMAN WITHIN SIX CITY BLOCKS INTO THE FORM OF MY CHOOSING!
SOON, IT WILL BREAK YOUR PATHETIC BONDS, COMPLETE ITS TASK, AND RETURN TO ME! AND THEN I'LL HAVE IT DEAL WITH YOU!

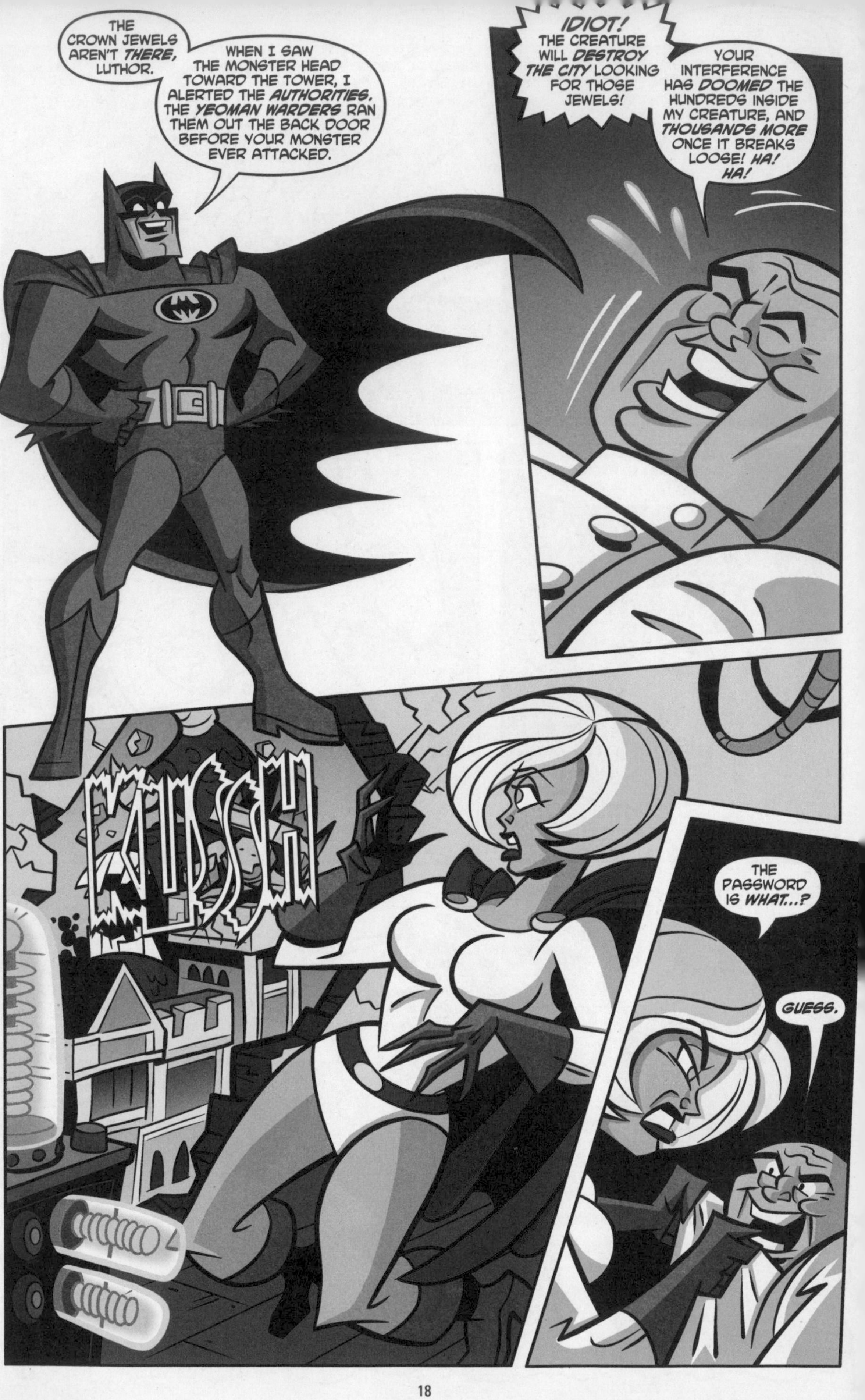
THE CROWN JEWELS AREN'T *THERE,* LUTHOR.
WHEN I SAW THE MONSTER HEAD TOWARD THE TOWER, I ALERTED THE *AUTHORITIES.* THE *YEOMAN WARDERS* RAN THEM OUT THE BACK DOOR BEFORE YOUR MONSTER EVER ATTACKED.
IDIOT! THE CREATURE WILL *DESTROY THE CITY* LOOKING FOR THOSE JEWELS!
YOUR INTERFERENCE HAS *DOOMED* THE HUNDREDS INSIDE MY CREATURE, AND *THOUSANDS MORE* ONCE IT BREAKS LOOSE! *HA! HA!*
THE PASSWORD IS *WHAT...?*
GUESS.

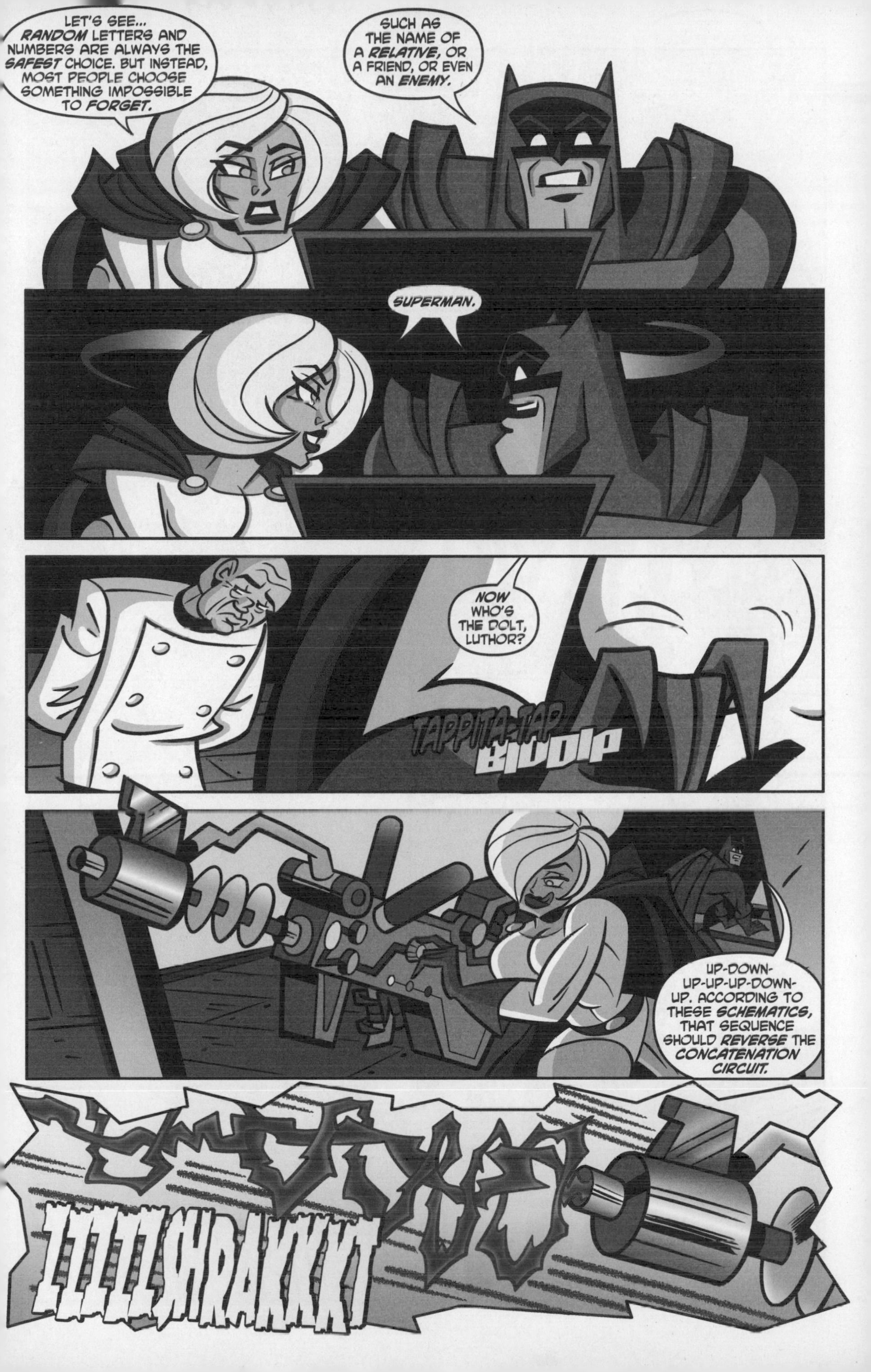
LET'S SEE... RANDOM LETTERS AND NUMBERS ARE ALWAYS THE SAFEST CHOICE. BUT INSTEAD, MOST PEOPLE CHOOSE SOMETHING IMPOSSIBLE TO FORGET.
SUCH AS THE NAME OF A RELATIVE, OR A FRIEND, OR EVEN AN ENEMY.
SUPERMAN.
NOW WHO'S THE DOLT, LUTHOR?
TAPPITA-TAP
BIDDIP
UP-DOWN-UP-UP-UP-DOWN-UP. ACCORDING TO THESE SCHEMATICS, THAT SEQUENCE SHOULD REVERSE THE CONCATENATION CIRCUIT.
ZZZZSHRAKKKT

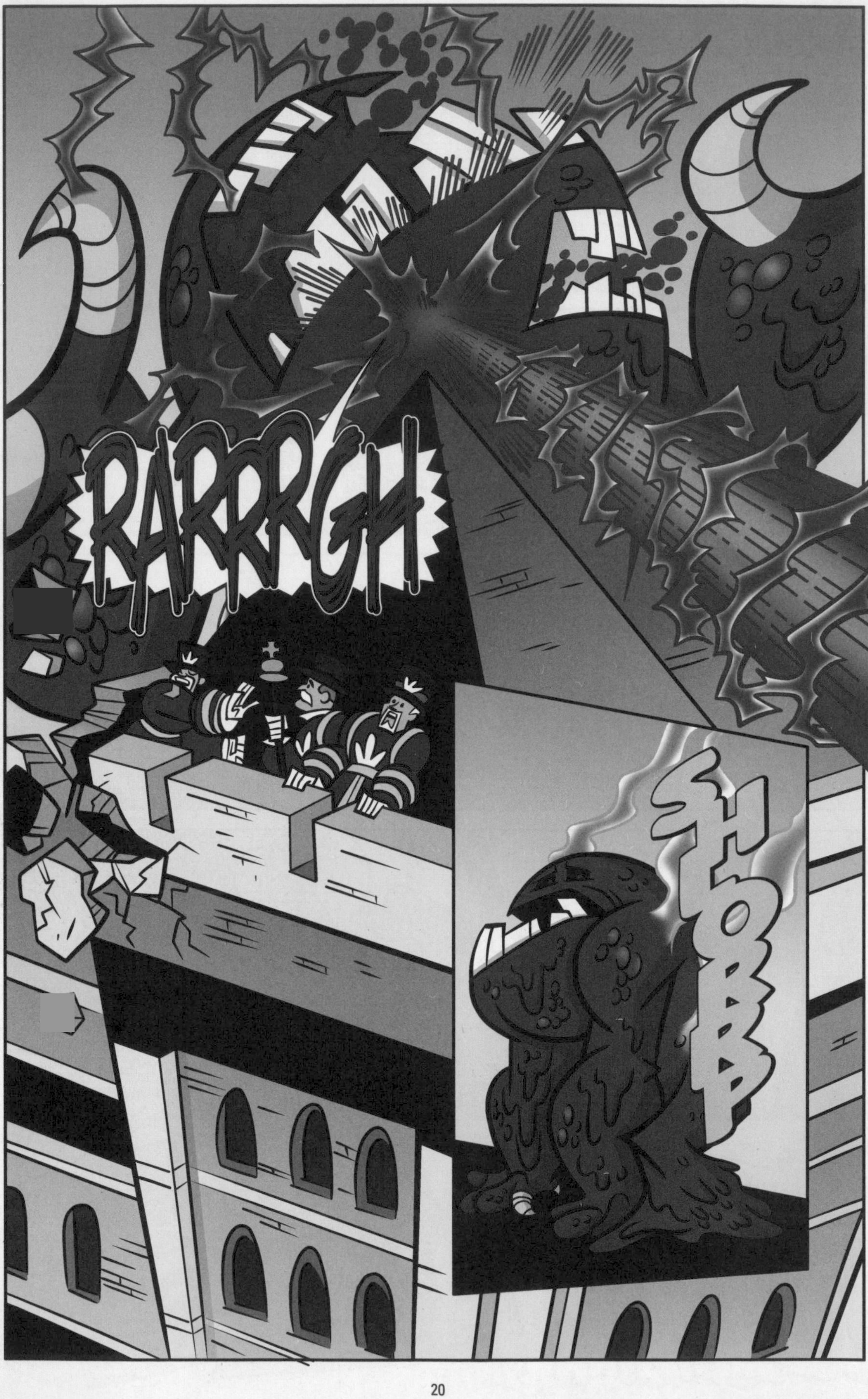
RARRRGH
SHLOBB

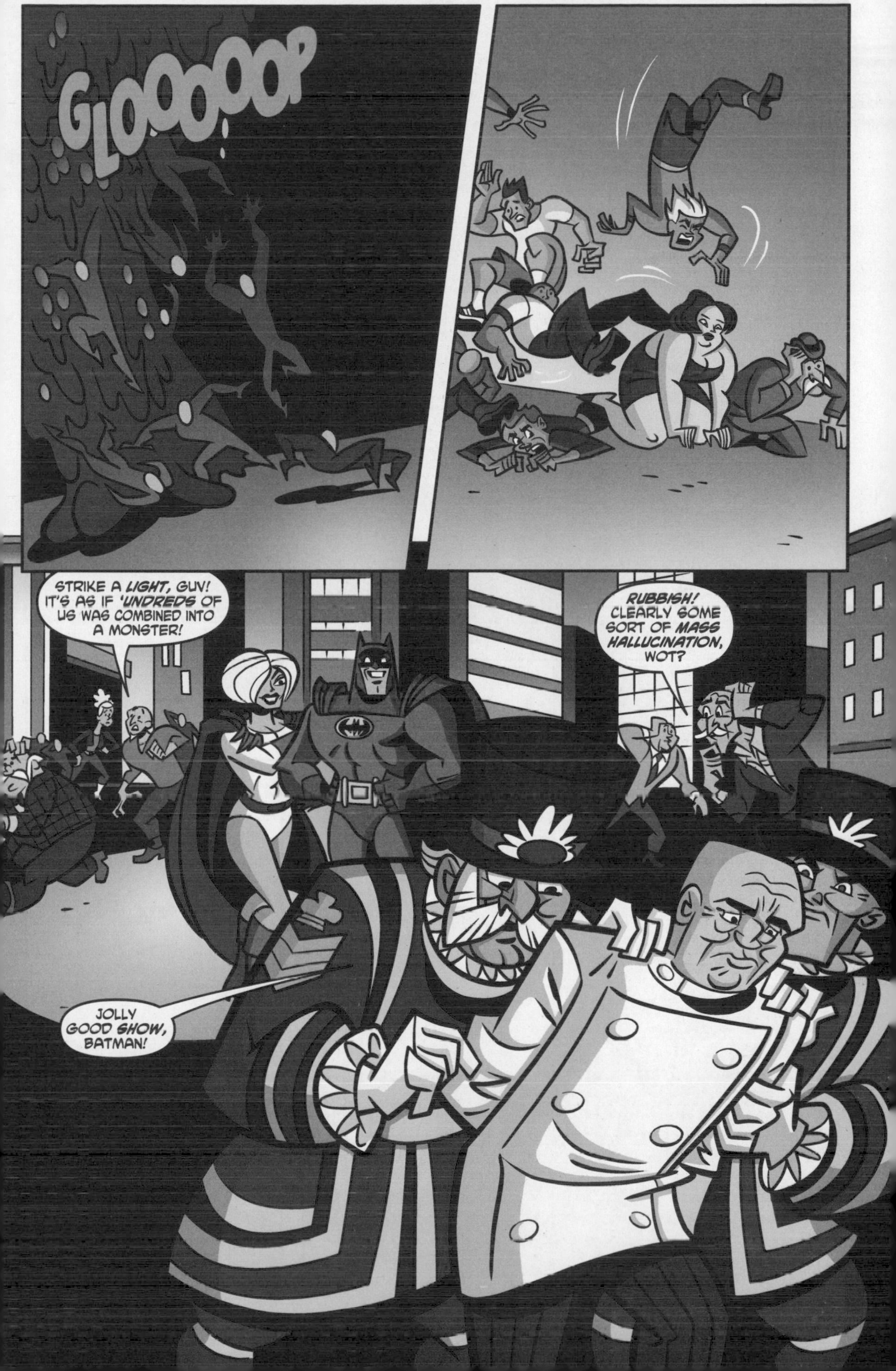
GLOOOOOP
STRIKE A LIGHT, GUV! IT'S AS IF 'UNDREDS OF US WAS COMBINED INTO A MONSTER!
RUBBISH! CLEARLY SOME SORT OF MASS HALLUCINATION, WOT?
JOLLY GOOD SHOW, BATMAN!

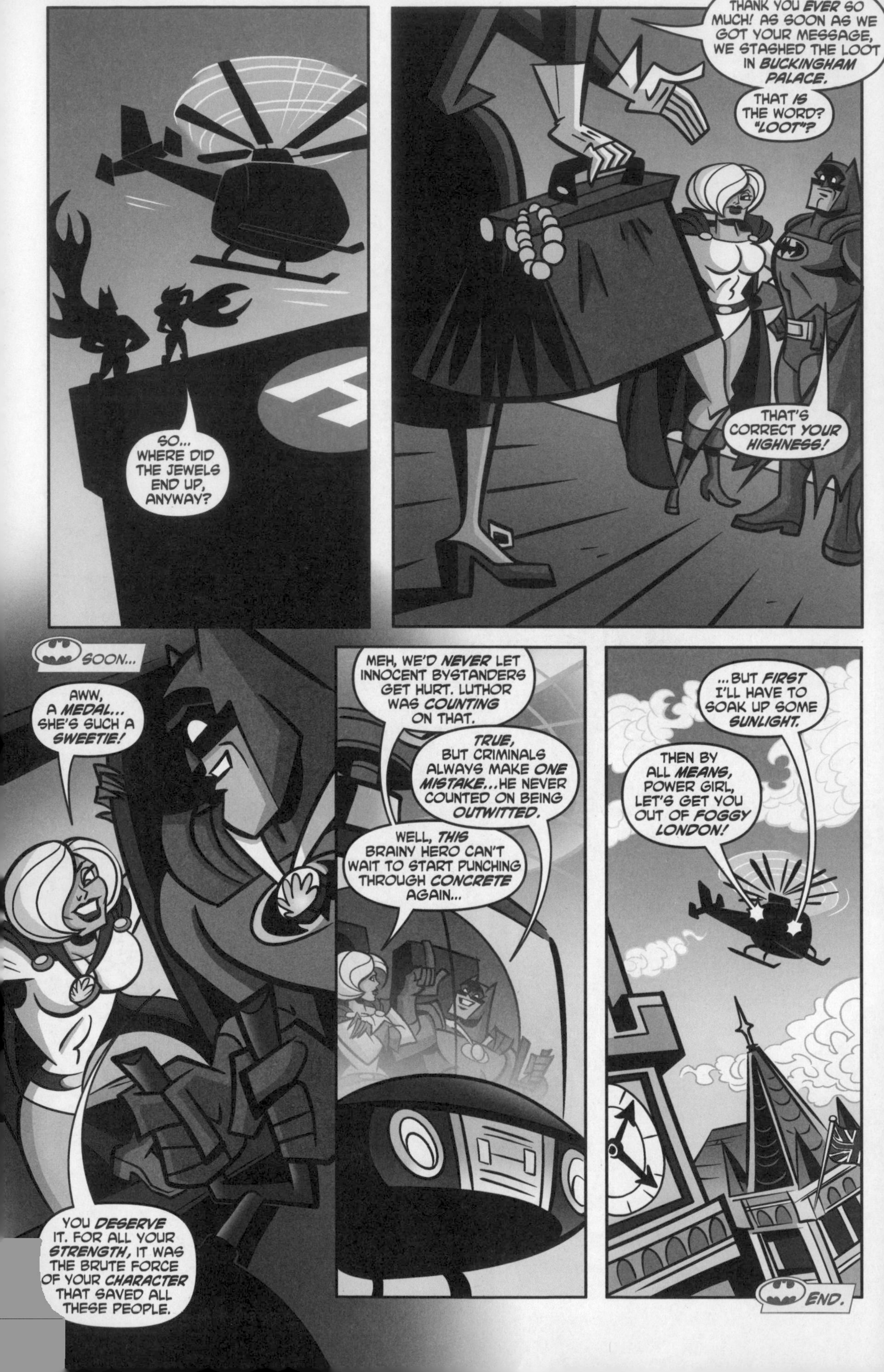
SO... WHERE DID THE JEWELS END UP, ANYWAY?
BATMAN! THANK YOU EVER SO MUCH! AS SOON AS WE GOT YOUR MESSAGE, WE STASHED THE LOOT IN BUCKINGHAM PALACE.
THAT IS THE WORD? "LOOT"?
THAT'S CORRECT YOUR HIGHNESS!
SOON...
AWW, A MEDAL... SHE'S SUCH A SWEETIE!
YOU DESERVE IT. FOR ALL YOUR STRENGTH, IT WAS THE BRUTE FORCE OF YOUR CHARACTER THAT SAVED ALL THESE PEOPLE.
MEH, WE'D NEVER LET INNOCENT BYSTANDERS GET HURT. LUTHOR WAS COUNTING ON THAT.
TRUE, BUT CRIMINALS ALWAYS MAKE ONE MISTAKE... HE NEVER COUNTED ON BEING OUTWITTED.
WELL, THIS BRAINY HERO CAN'T WAIT TO START PUNCHING THROUGH CONCRETE AGAIN...
...BUT FIRST I'LL HAVE TO SOAK UP SOME SUNLIGHT.
THEN BY ALL MEANS, POWER GIRL, LET'S GET YOU OUT OF FOGGY LONDON!
END.

LEX LUTHOR

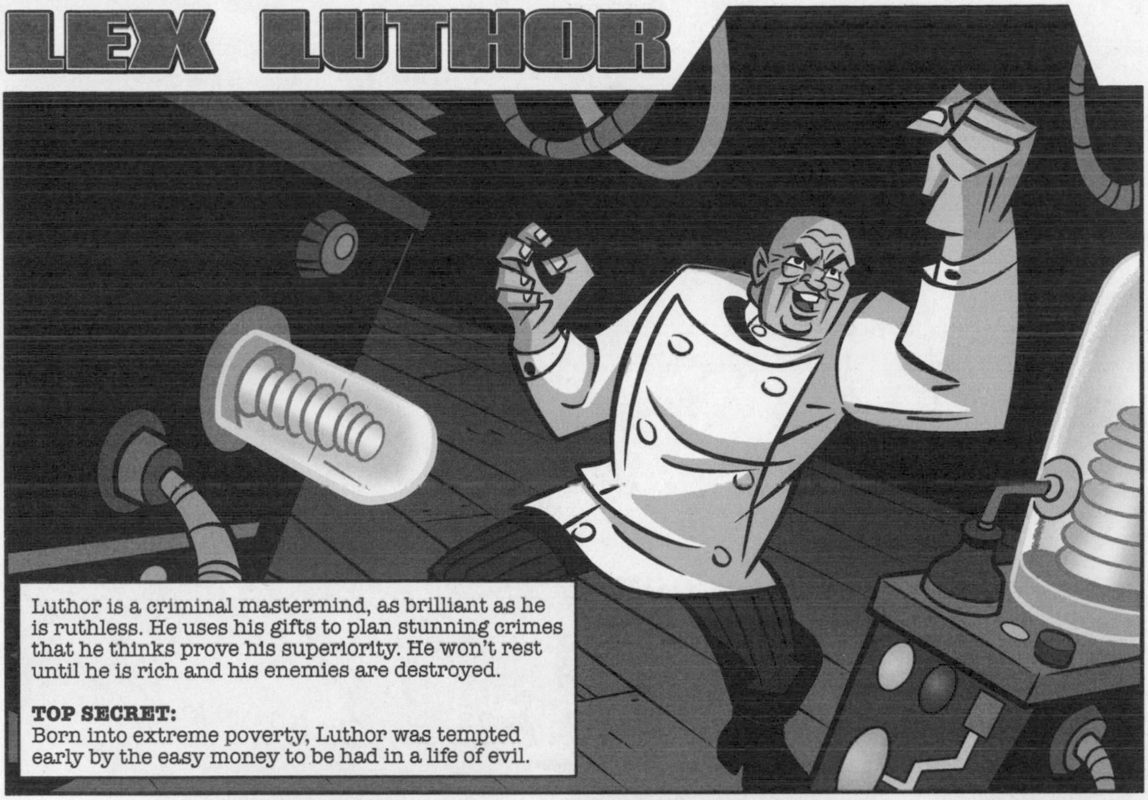
Luthor is a criminal mastermind, as brilliant as he is ruthless. He uses his gifts to plan stunning crimes that he thinks prove his superiority. He won't rest until he is rich and his enemies are destroyed.
TOP SECRET:
Born into extreme poverty, Luthor was tempted early by the easy money to be had in a life of evil.

POWER GIRL

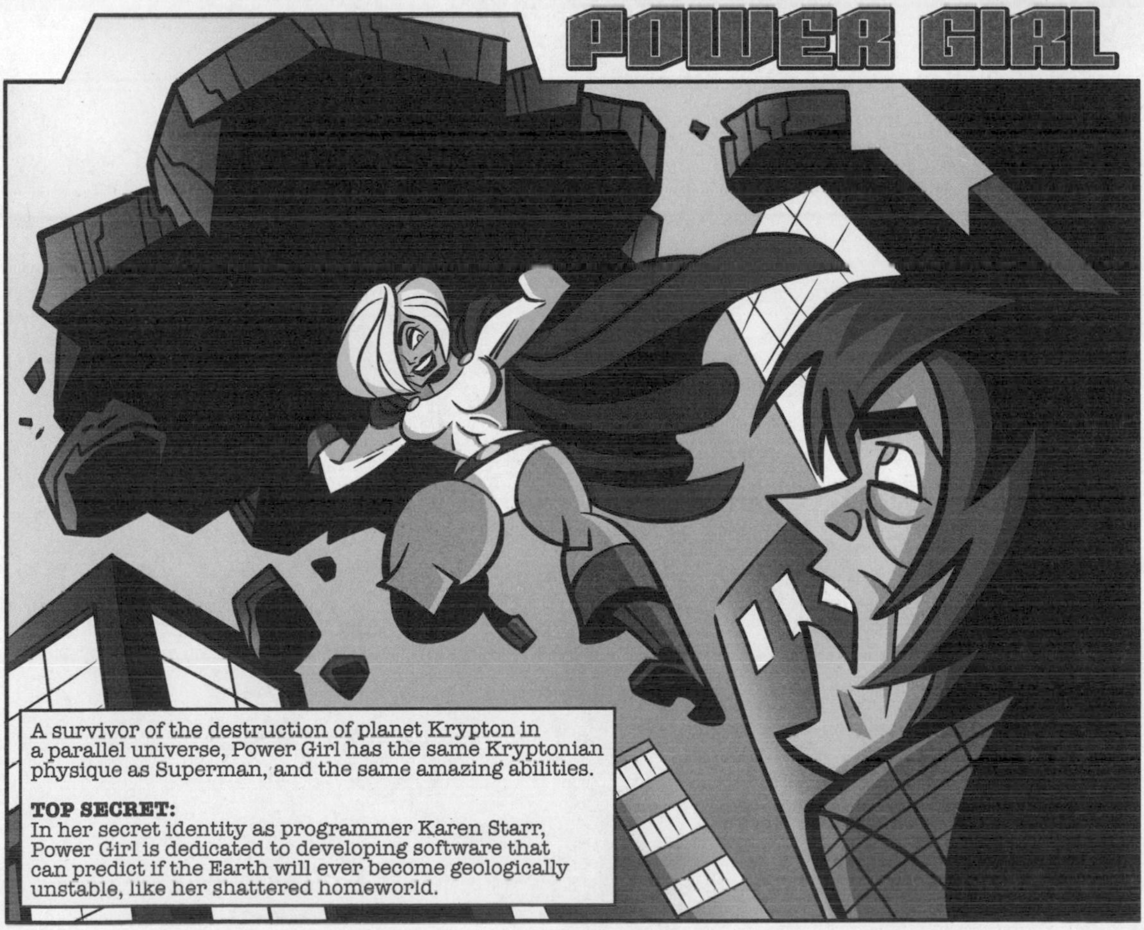
A survivor of the destruction of planet Krypton in a parallel universe, Power Girl has the same Kryptonian physique as Superman, and the same amazing abilities.
TOP SECRET:
In her secret identity as programmer Karen Starr, Power Girl is dedicated to developing software that can predict if the Earth will ever become geologically unstable, like her shattered homeworld.

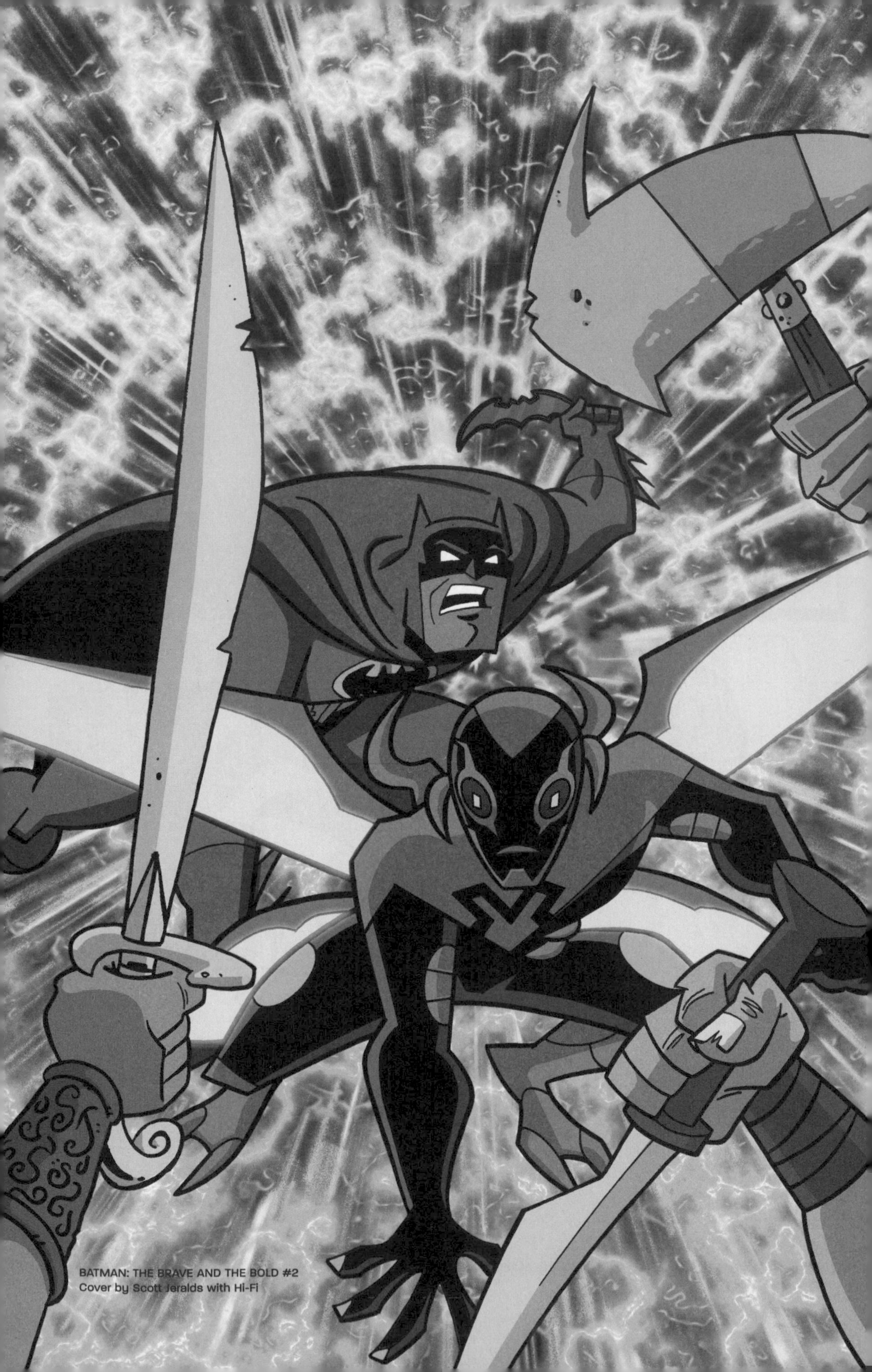

BATMAN: THE BRAVE AND THE BOLD #2
Cover by Scott Jeralds with Hi-Fi

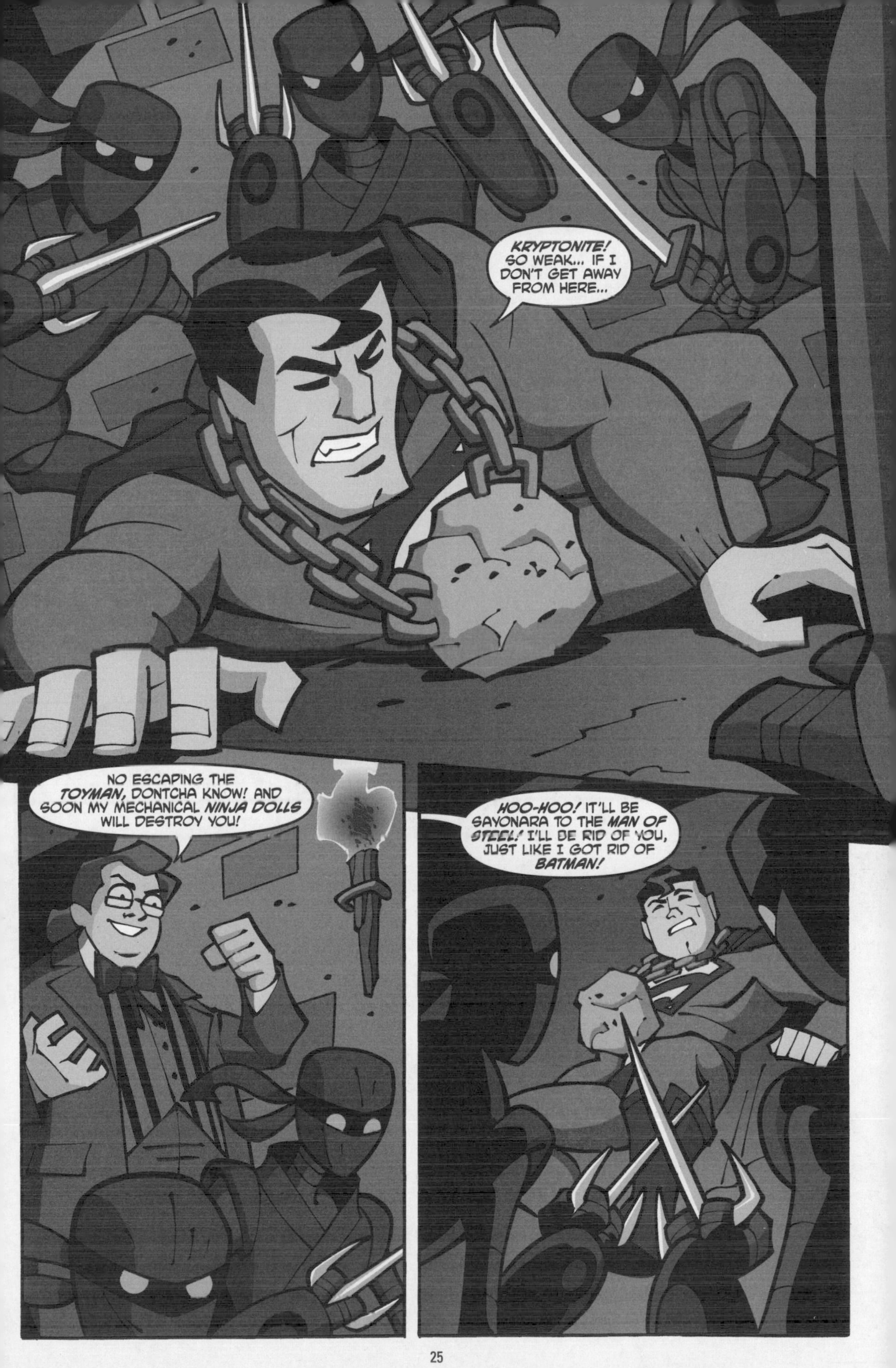
KRYPTONITE! SO WEAK... IF I DON'T GET AWAY FROM HERE...
NO ESCAPING THE TOYMAN, DONTCHA KNOW! AND SOON MY MECHANICAL NINJA DOLLS WILL DESTROY YOU!
HOO-HOO! IT'LL BE SAYONARA TO THE MAN OF STEEL! I'LL BE RID OF YOU, JUST LIKE I GOT RID OF BATMAN!

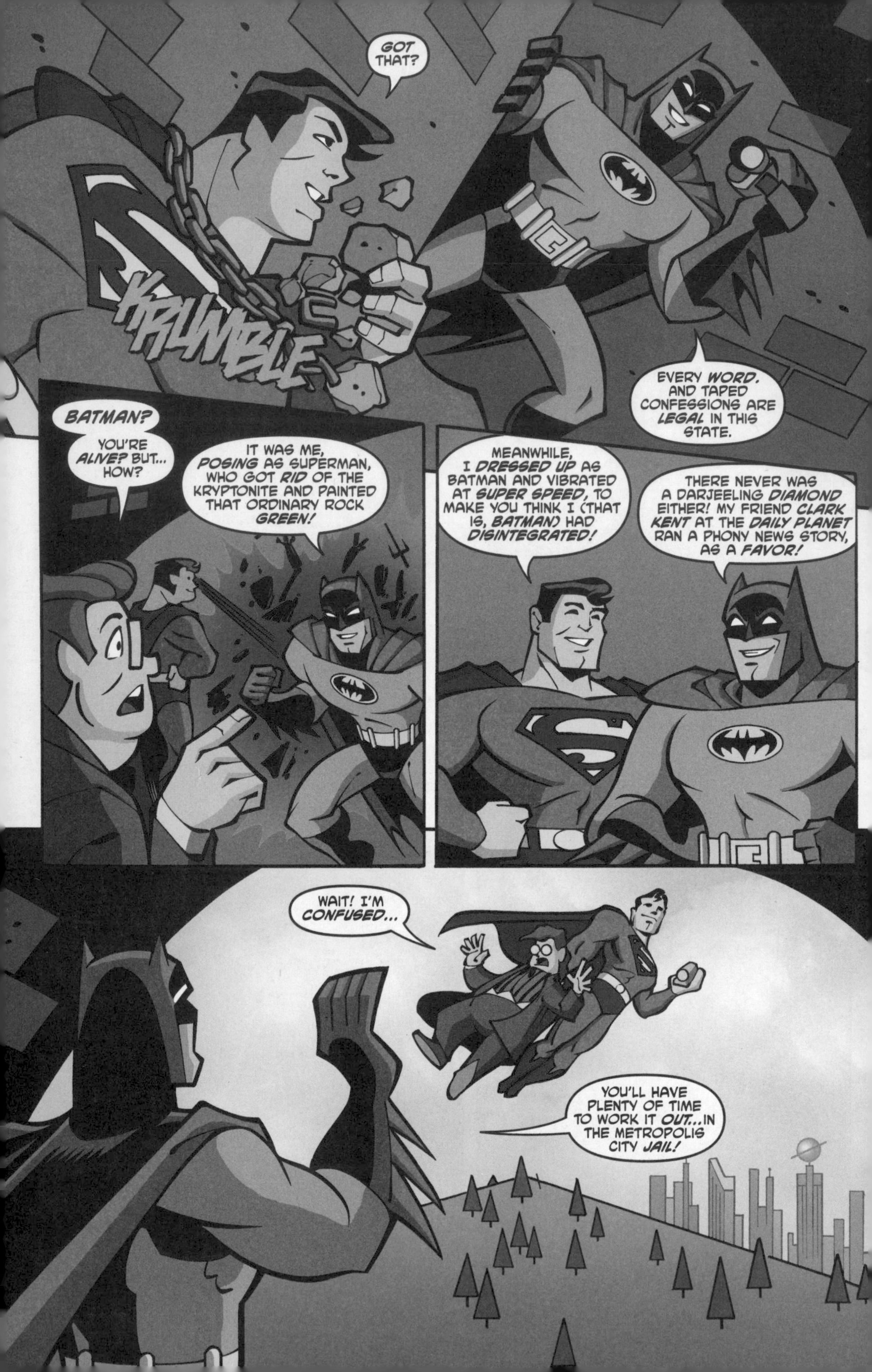
GOT THAT?
KRUMBLE
EVERY WORD. AND TAPED CONFESSIONS ARE LEGAL IN THIS STATE.
BATMAN?
YOU'RE ALIVE? BUT... HOW?
IT WAS ME, POSING AS SUPERMAN, WHO GOT RID OF THE KRYPTONITE AND PAINTED THAT ORDINARY ROCK GREEN!
MEANWHILE, I DRESSED UP AS BATMAN AND VIBRATED AT SUPER SPEED, TO MAKE YOU THINK I (THAT IS, BATMAN) HAD DISINTEGRATED!
THERE NEVER WAS A DARJEELING DIAMOND EITHER! MY FRIEND CLARK KENT AT THE DAILY PLANET RAN A PHONY NEWS STORY, AS A FAVOR!
WAIT! I'M CONFUSED...
YOU'LL HAVE PLENTY OF TIME TO WORK IT OUT...IN THE METROPOLIS CITY JAIL!

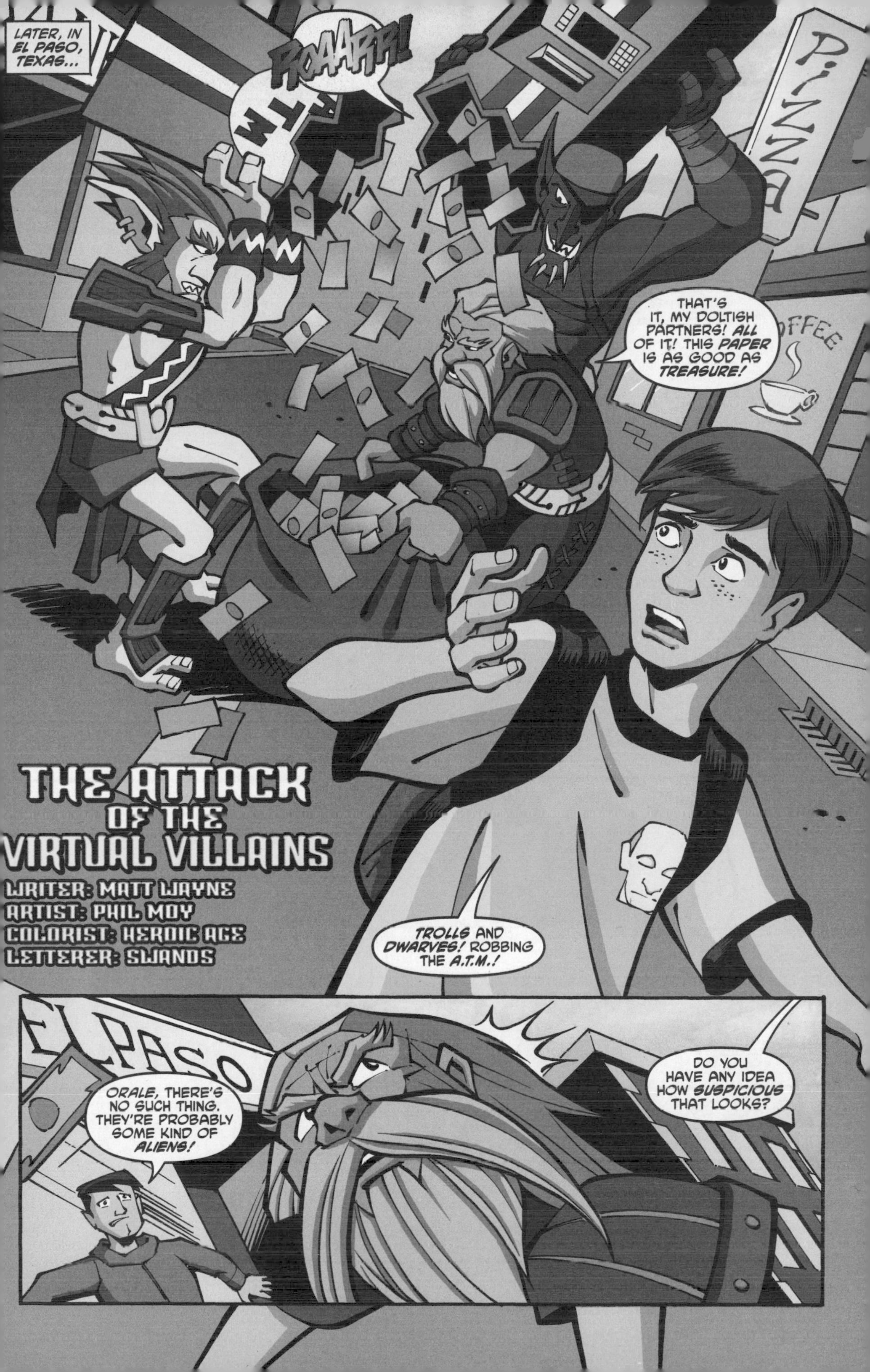

LATER, IN EL PASO, TEXAS...
ROAARR!
THAT'S IT, MY DOLTISH PARTNERS! ALL OF IT! THIS PAPER IS AS GOOD AS TREASURE!
THE ATTACK OF THE VIRTUAL VILLAINS
WRITER: MATT WAYNE
ARTIST: PHIL MOY
COLORIST: HEROIC AGE
LETTERER: SWANDS
TROLLS AND DWARVES! ROBBING THE A.T.M.!
EL PASO
ORALE, THERE'S NO SUCH THING. THEY'RE PROBABLY SOME KIND OF ALIENS!
DO YOU HAVE ANY IDEA HOW SUSPICIOUS THAT LOOKS?

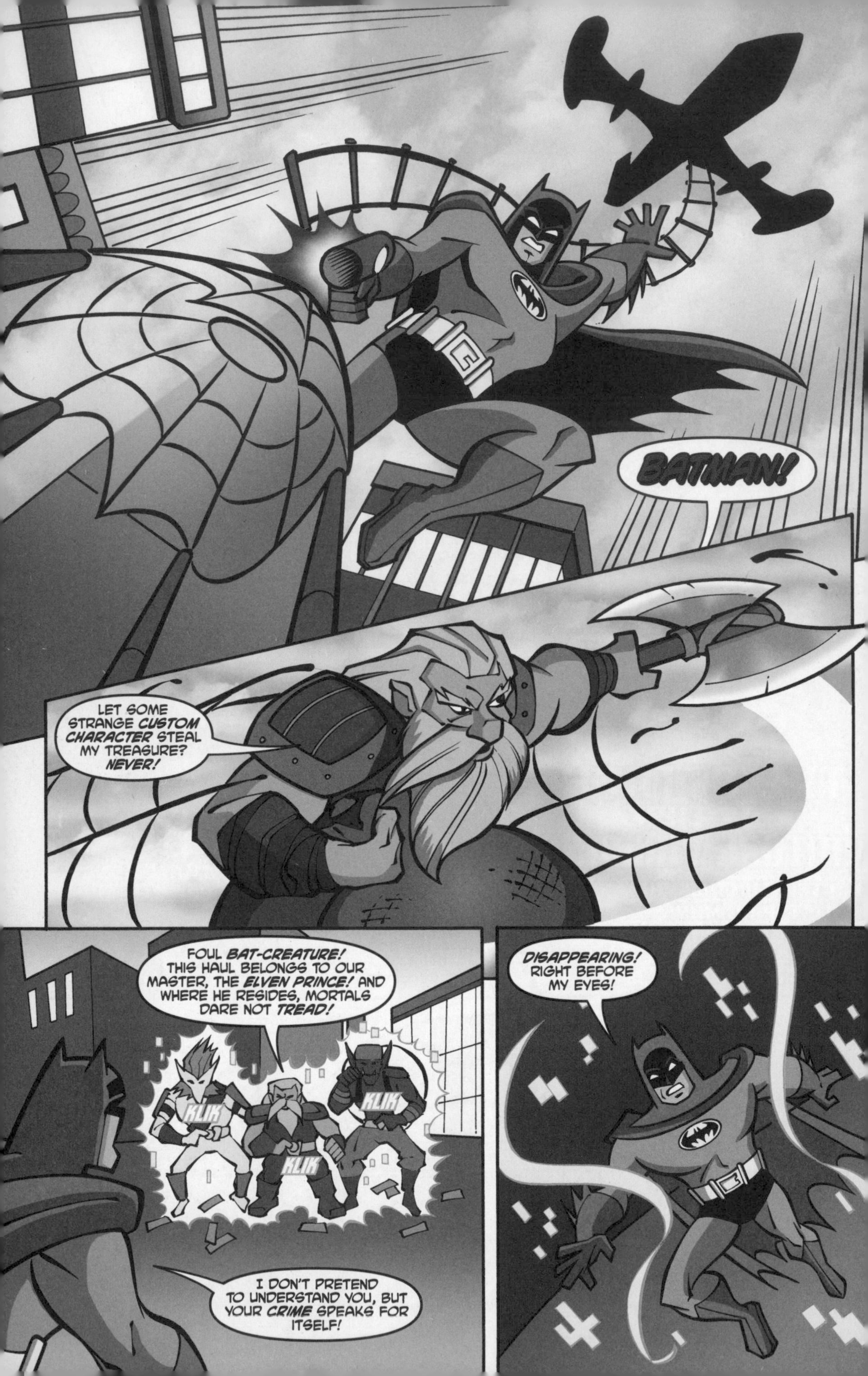
BATMAN!
LET SOME STRANGE CUSTOM CHARACTER STEAL MY TREASURE? NEVER!
FOUL BAT-CREATURE! THIS HAUL BELONGS TO OUR MASTER, THE ELVEN PRINCE! AND WHERE HE RESIDES, MORTALS DARE NOT TREAD!
KLIK
KLIK
KLIK
I DON'T PRETEND TO UNDERSTAND YOU, BUT YOUR CRIME SPEAKS FOR ITSELF!
DISAPPEARING! RIGHT BEFORE MY EYES!

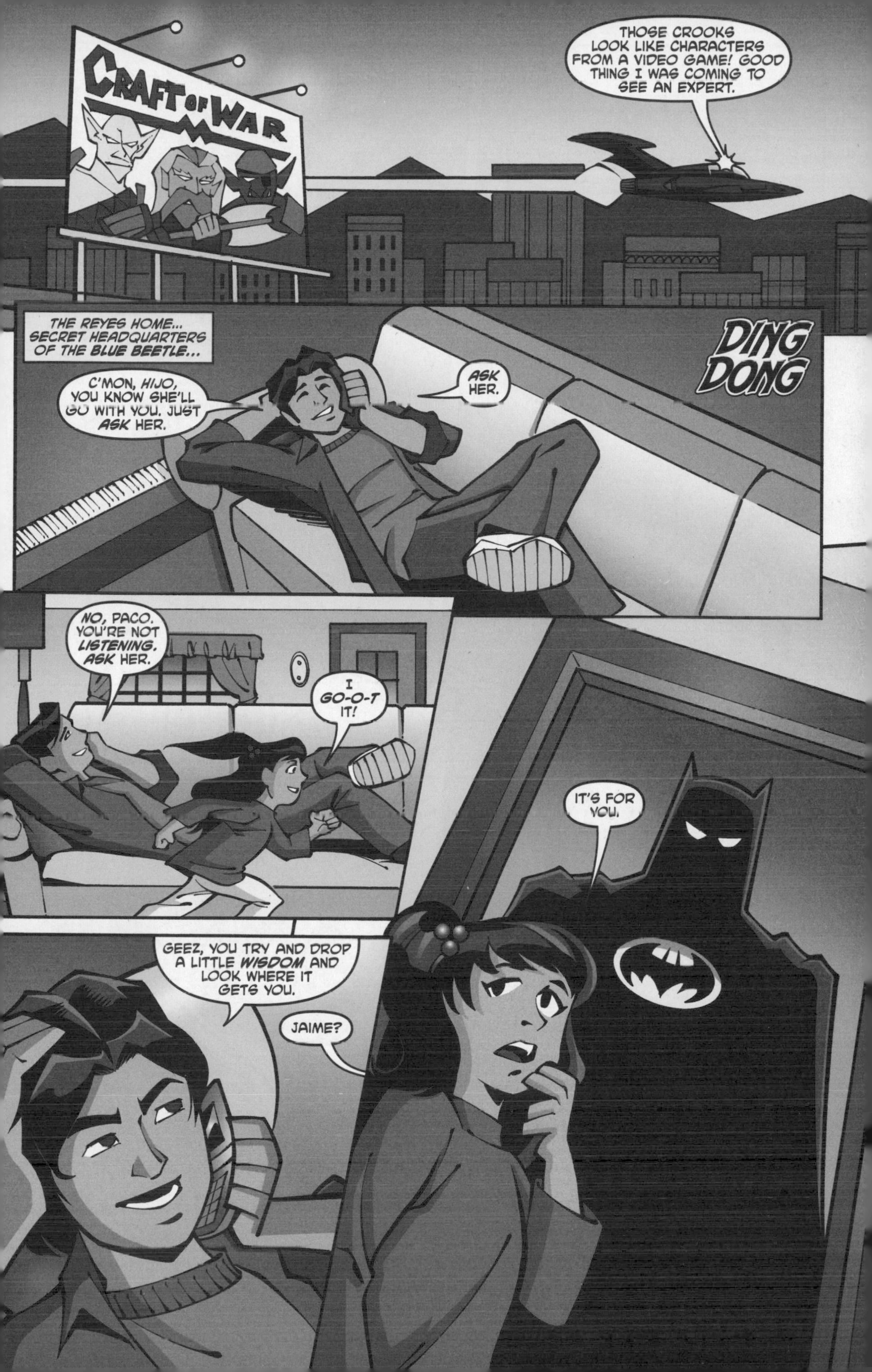
CRAFT OF WAR
THOSE CROOKS LOOK LIKE CHARACTERS FROM A VIDEO GAME! GOOD THING I WAS COMING TO SEE AN EXPERT.
THE REYES HOME... SECRET HEADQUARTERS OF THE BLUE BEETLE...
C'MON, HIJO, YOU KNOW SHE'LL GO WITH YOU. JUST ASK HER.
ASK HER.
DING DONG
NO, PACO. YOU'RE NOT LISTENING. ASK HER.
I GO-O-T IT!
IT'S FOR YOU.
GEEZ, YOU TRY AND DROP A LITTLE WISDOM AND LOOK WHERE IT GETS YOU.
JAIME?

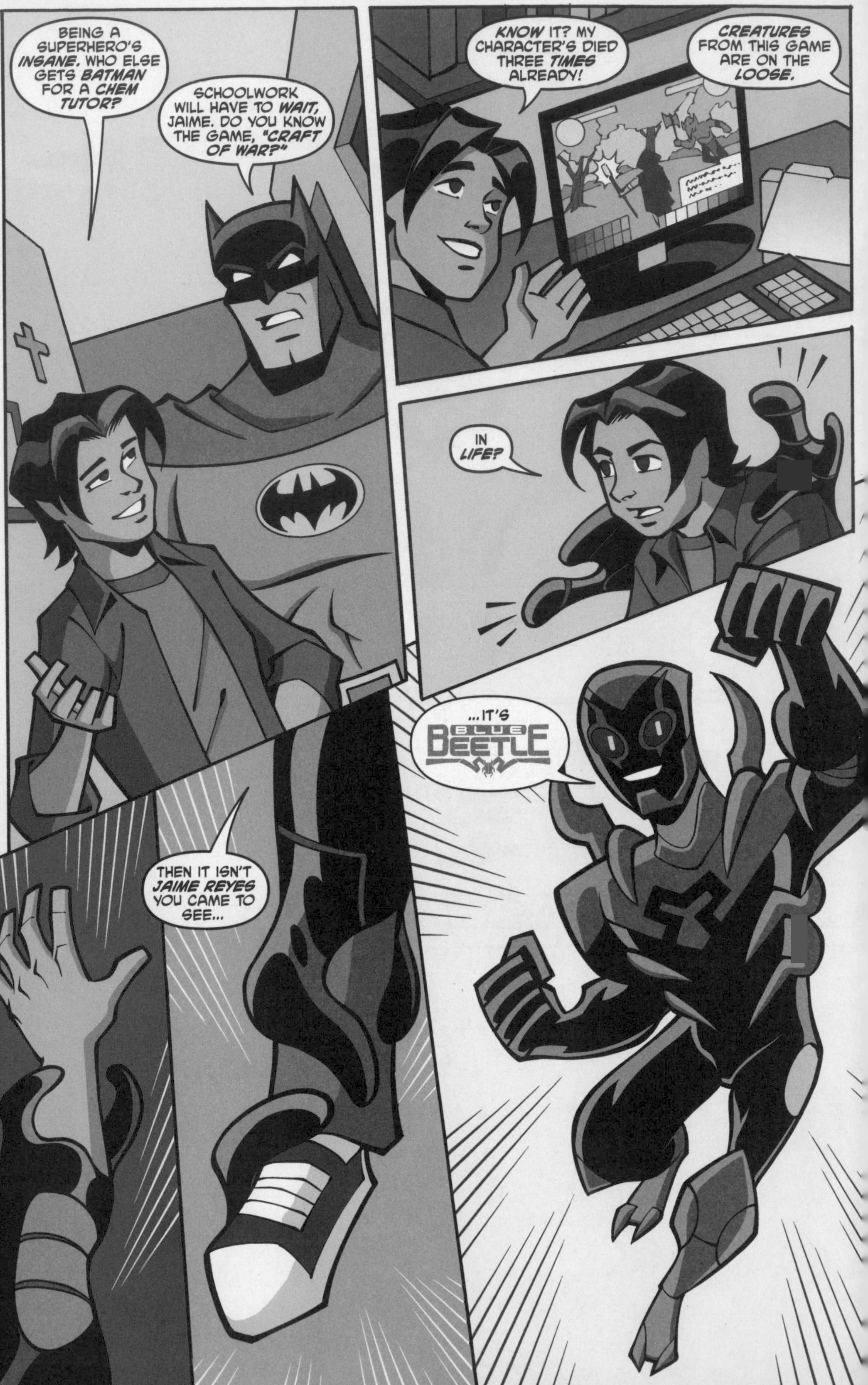
BEING A SUPERHERO'S *INSANE*. WHO ELSE GETS *BATMAN* FOR A *CHEM TUTOR?*
SCHOOLWORK WILL HAVE TO *WAIT*, JAIME. DO YOU KNOW THE GAME, *"CRAFT OF WAR?"*
KNOW IT? MY CHARACTER'S DIED THREE *TIMES* ALREADY!
CREATURES FROM THIS GAME ARE ON THE *LOOSE*.
IN *LIFE?*
THEN IT ISN'T *JAIME REYES* YOU CAME TO SEE...
...IT'S BLUE BEETLE

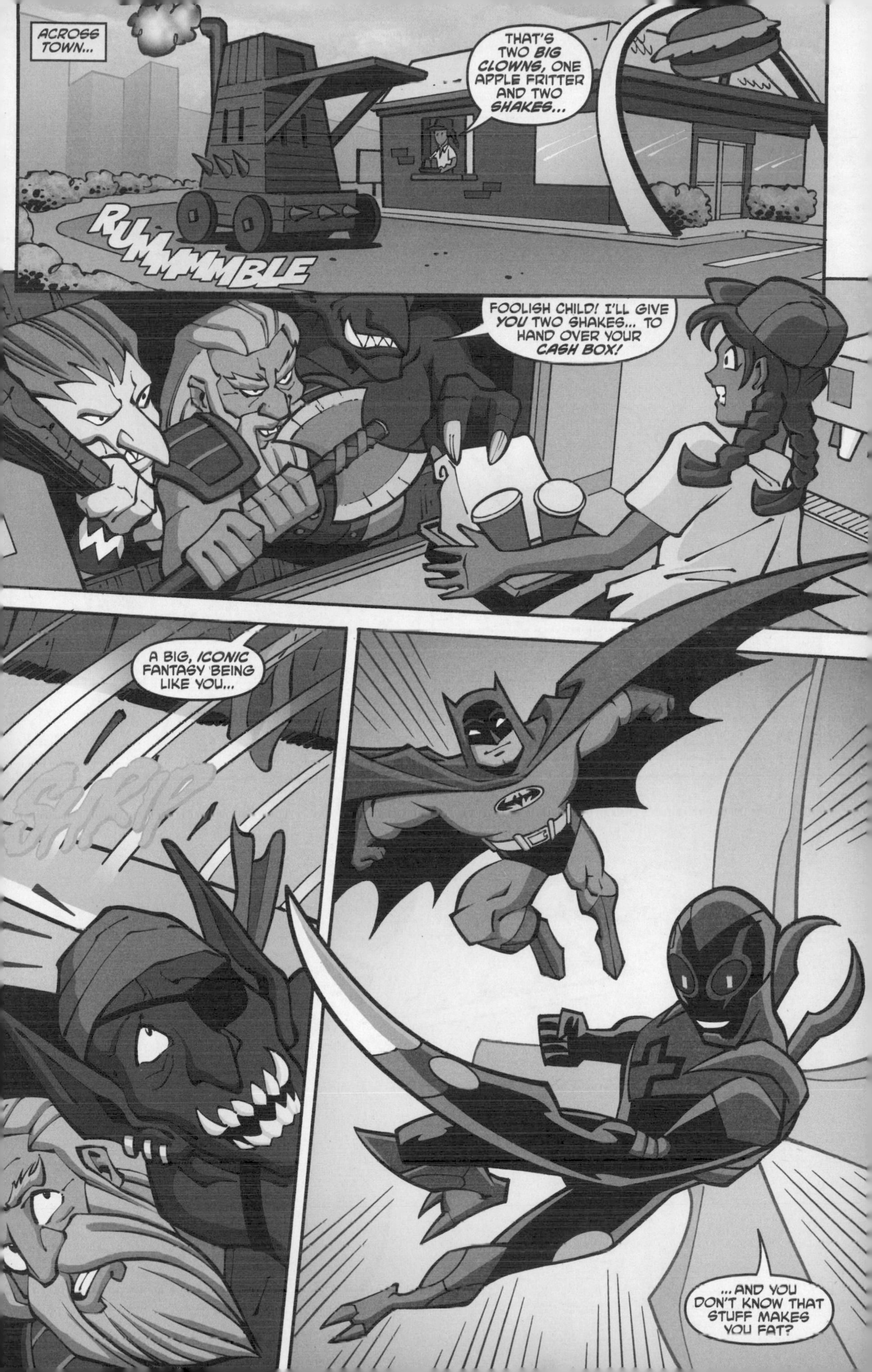
ACROSS TOWN...
THAT'S TWO BIG CLOWNS, ONE APPLE FRITTER AND TWO SHAKES...
RUMMMMBLE
FOOLISH CHILD! I'LL GIVE YOU TWO SHAKES... TO HAND OVER YOUR CASH BOX!
A BIG, ICONIC FANTASY BEING LIKE YOU...
SHRIP
...AND YOU DON'T KNOW THAT STUFF MAKES YOU FAT?

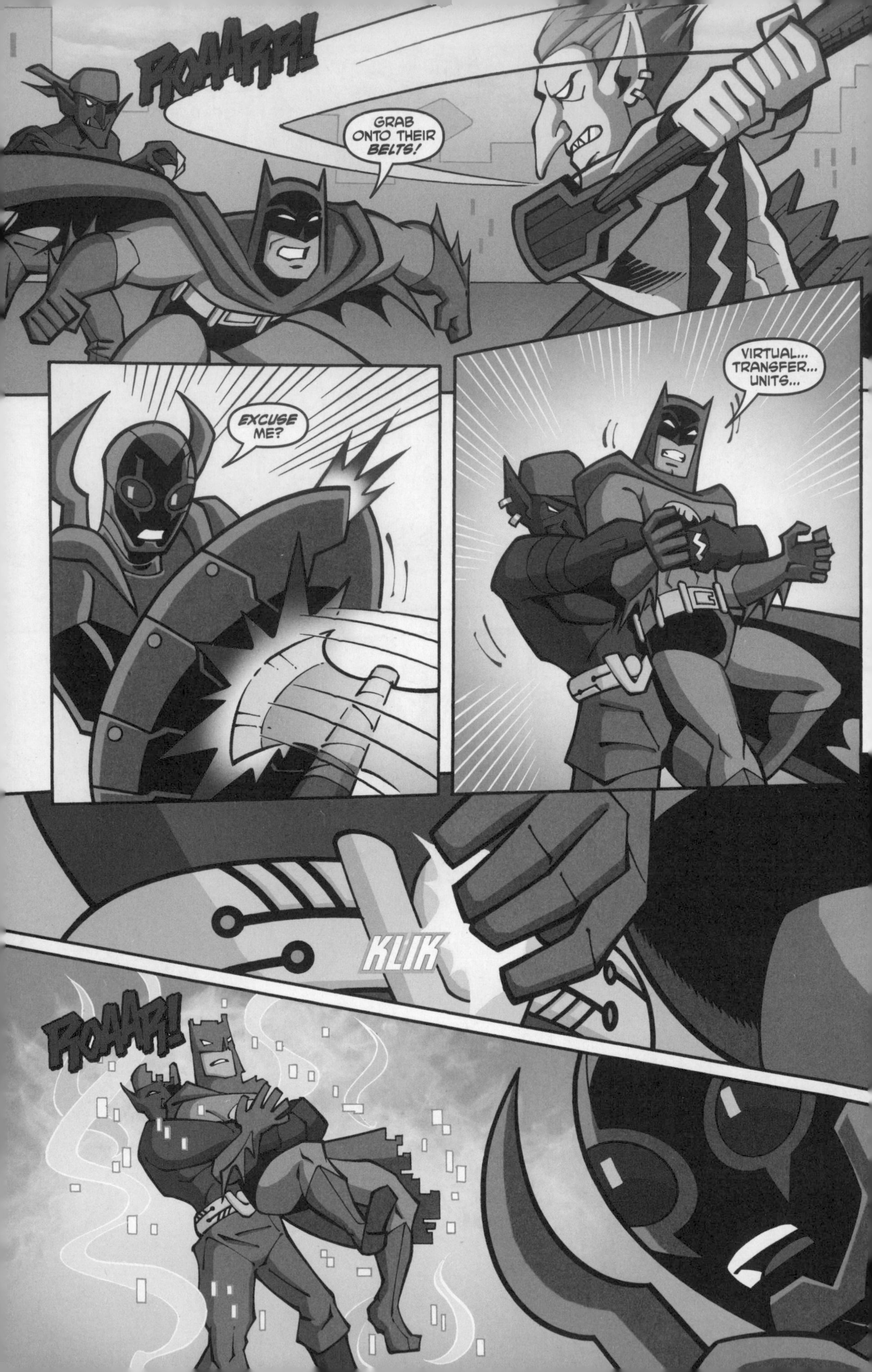
ROAAARR!
GRAB ONTO THEIR BELTS!
EXCUSE ME?
VIRTUAL... TRANSFER... UNITS...
KLIK
ROAAR!

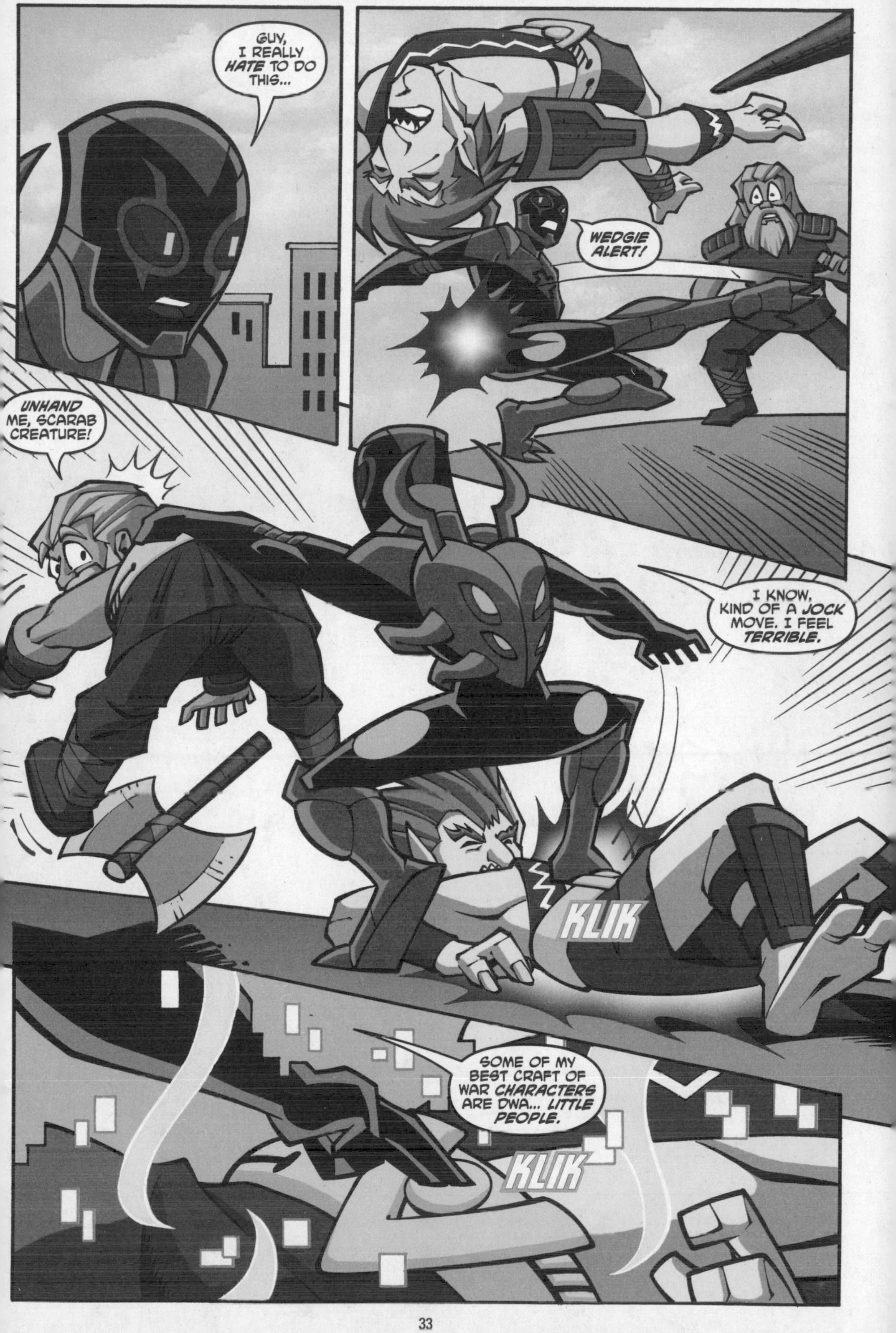
GUY, I REALLY *HATE* TO DO THIS...
WEDGIE ALERT!
UNHAND ME, SCARAB CREATURE!
I KNOW, KIND OF A *JOCK* MOVE. I FEEL *TERRIBLE.*
KLIK
SOME OF MY BEST CRAFT OF WAR *CHARACTERS* ARE DWA... *LITTLE PEOPLE.*
KLIK

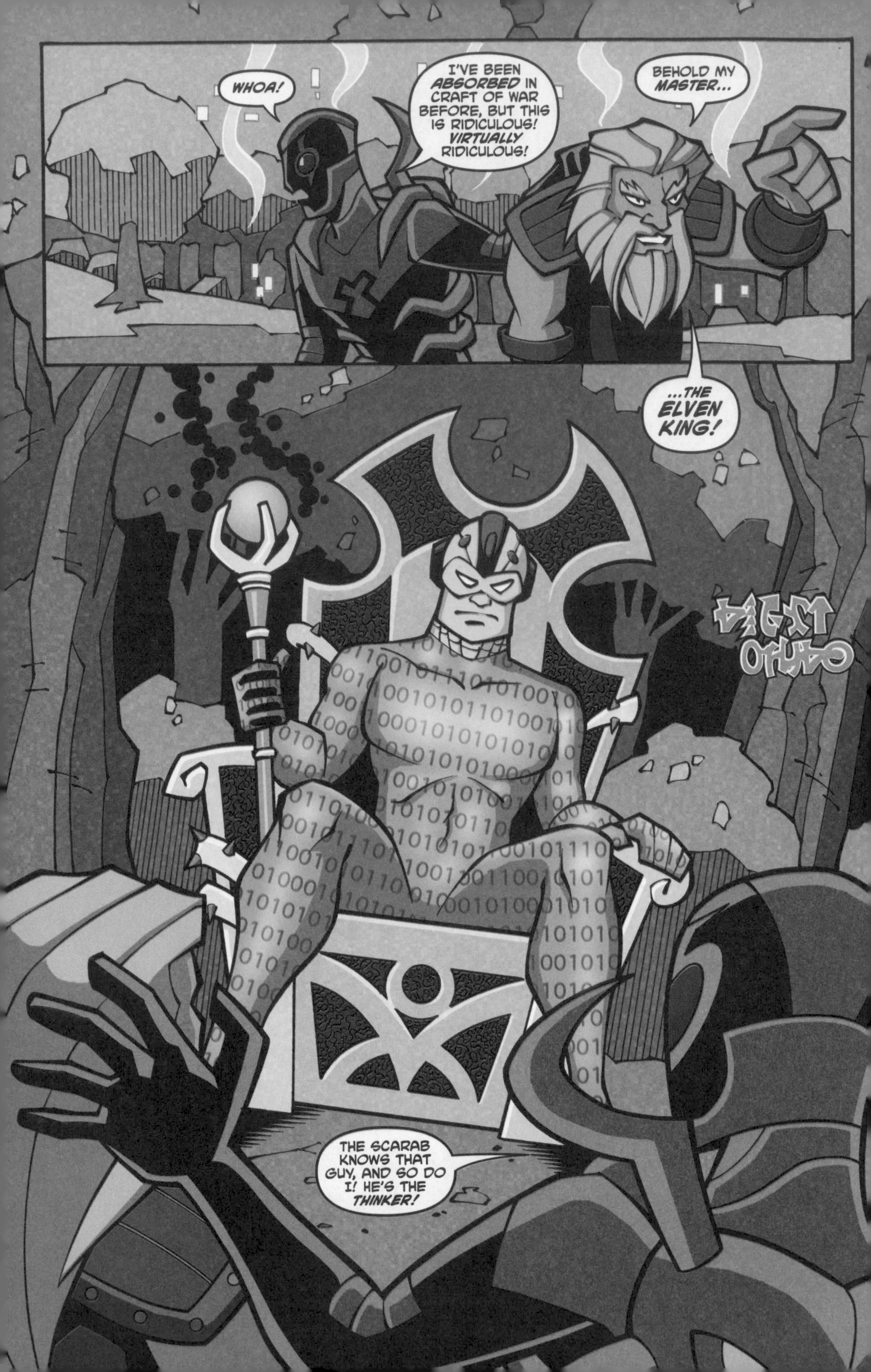
WHOA!
I'VE BEEN ABSORBED IN CRAFT OF WAR BEFORE, BUT THIS IS RIDICULOUS! VIRTUALLY RIDICULOUS!
BEHOLD MY MASTER...
...THE ELVEN KING!
THE SCARAB KNOWS THAT GUY, AND SO DO I! HE'S THE THINKER!

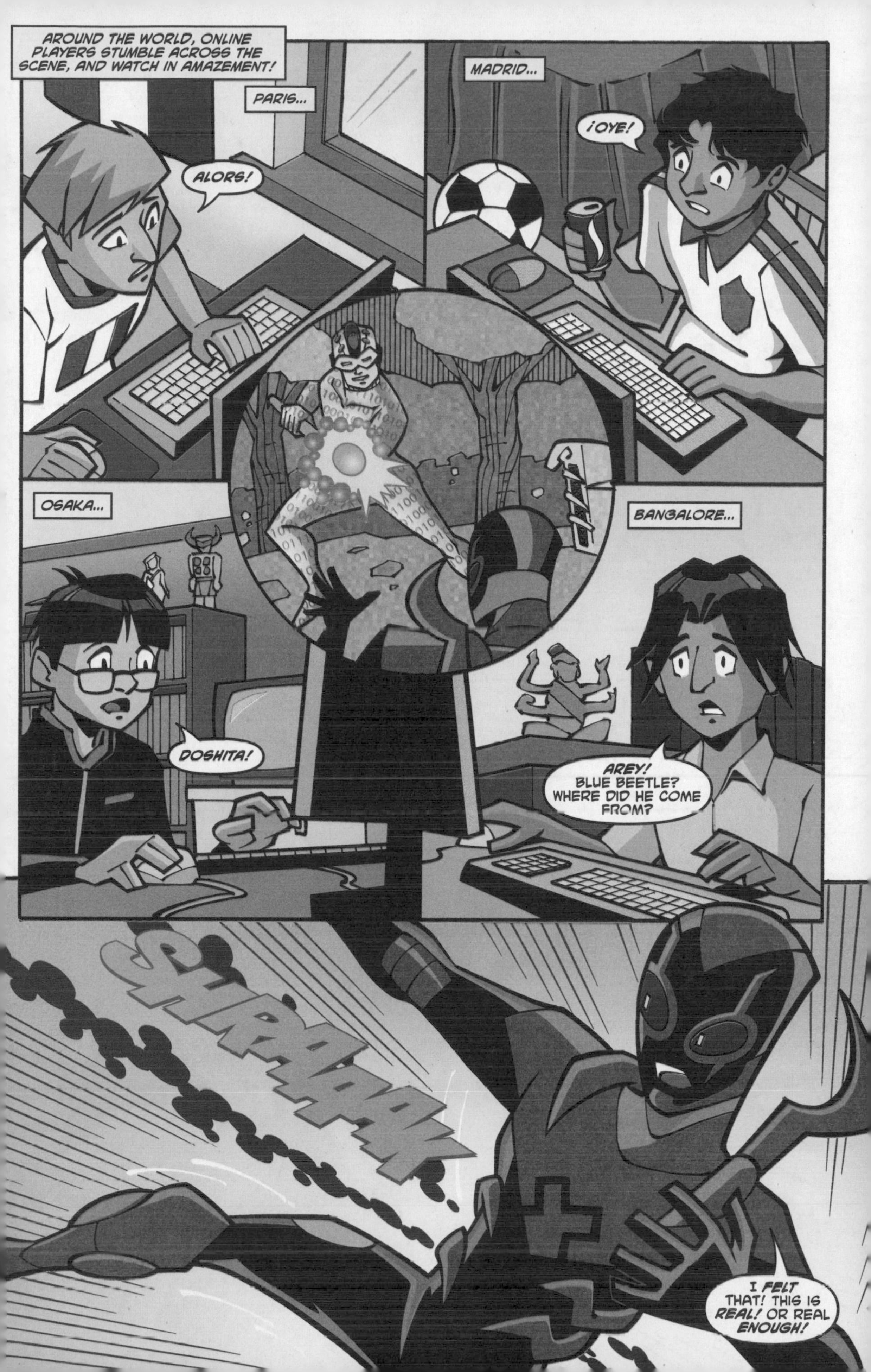
AROUND THE WORLD, ONLINE PLAYERS STUMBLE ACROSS THE SCENE, AND WATCH IN AMAZEMENT!
PARIS...
ALORS!
MADRID...
¡OYE!
OSAKA...
DOSHITA!
BANGALORE...
AREY! BLUE BEETLE? WHERE DID HE COME FROM?
SHRAAAK
I FELT THAT! THIS IS REAL! OR REAL ENOUGH!

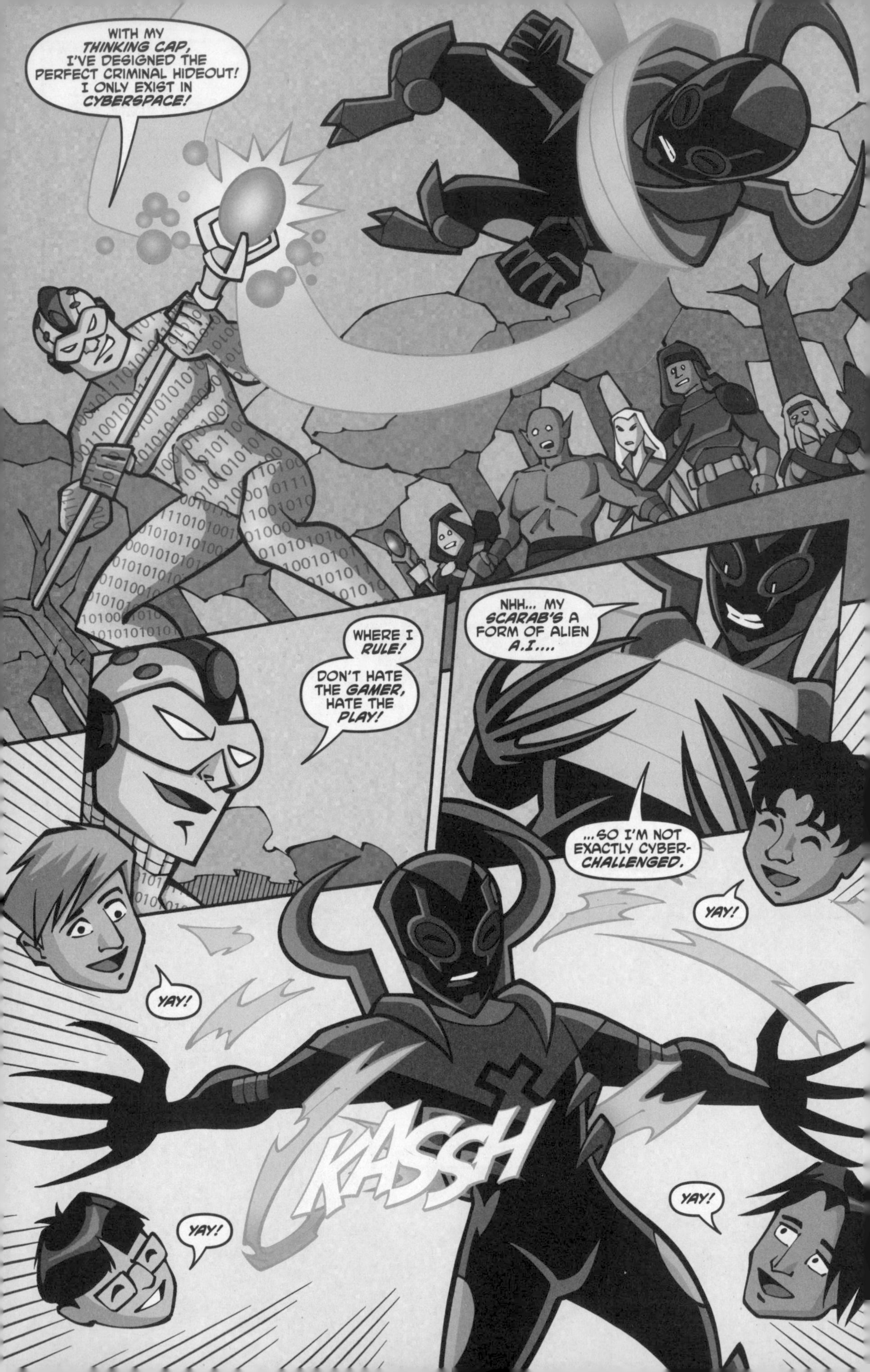
WITH MY THINKING CAP, I'VE DESIGNED THE PERFECT CRIMINAL HIDEOUT! I ONLY EXIST IN CYBERSPACE!
WHERE I RULE!
DON'T HATE THE GAMER, HATE THE PLAY!
NHH... MY SCARAB'S A FORM OF ALIEN A.I....
...SO I'M NOT EXACTLY CYBER-CHALLENGED.
YAY!
YAY!
KASSH
YAY!
YAY!

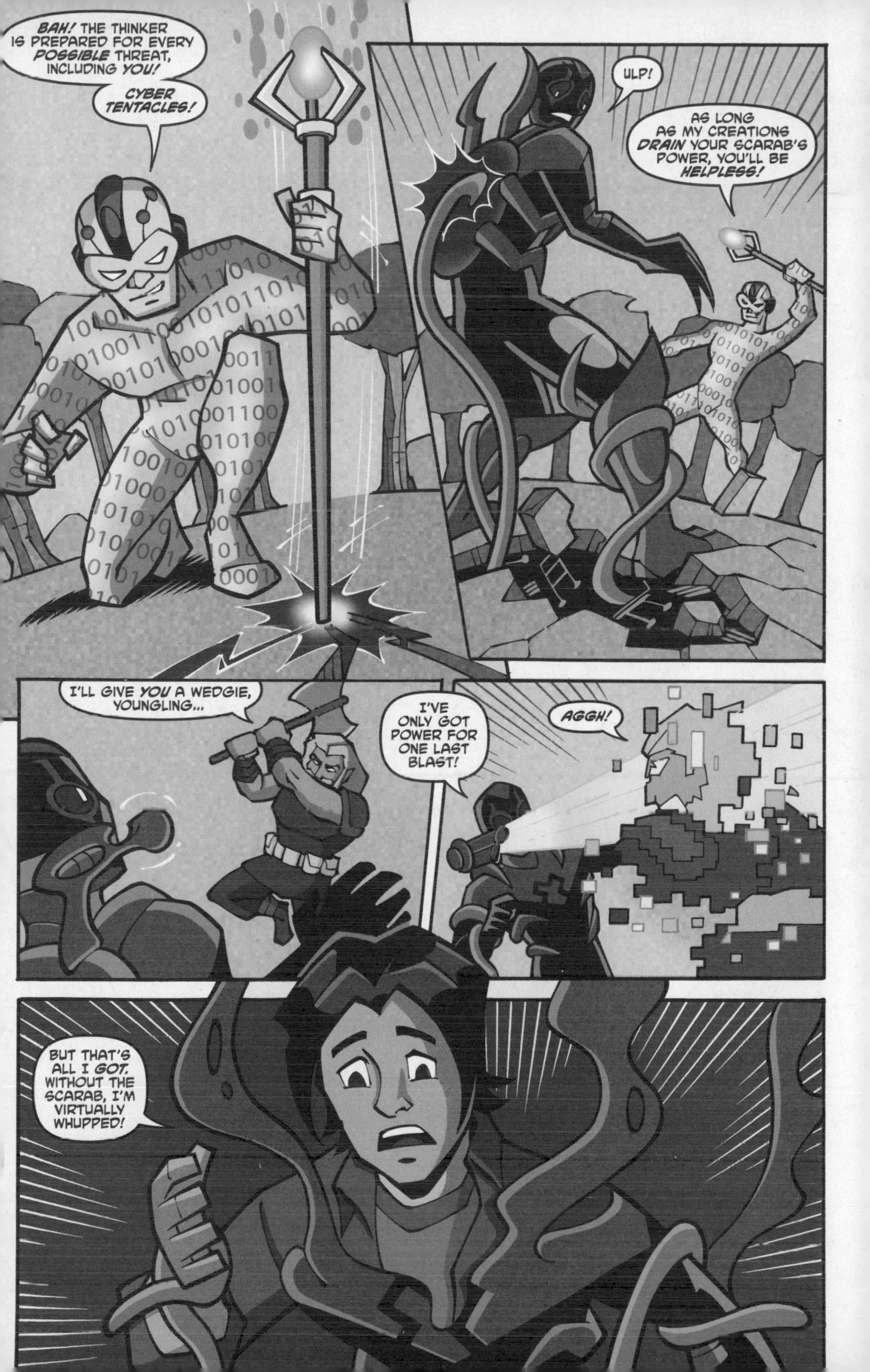
BAH! THE THINKER IS PREPARED FOR EVERY POSSIBLE THREAT, INCLUDING YOU!
CYBER TENTACLES!
ULP!
AS LONG AS MY CREATIONS DRAIN YOUR SCARAB'S POWER, YOU'LL BE HELPLESS!
I'LL GIVE YOU A WEDGIE, YOUNGLING...
I'VE ONLY GOT POWER FOR ONE LAST BLAST!
AGGH!
BUT THAT'S ALL I GOT. WITHOUT THE SCARAB, I'M VIRTUALLY WHUPPED!

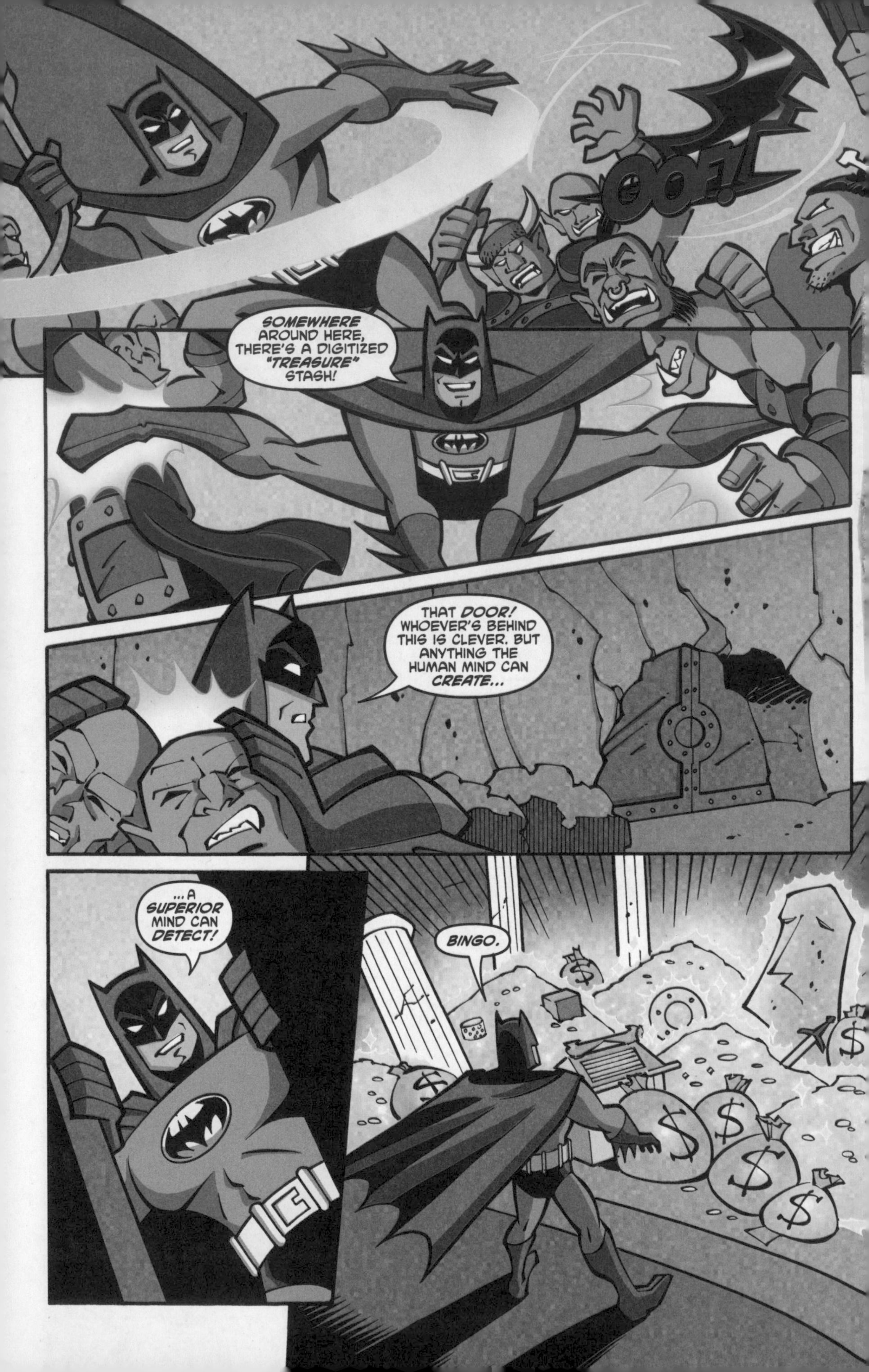
OOF!
SOMEWHERE AROUND HERE, THERE'S A DIGITIZED "TREASURE" STASH!
THAT DOOR! WHOEVER'S BEHIND THIS IS CLEVER. BUT ANYTHING THE HUMAN MIND CAN CREATE...
...A SUPERIOR MIND CAN DETECT!
BINGO.

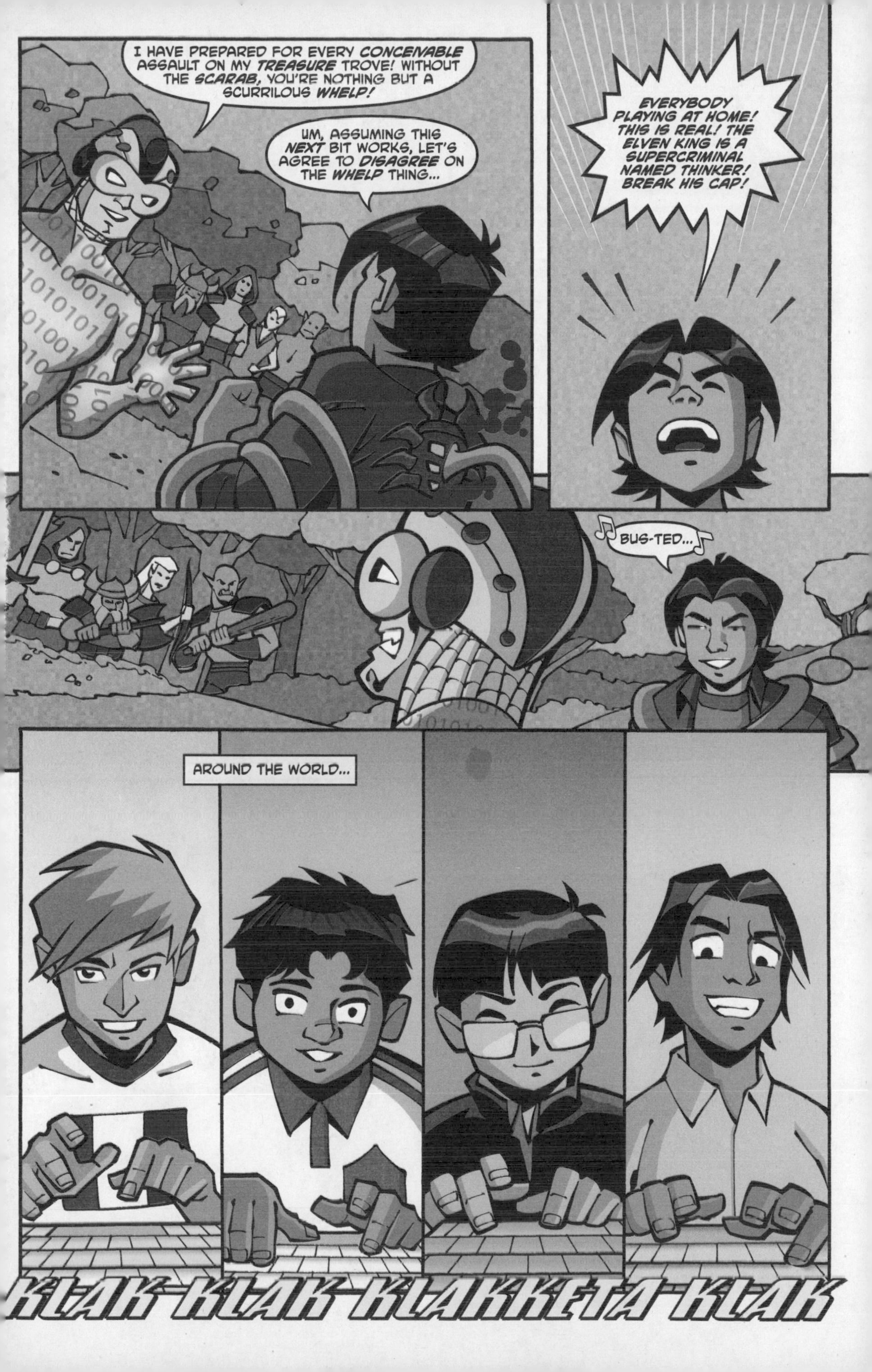
I HAVE PREPARED FOR EVERY CONCEIVABLE ASSAULT ON MY TREASURE TROVE! WITHOUT THE SCARAB, YOU'RE NOTHING BUT A SCURRILOUS WHELP!
UM, ASSUMING THIS NEXT BIT WORKS, LET'S AGREE TO DISAGREE ON THE WHELP THING...
EVERYBODY PLAYING AT HOME! THIS IS REAL! THE ELVEN KING IS A SUPERCRIMINAL NAMED THINKER! BREAK HIS CAP!
BUS-TED...
AROUND THE WORLD...
KLAK KLAK KLAKKETA KLAK

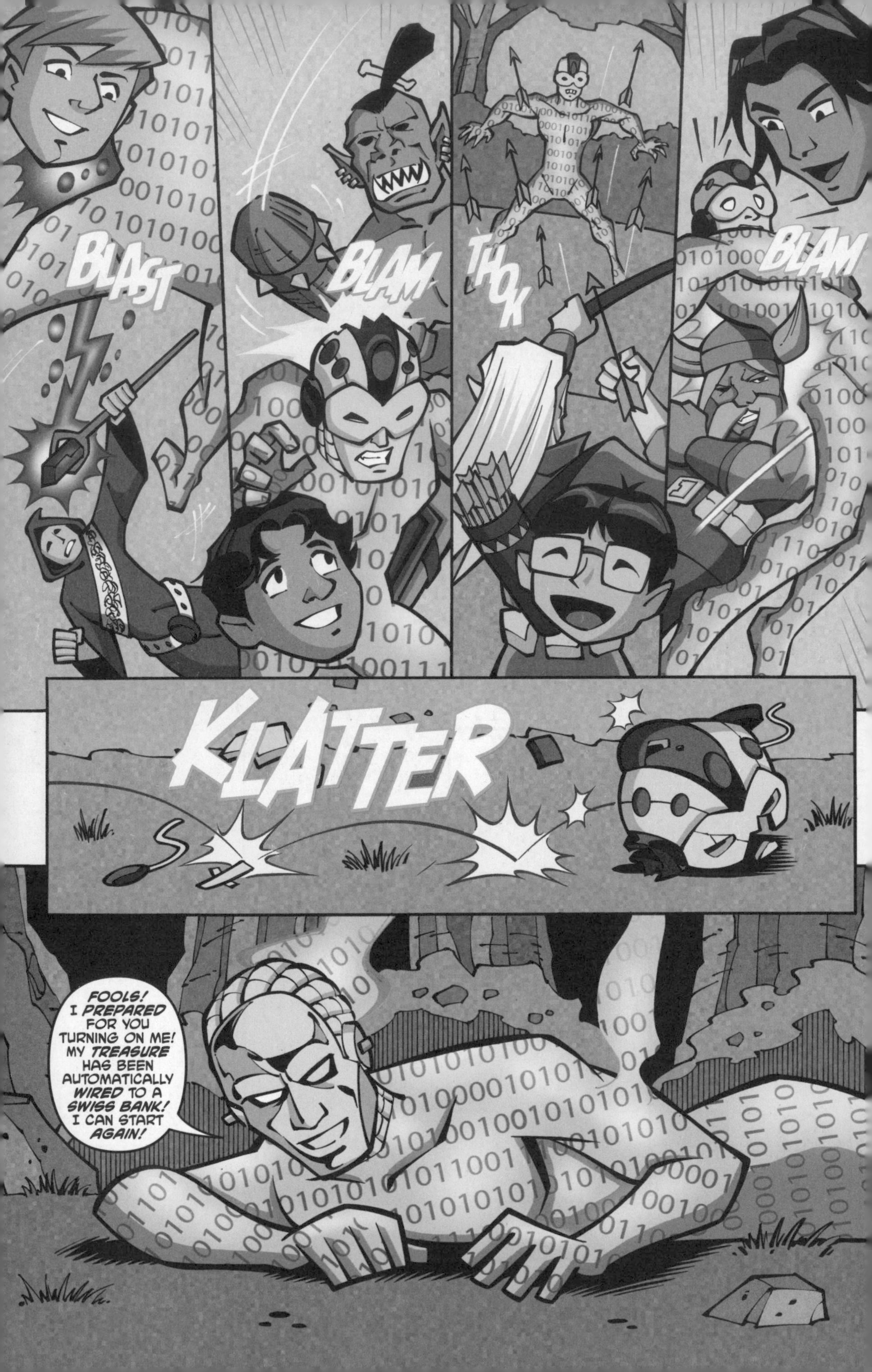
BLAST
BLAM
THOK
BLAM
KLATTER
FOOLS! I PREPARED FOR YOU TURNING ON ME! MY TREASURE HAS BEEN AUTOMATICALLY WIRED TO A SWISS BANK! I CAN START AGAIN!

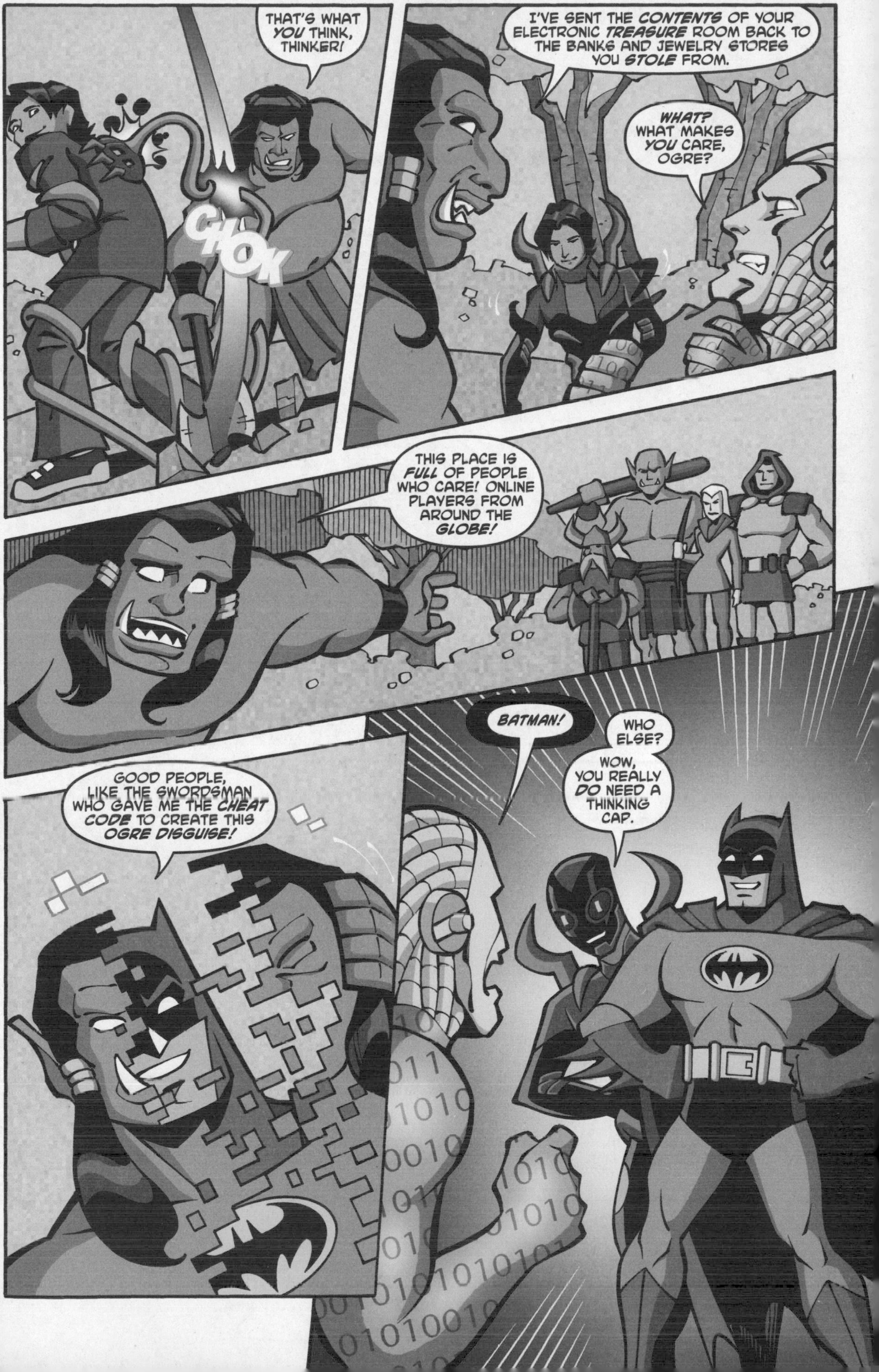
THAT'S WHAT *YOU* THINK, THINKER!
CHOK
I'VE SENT THE *CONTENTS* OF YOUR ELECTRONIC *TREASURE* ROOM BACK TO THE BANKS AND JEWELRY STORES YOU *STOLE* FROM.
WHAT? WHAT MAKES *YOU* CARE, OGRE?
THIS PLACE IS *FULL* OF PEOPLE WHO CARE! ONLINE PLAYERS FROM AROUND THE *GLOBE!*
GOOD PEOPLE, LIKE THE SWORDSMAN WHO GAVE ME THE *CHEAT CODE* TO CREATE THIS *OGRE DISGUISE!*
BATMAN!
WHO ELSE?
WOW, YOU REALLY *DO* NEED A THINKING CAP.

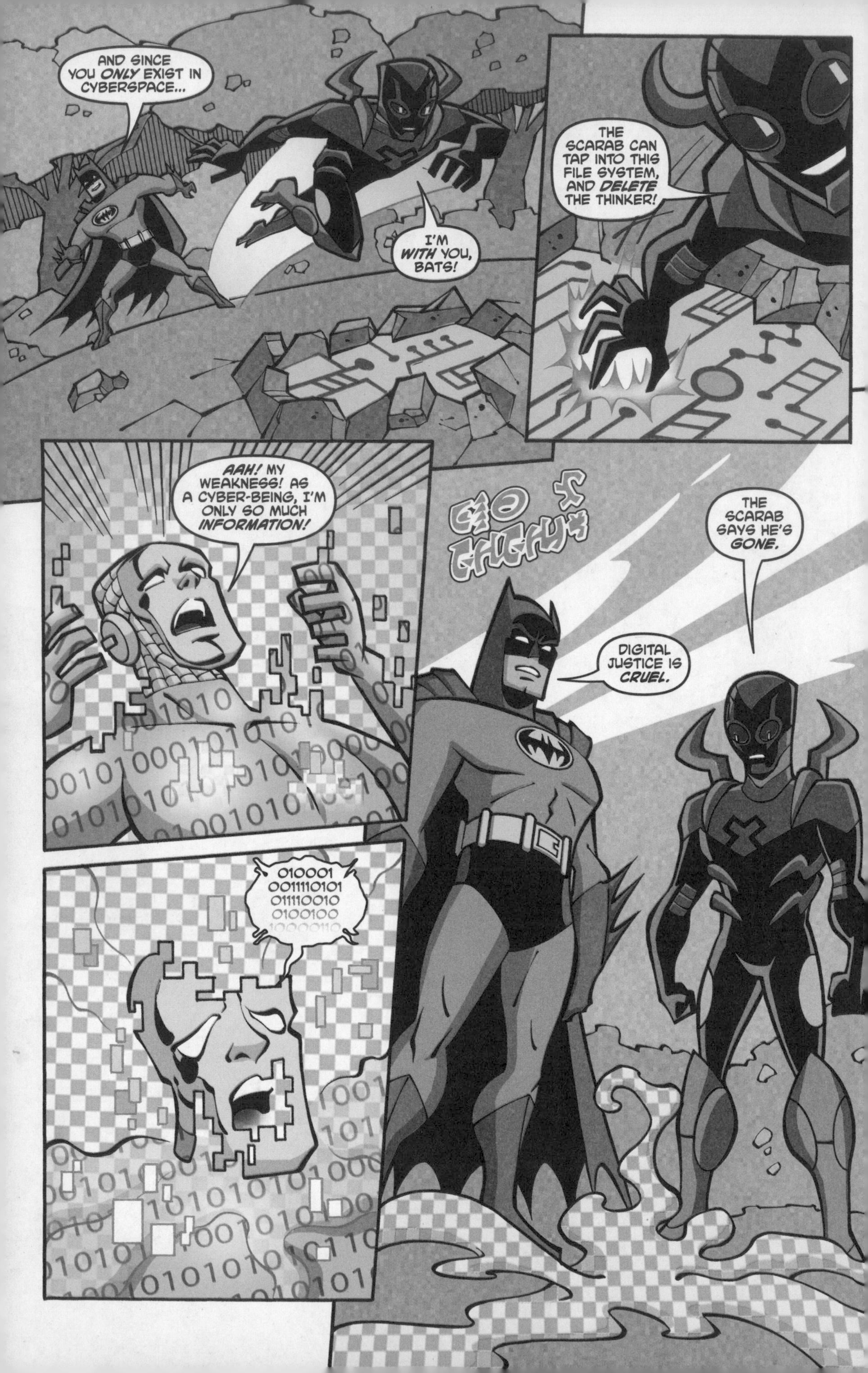
AND SINCE YOU ONLY EXIST IN CYBERSPACE...
I'M WITH YOU, BATS!
THE SCARAB CAN TAP INTO THIS FILE SYSTEM, AND DELETE THE THINKER!
AAH! MY WEAKNESS! AS A CYBER-BEING, I'M ONLY SO MUCH INFORMATION!
010001
0011110101
011110010
0100100
THE SCARAB SAYS HE'S GONE.
DIGITAL JUSTICE IS CRUEL.

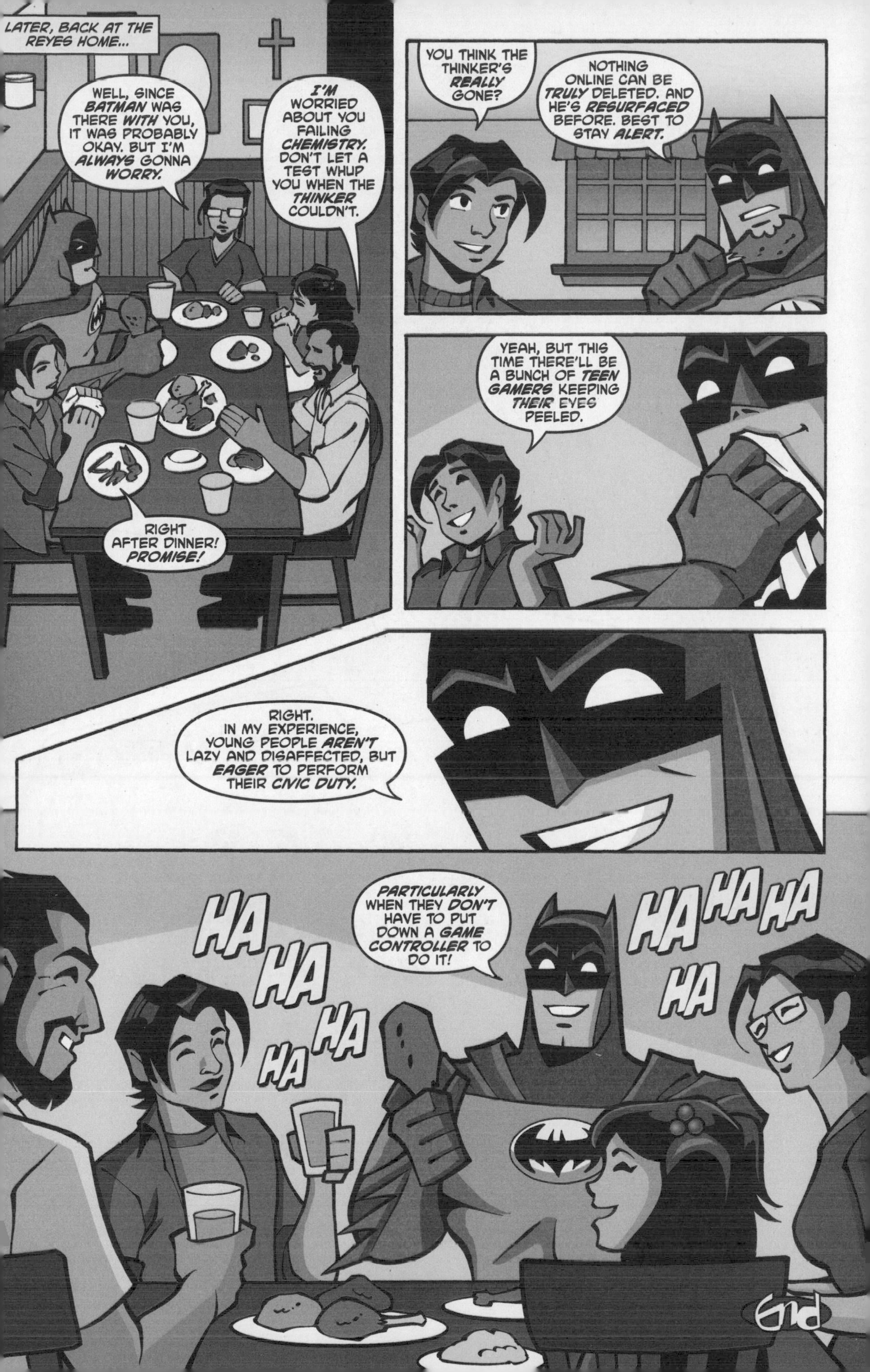
LATER, BACK AT THE REYES HOME...
WELL, SINCE BATMAN WAS THERE WITH YOU, IT WAS PROBABLY OKAY. BUT I'M ALWAYS GONNA WORRY.
I'M WORRIED ABOUT YOU FAILING CHEMISTRY. DON'T LET A TEST WHUP YOU WHEN THE THINKER COULDN'T.
RIGHT AFTER DINNER! PROMISE!
YOU THINK THE THINKER'S REALLY GONE?
NOTHING ONLINE CAN BE TRULY DELETED. AND HE'S RESURFACED BEFORE. BEST TO STAY ALERT.
YEAH, BUT THIS TIME THERE'LL BE A BUNCH OF TEEN GAMERS KEEPING THEIR EYES PEELED.
RIGHT. IN MY EXPERIENCE, YOUNG PEOPLE AREN'T LAZY AND DISAFFECTED, BUT EAGER TO PERFORM THEIR CIVIC DUTY.
HA HA HA HA HA
PARTICULARLY WHEN THEY DON'T HAVE TO PUT DOWN A GAME CONTROLLER TO DO IT!
HA HA HA HA HA
End

THE THINKER:

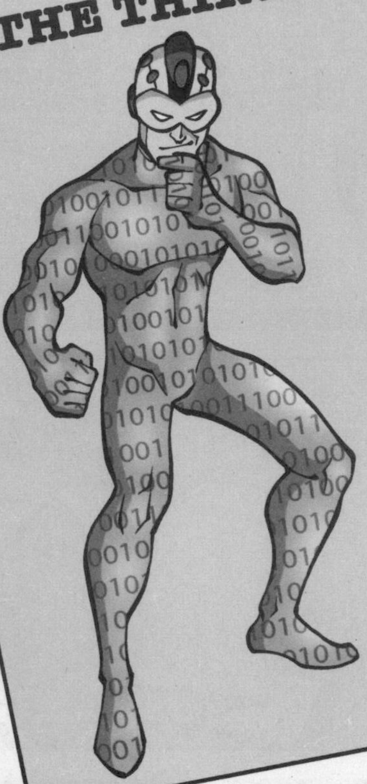

The Thinker stole his thinking cap from a government agency– the first of many bad ideas. He soon found his mental capacity greatly increased. But he still wasn't smart enough to turn down a life of crime.

TOP SECRET:
A heist gone bad left the Thinker without a physical body. He now only exists in cyberspace.

BLUE BEETLE:

An American teen living in El Paso, JAIME REYES is the third hero to call himself BLUE BEETLE. The "scarab" attached to the base of Beetle's spine is an alien artifical-intelligence creature called Khadji-Da, which can grow armor and a slew of different wings, blades and energy weapons.

TOP SECRET:
In winter when the sun goes down early, Jaime takes the trash out for his sister, because she is secretly afraid of the dark.

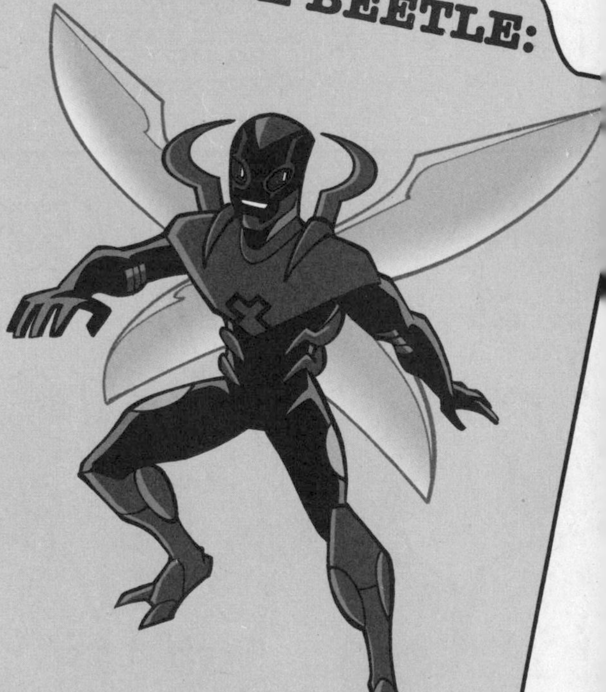

BATMAN: THE BRAVE AND THE BOLD #3
Cover by Scott Jeralds with Hi-Fi

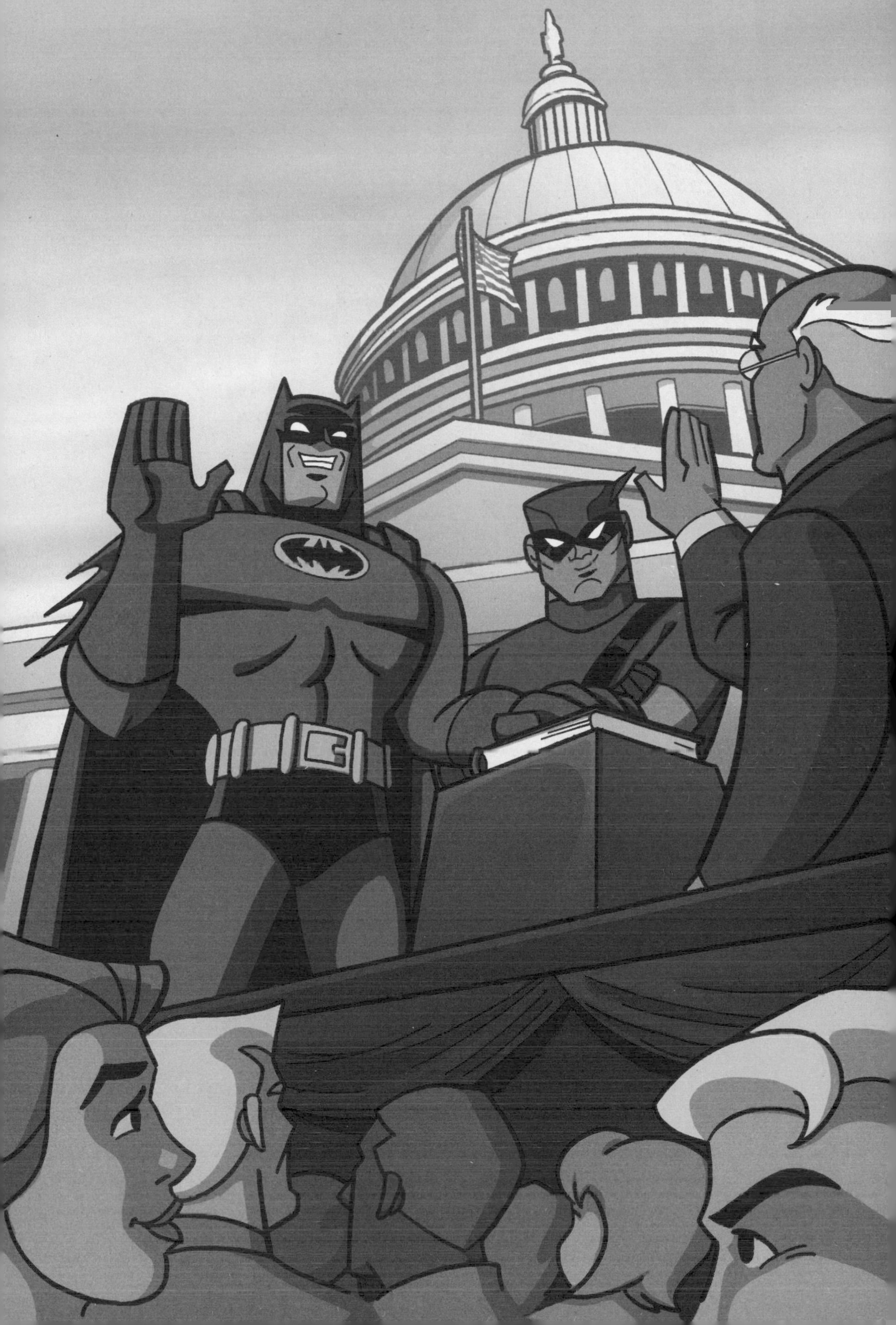

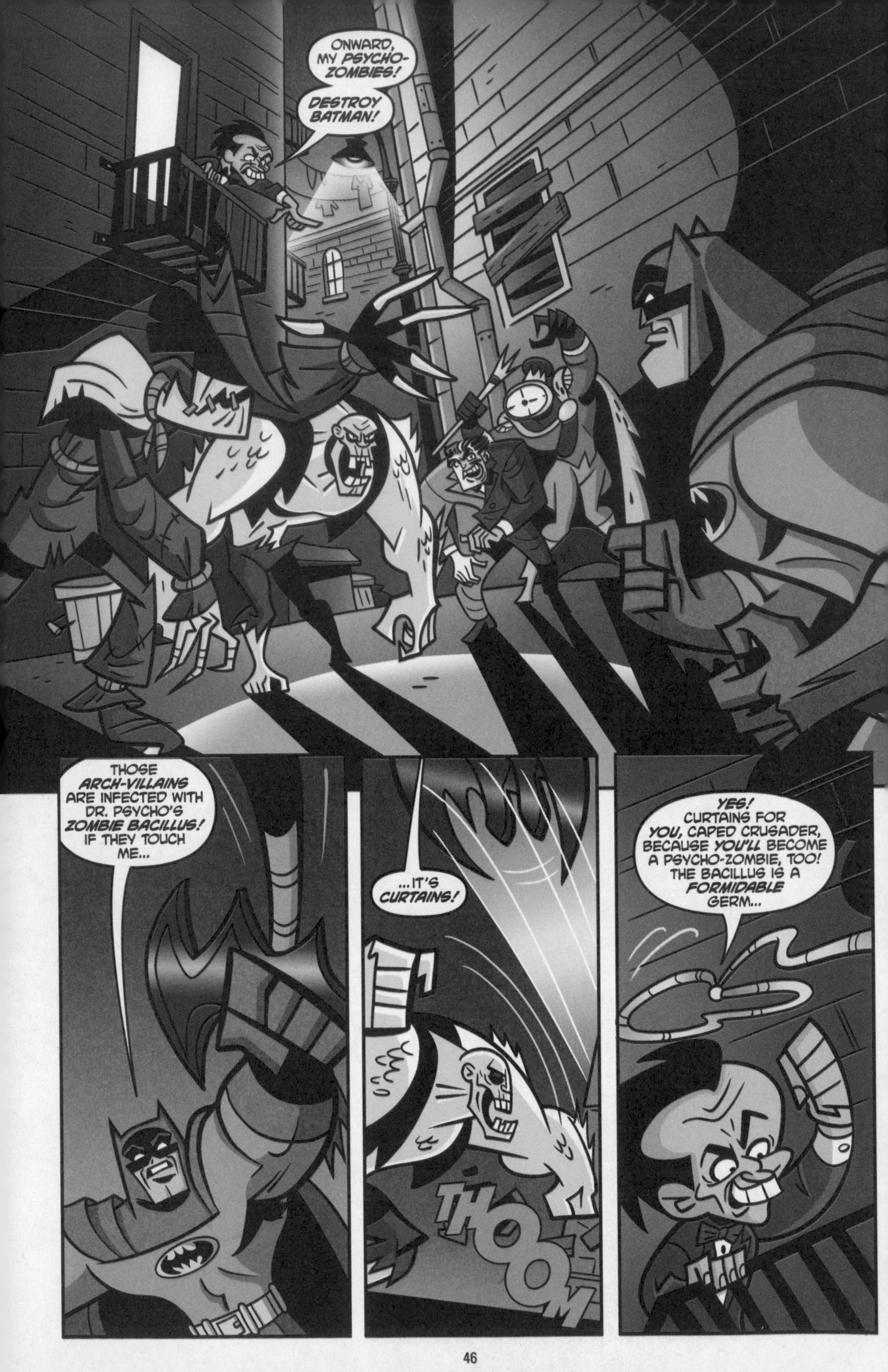
ONWARD, MY PSYCHO-ZOMBIES!
DESTROY BATMAN!
THOSE ARCH-VILLAINS ARE INFECTED WITH DR. PSYCHO'S ZOMBIE BACILLUS! IF THEY TOUCH ME...
...IT'S CURTAINS!
THOOOM
YES! CURTAINS FOR YOU, CAPED CRUSADER, BECAUSE YOU'LL BECOME A PSYCHO-ZOMBIE, TOO! THE BACILLUS IS A FORMIDABLE GERM...

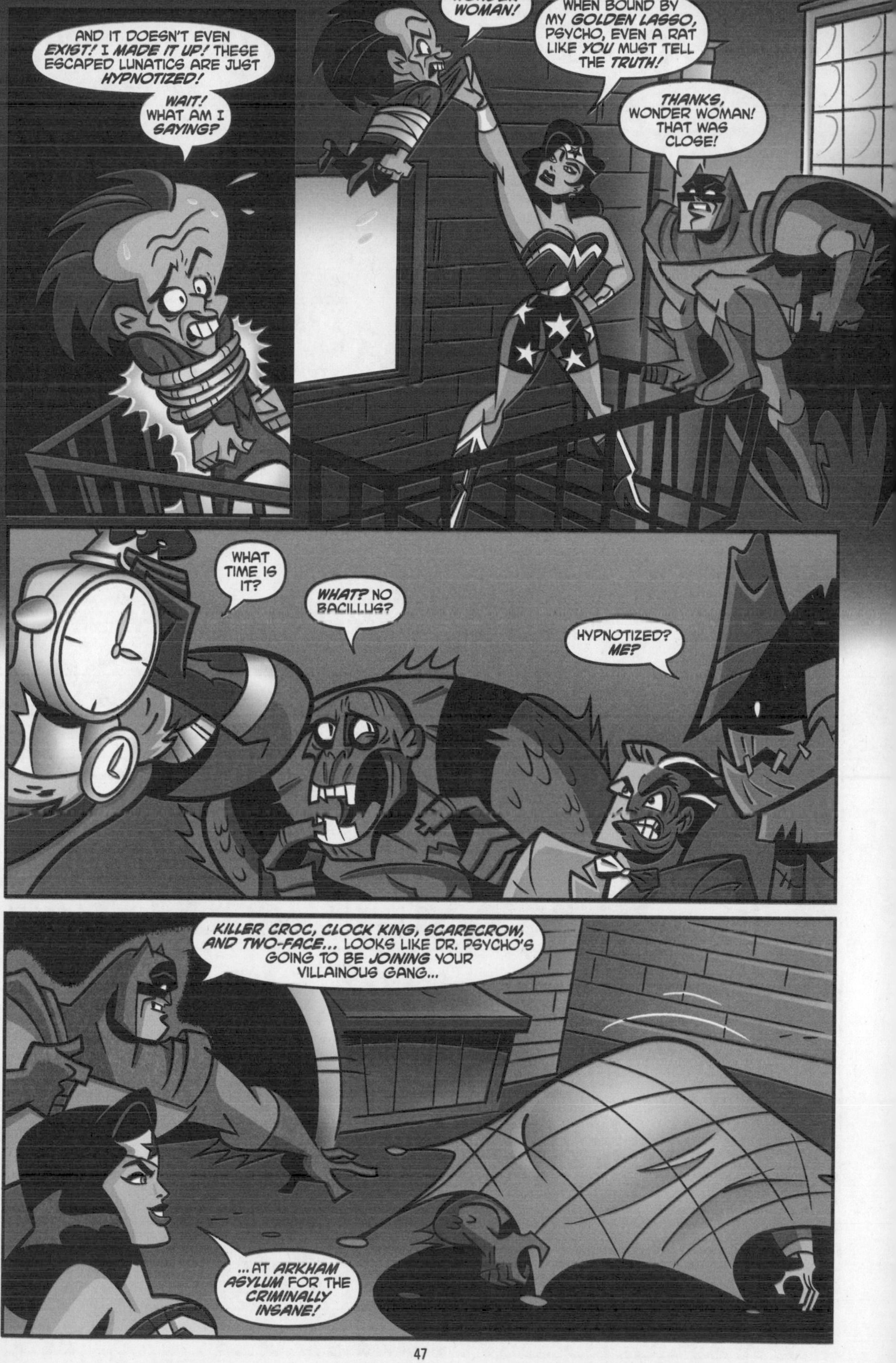
AND IT DOESN'T EVEN EXIST! I MADE IT UP! THESE ESCAPED LUNATICS ARE JUST HYPNOTIZED!
WAIT! WHAT AM I SAYING?
WONDER WOMAN!
WHEN BOUND BY MY GOLDEN LASSO, PSYCHO, EVEN A RAT LIKE YOU MUST TELL THE TRUTH!
THANKS, WONDER WOMAN! THAT WAS CLOSE!
WHAT TIME IS IT?
WHAT? NO BACILLUS?
HYPNOTIZED? ME?
KILLER CROC, CLOCK KING, SCARECROW, AND TWO-FACE... LOOKS LIKE DR. PSYCHO'S GOING TO BE JOINING YOUR VILLAINOUS GANG...
...AT ARKHAM ASYLUM FOR THE CRIMINALLY INSANE!

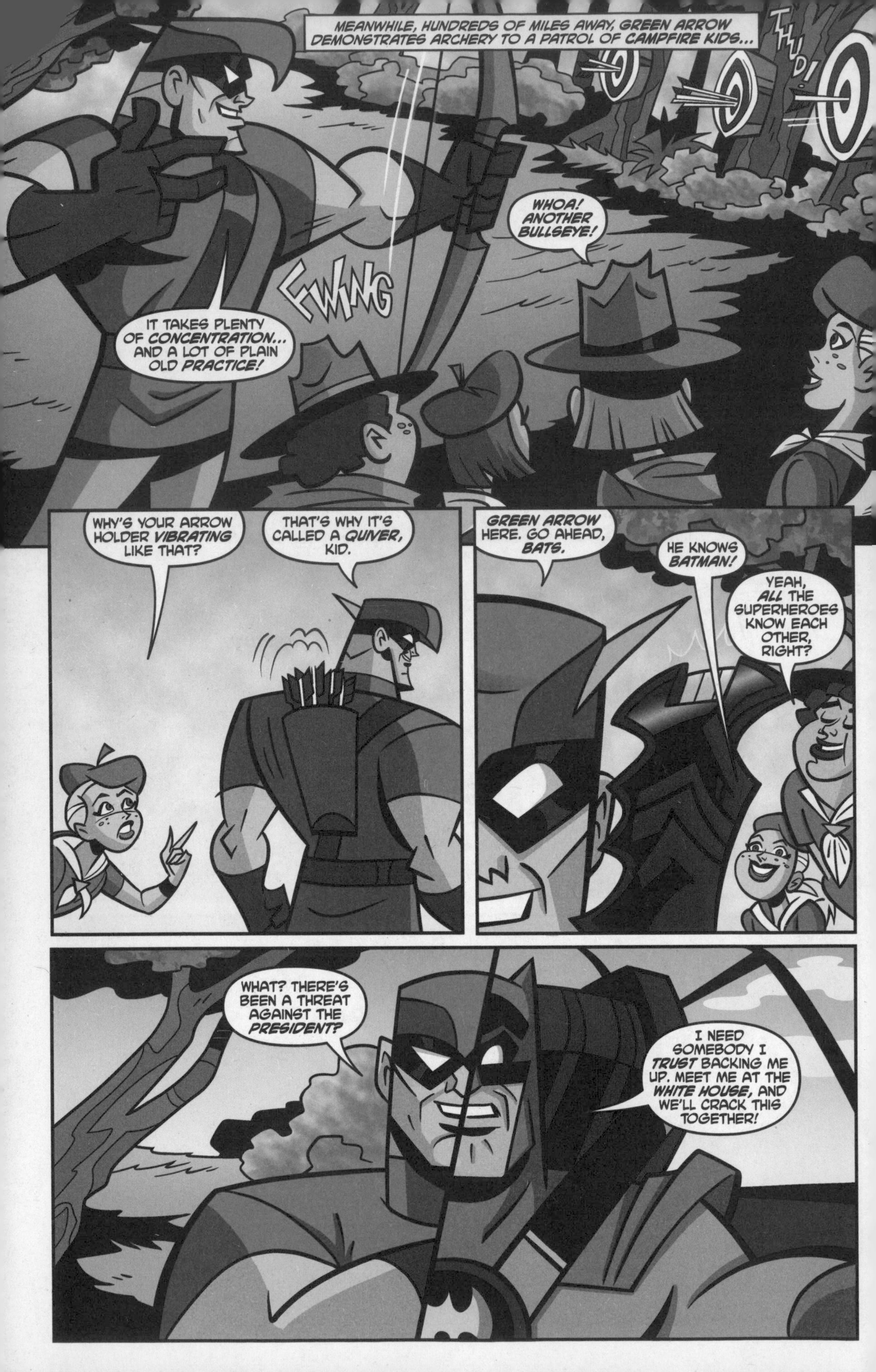

MEANWHILE, HUNDREDS OF MILES AWAY, GREEN ARROW DEMONSTRATES ARCHERY TO A PATROL OF CAMPFIRE KIDS...
THUD!
FWING
WHOA! ANOTHER BULLSEYE!
IT TAKES PLENTY OF CONCENTRATION... AND A LOT OF PLAIN OLD PRACTICE!
WHY'S YOUR ARROW HOLDER VIBRATING LIKE THAT?
THAT'S WHY IT'S CALLED A QUIVER, KID.
GREEN ARROW HERE. GO AHEAD, BATS.
HE KNOWS BATMAN!
YEAH, ALL THE SUPERHEROES KNOW EACH OTHER, RIGHT?
WHAT? THERE'S BEEN A THREAT AGAINST THE PRESIDENT?
I NEED SOMEBODY I TRUST BACKING ME UP. MEET ME AT THE WHITE HOUSE, AND WE'LL CRACK THIS TOGETHER!

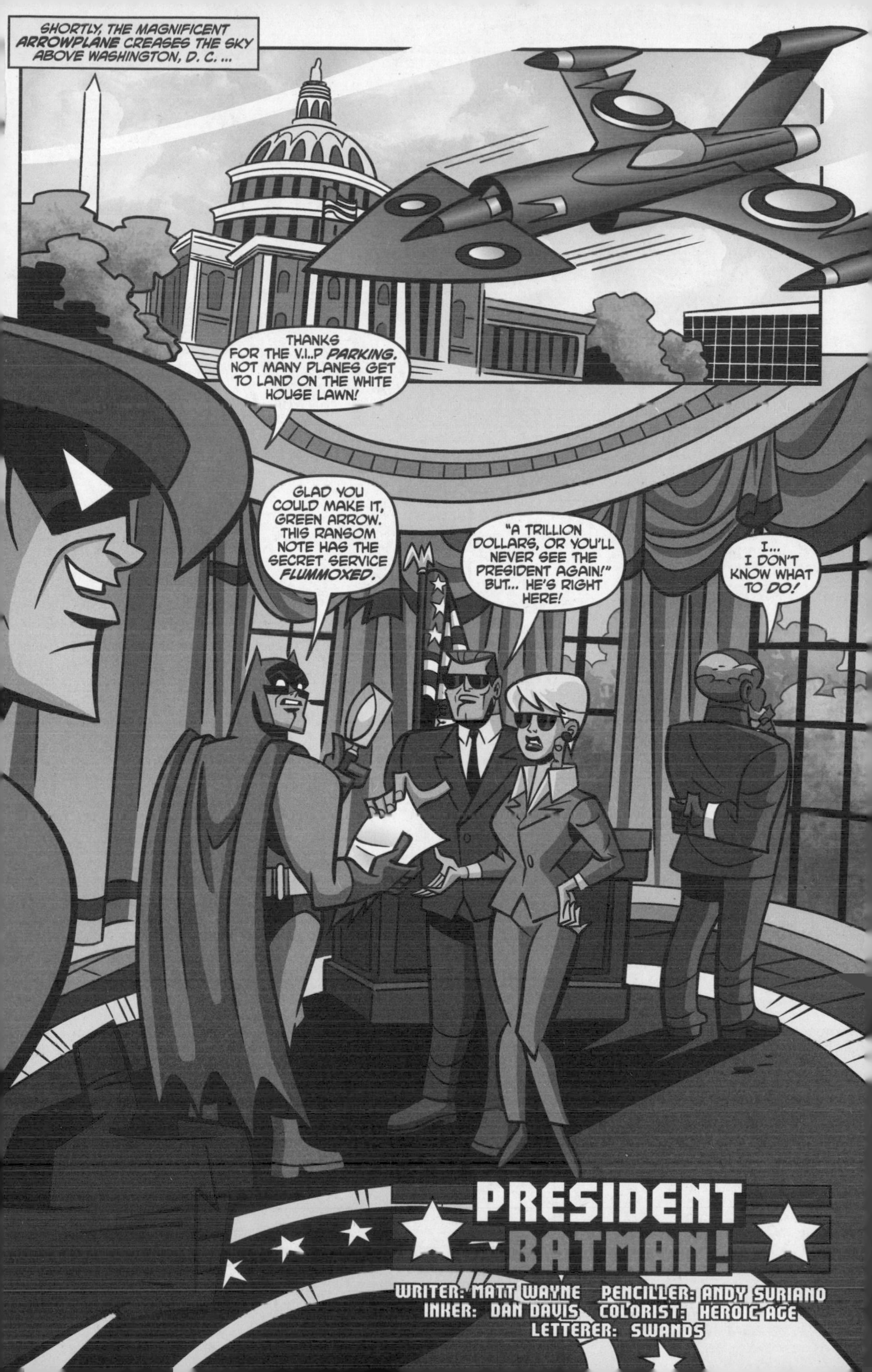
SHORTLY, THE MAGNIFICENT ARROWPLANE CREASES THE SKY ABOVE WASHINGTON, D. C. ...
THANKS FOR THE V.I.P PARKING. NOT MANY PLANES GET TO LAND ON THE WHITE HOUSE LAWN!
GLAD YOU COULD MAKE IT, GREEN ARROW. THIS RANSOM NOTE HAS THE SECRET SERVICE FLUMMOXED.
"A TRILLION DOLLARS, OR YOU'LL NEVER SEE THE PRESIDENT AGAIN!" BUT... HE'S RIGHT HERE!
I... I DON'T KNOW WHAT TO DO!
PRESIDENT BATMAN!
WRITER: MATT WAYNE PENCILLER: ANDY SURIANO
INKER: DAN DAVIS COLORIST: HEROIC AGE
LETTERER: SWANDS

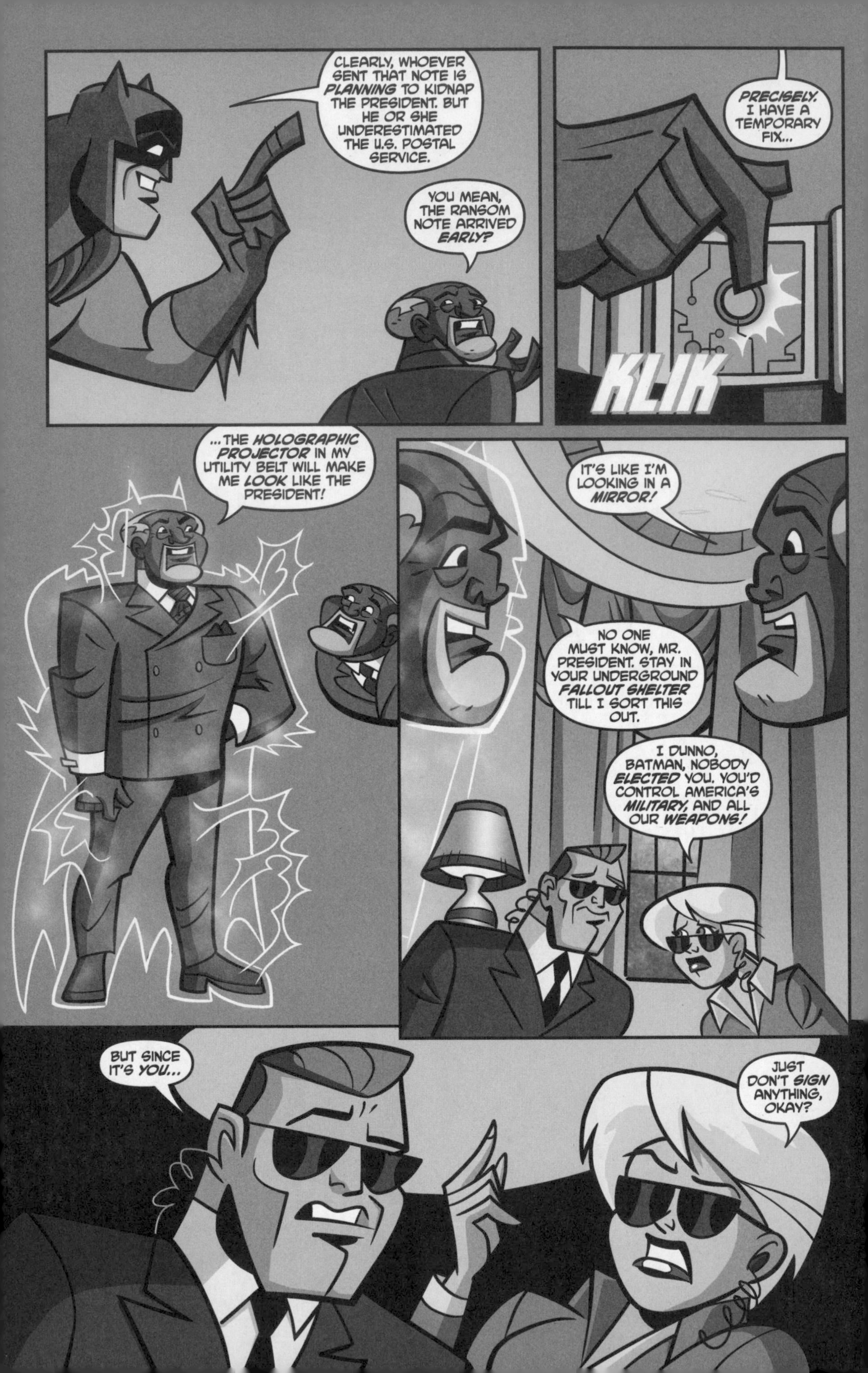
CLEARLY, WHOEVER SENT THAT NOTE IS PLANNING TO KIDNAP THE PRESIDENT. BUT HE OR SHE UNDERESTIMATED THE U.S. POSTAL SERVICE.
YOU MEAN, THE RANSOM NOTE ARRIVED EARLY?
PRECISELY. I HAVE A TEMPORARY FIX...
KLIK
...THE HOLOGRAPHIC PROJECTOR IN MY UTILITY BELT WILL MAKE ME LOOK LIKE THE PRESIDENT!
IT'S LIKE I'M LOOKING IN A MIRROR!
NO ONE MUST KNOW, MR. PRESIDENT. STAY IN YOUR UNDERGROUND FALLOUT SHELTER TILL I SORT THIS OUT.
I DUNNO, BATMAN, NOBODY ELECTED YOU. YOU'D CONTROL AMERICA'S MILITARY, AND ALL OUR WEAPONS!
BUT SINCE IT'S YOU...
JUST DON'T SIGN ANYTHING, OKAY?

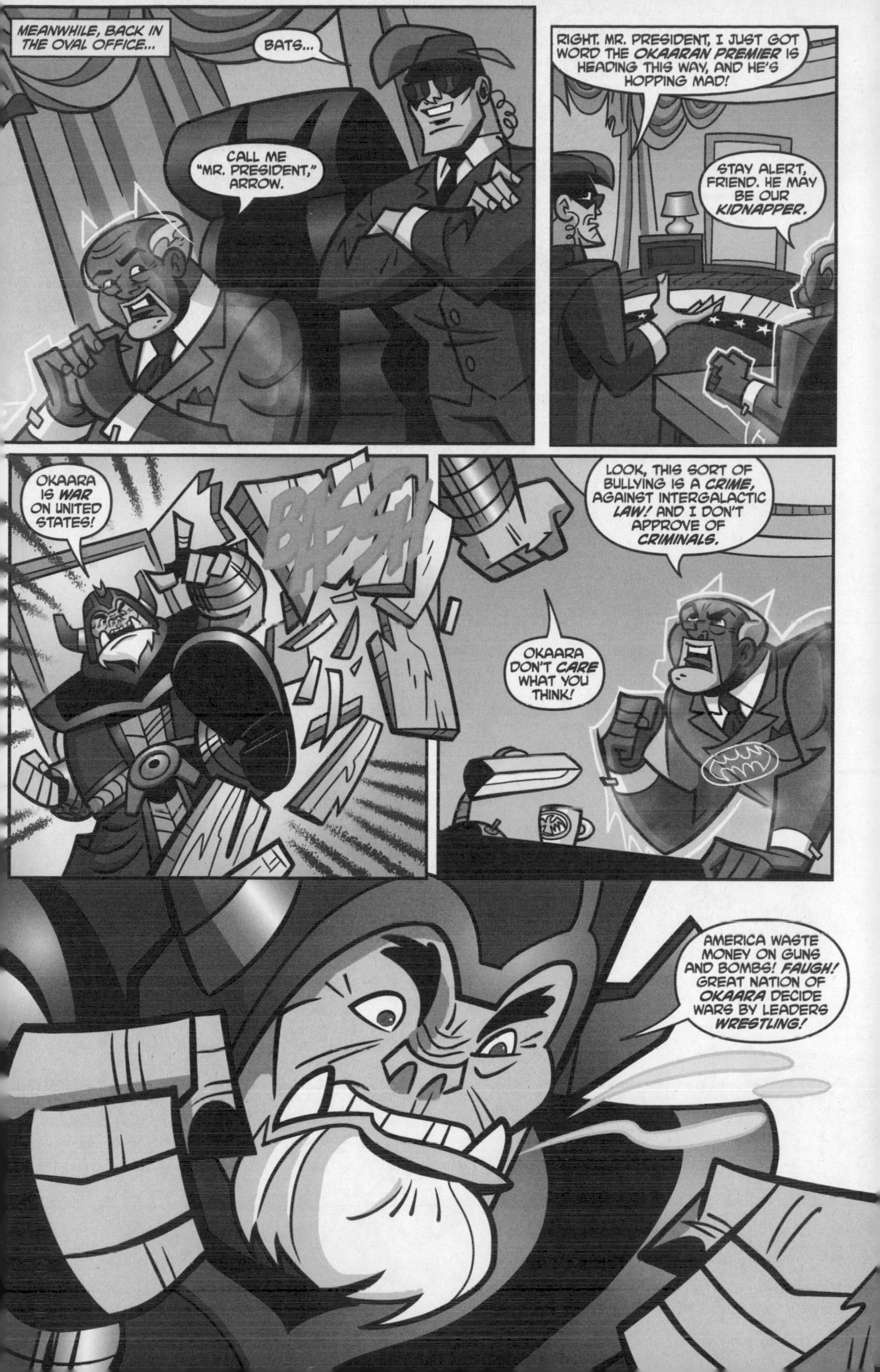

MEANWHILE, BACK IN THE OVAL OFFICE...
BATS...
CALL ME "MR. PRESIDENT," ARROW.
RIGHT. MR. PRESIDENT, I JUST GOT WORD THE OKAARAN PREMIER IS HEADING THIS WAY, AND HE'S HOPPING MAD!
STAY ALERT, FRIEND. HE MAY BE OUR KIDNAPPER.
OKAARA IS WAR ON UNITED STATES!
BASGH
LOOK, THIS SORT OF BULLYING IS A CRIME, AGAINST INTERGALACTIC LAW! AND I DON'T APPROVE OF CRIMINALS.
OKAARA DON'T CARE WHAT YOU THINK!
AMERICA WASTE MONEY ON GUNS AND BOMBS! FAUGH! GREAT NATION OF OKAARA DECIDE WARS BY LEADERS WRESTLING!

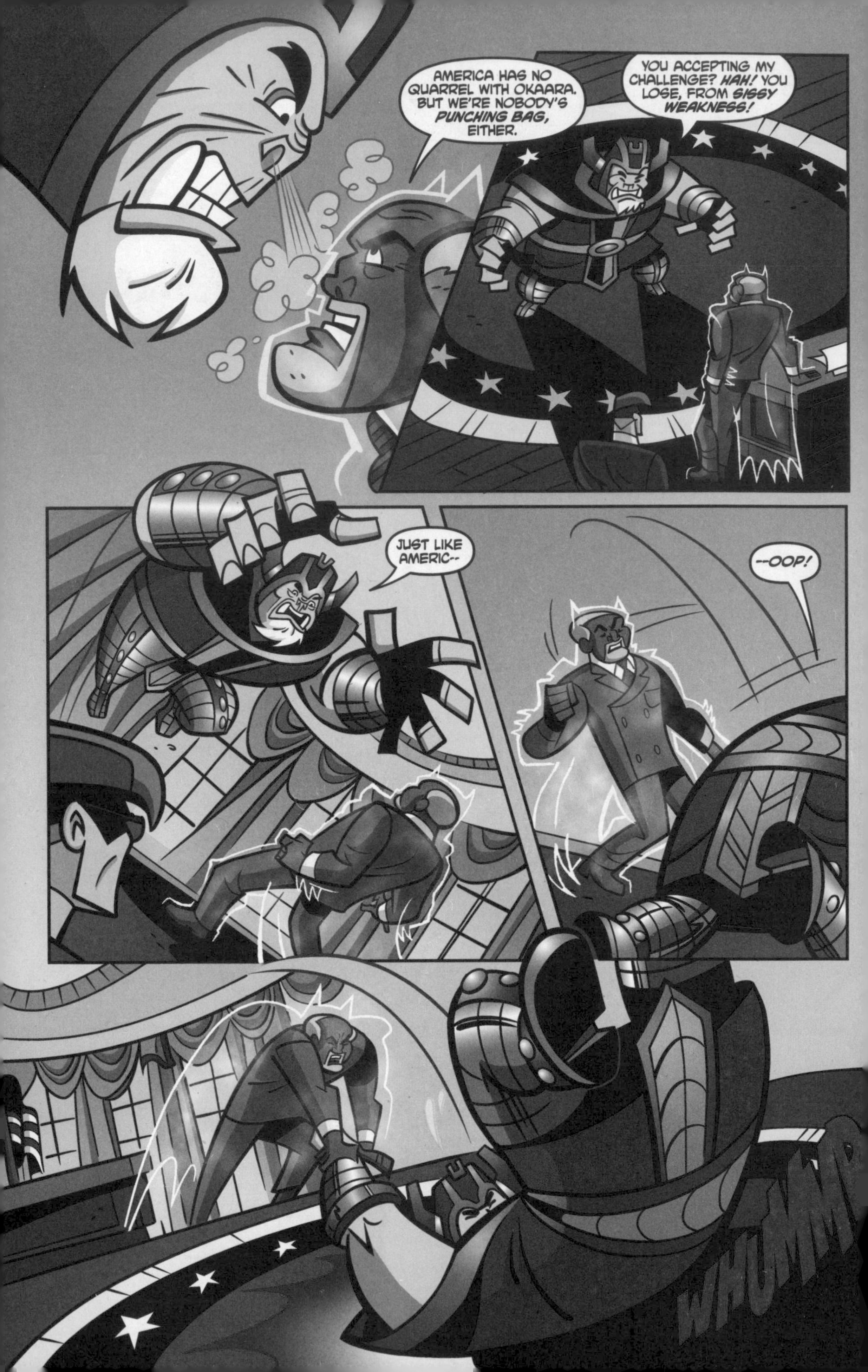
AMERICA HAS NO QUARREL WITH OKAARA. BUT WE'RE NOBODY'S *PUNCHING BAG,* EITHER.
YOU ACCEPTING MY CHALLENGE? *HAH!* YOU LOSE, FROM *SISSY WEAKNESS!*
JUST LIKE AMERIC--
--OOP!
WHUMMP

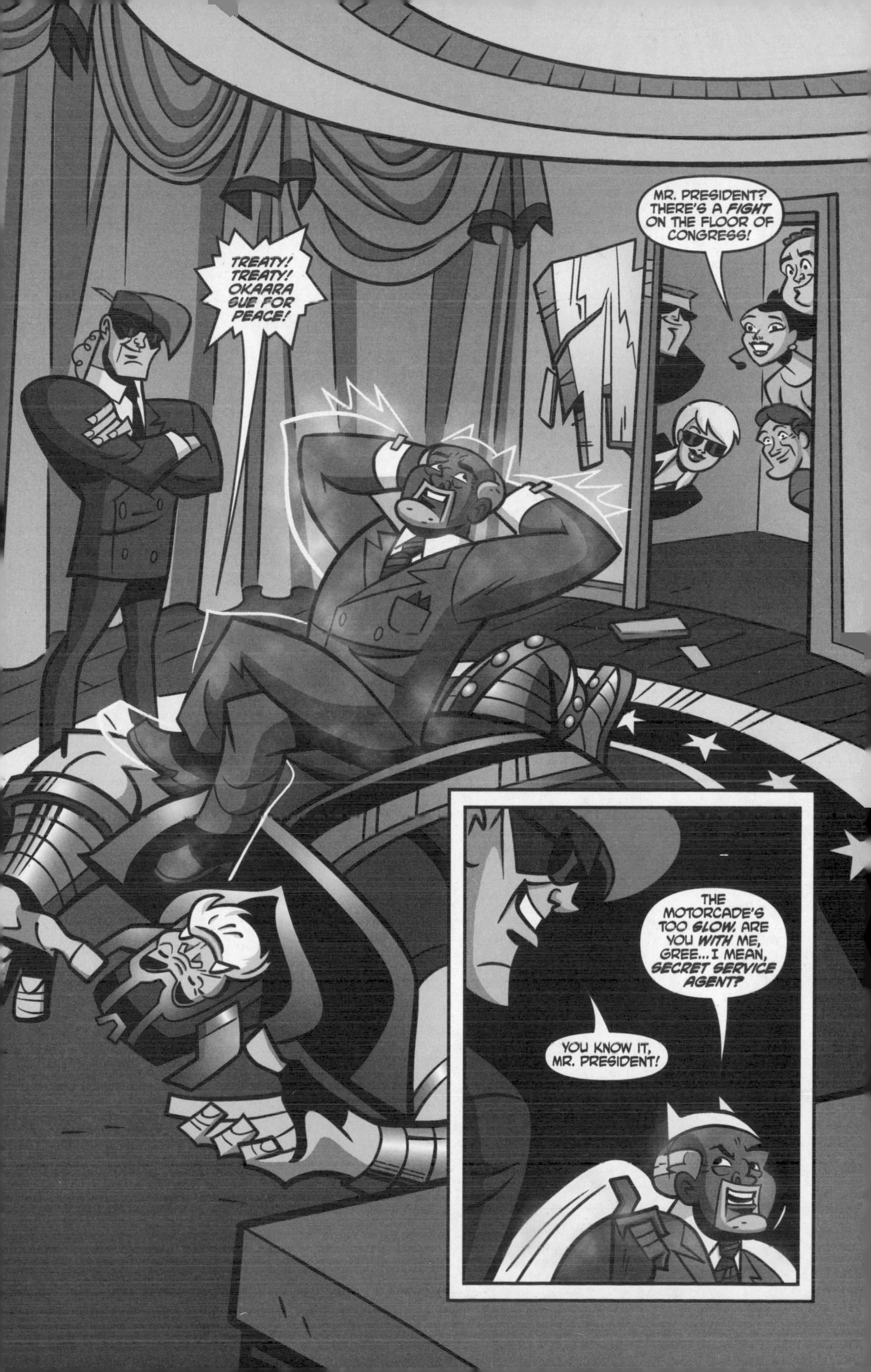
TREATY! TREATY! OKAARA SUE FOR PEACE!
MR. PRESIDENT? THERE'S A *FIGHT* ON THE FLOOR OF CONGRESS!
THE MOTORCADE'S TOO *SLOW.* ARE YOU *WITH* ME, GREE... I MEAN, *SECRET SERVICE AGENT?*
YOU KNOW IT, MR. PRESIDENT!

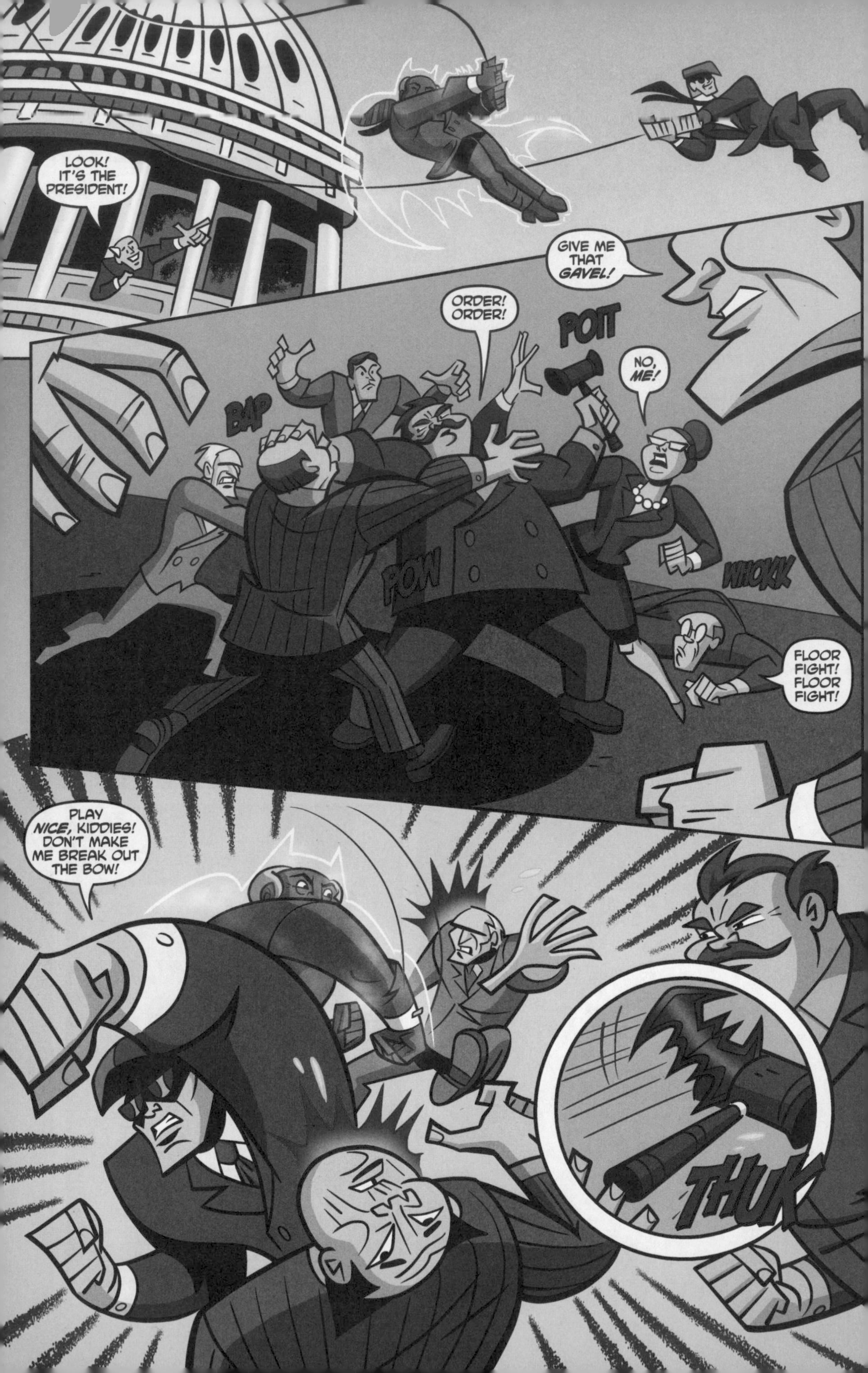
LOOK! IT'S THE PRESIDENT!
GIVE ME THAT GAVEL!
ORDER! ORDER!
POIT
NO, ME!
BAP
POW
WHOKK
FLOOR FIGHT! FLOOR FIGHT!
PLAY NICE, KIDDIES! DON'T MAKE ME BREAK OUT THE BOW!
THUK

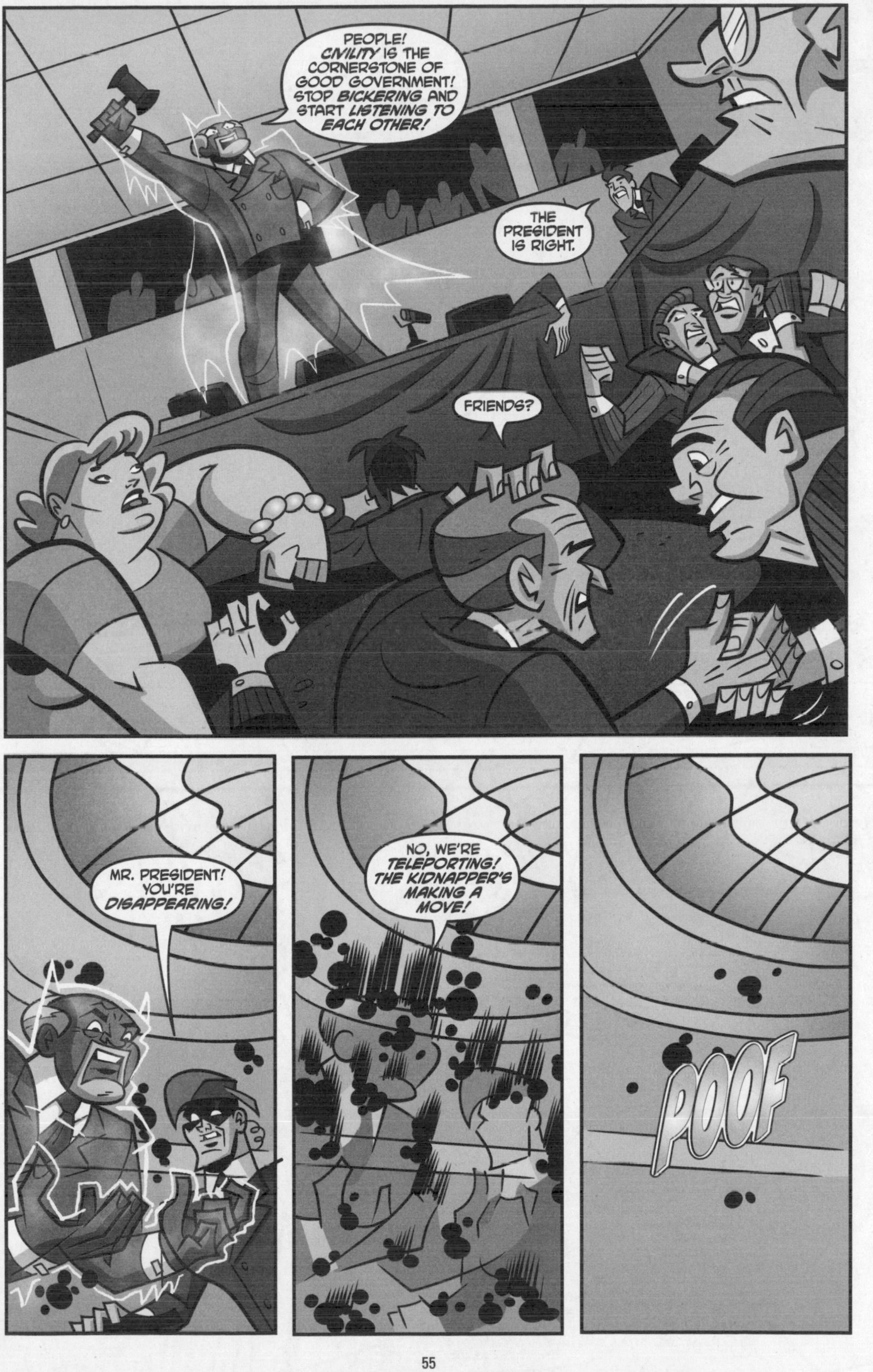
PEOPLE! CIVILITY IS THE CORNERSTONE OF GOOD GOVERNMENT! STOP BICKERING AND START LISTENING TO EACH OTHER!
THE PRESIDENT IS RIGHT.
FRIENDS?
MR. PRESIDENT! YOU'RE DISAPPEARING!
NO, WE'RE TELEPORTING! THE KIDNAPPER'S MAKING A MOVE!
POOF

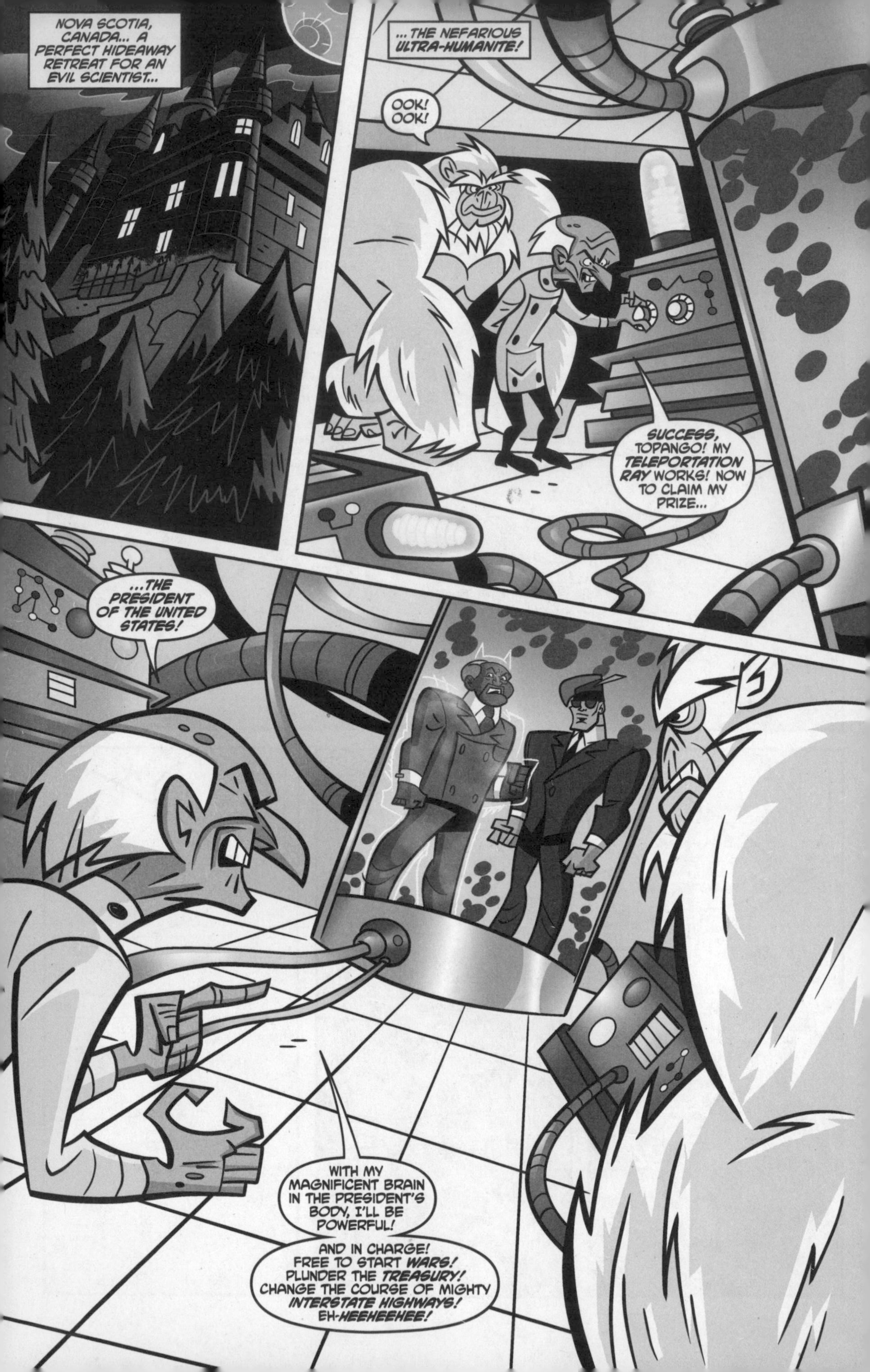
NOVA SCOTIA, CANADA... A PERFECT HIDEAWAY RETREAT FOR AN EVIL SCIENTIST...
...THE NEFARIOUS ULTRA-HUMANITE!
OOK! OOK!
SUCCESS, TOPANGO! MY TELEPORTATION RAY WORKS! NOW TO CLAIM MY PRIZE...
...THE PRESIDENT OF THE UNITED STATES!
WITH MY MAGNIFICENT BRAIN IN THE PRESIDENT'S BODY, I'LL BE POWERFUL!
AND IN CHARGE! FREE TO START WARS! PLUNDER THE TREASURY! CHANGE THE COURSE OF MIGHTY INTERSTATE HIGHWAYS! EH-HEEHEEHEE!

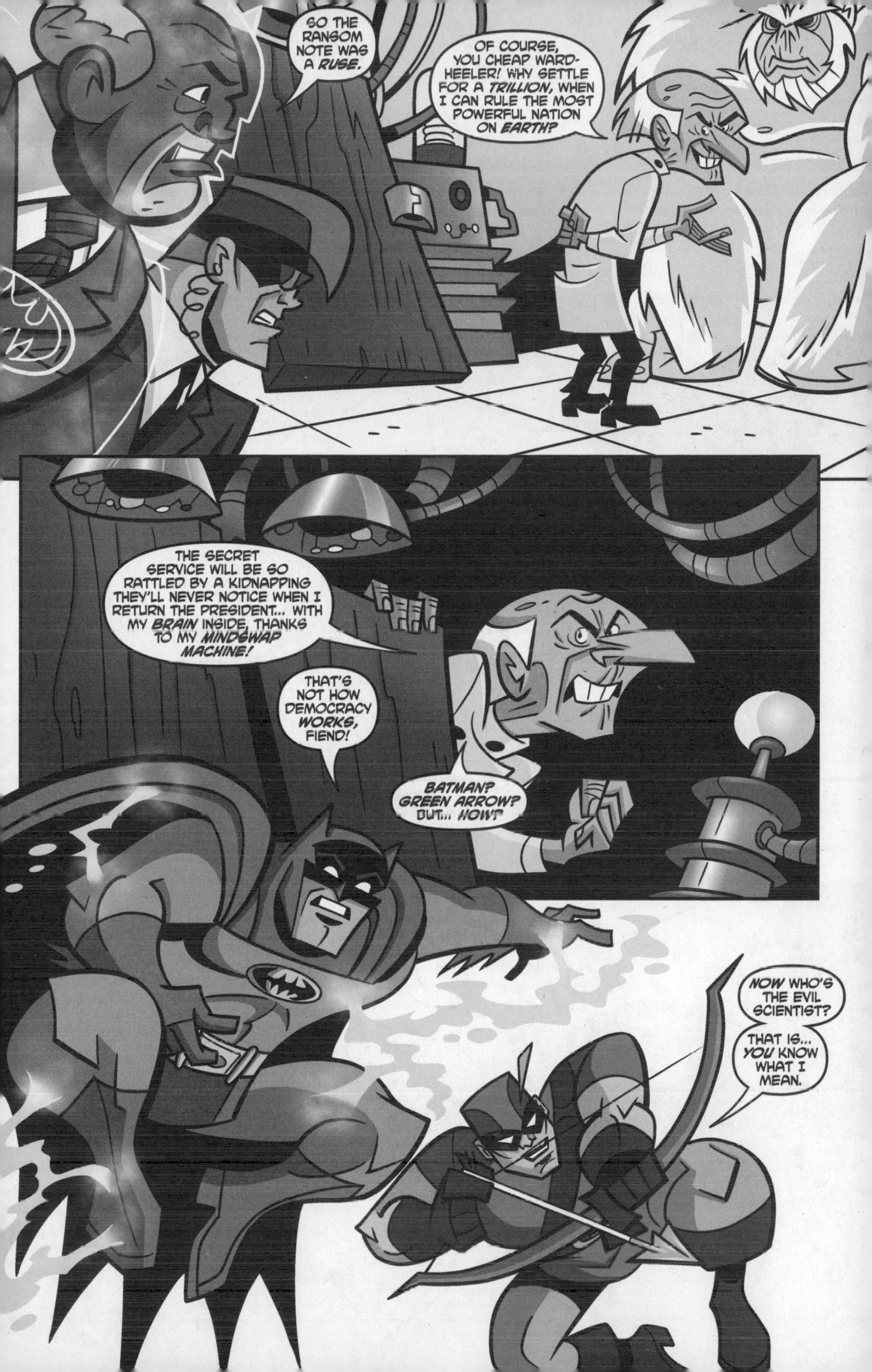
SO THE RANSOM NOTE WAS A *RUSE*.
OF COURSE, YOU CHEAP WARD-HEELER! WHY SETTLE FOR A *TRILLION*, WHEN I CAN RULE THE MOST POWERFUL NATION ON *EARTH*?
THE SECRET SERVICE WILL BE SO RATTLED BY A KIDNAPPING THEY'LL NEVER NOTICE WHEN I RETURN THE PRESIDENT... WITH MY *BRAIN* INSIDE, THANKS TO MY *MINDSWAP MACHINE!*
THAT'S NOT HOW DEMOCRACY *WORKS*, FIEND!
BATMAN? GREEN ARROW? BUT... HOW?
NOW WHO'S THE EVIL SCIENTIST?
THAT IS... *YOU* KNOW WHAT I MEAN.

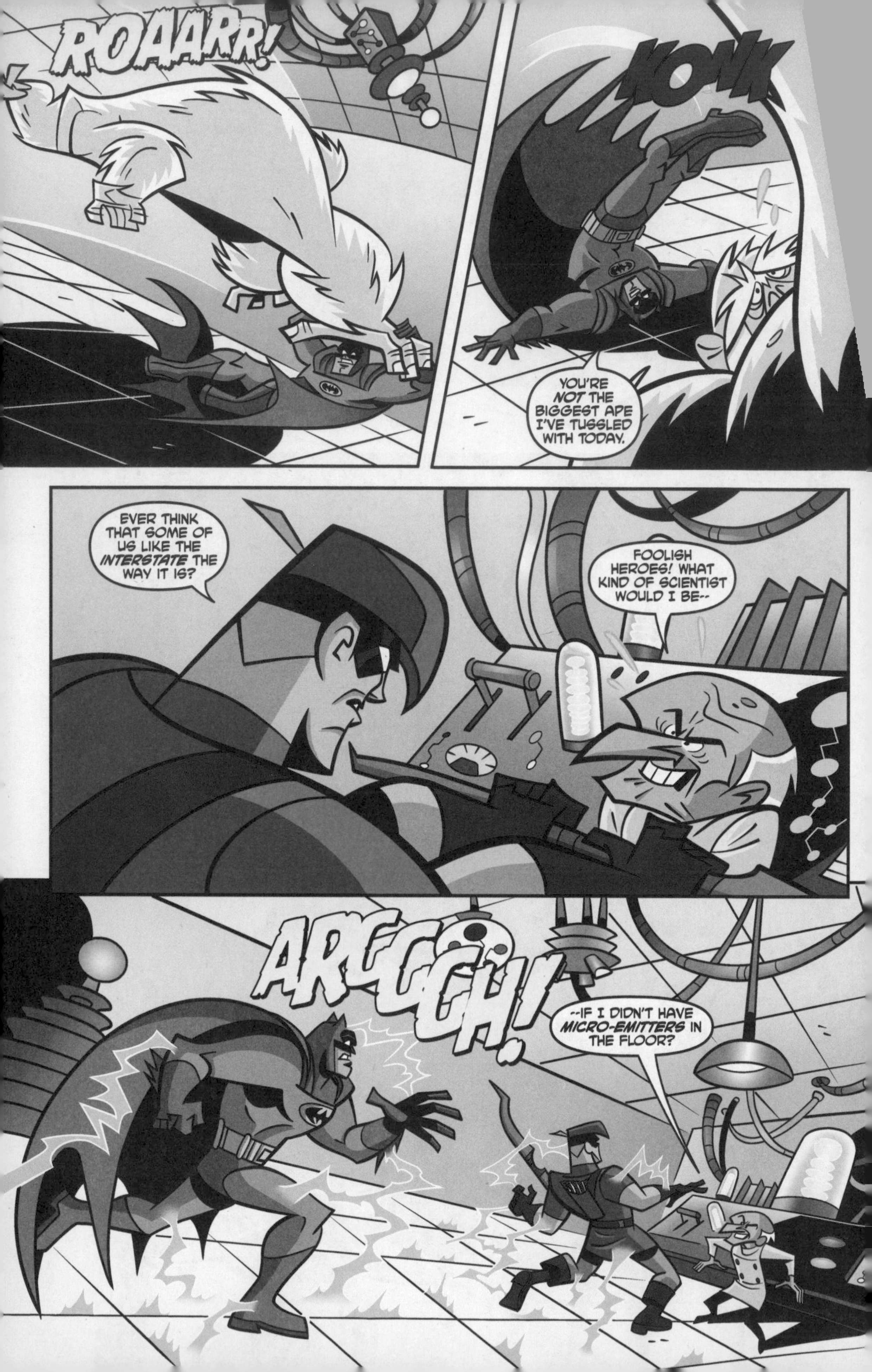
ROOAARR!
KONK
YOU'RE *NOT* THE BIGGEST APE I'VE TUSSLED WITH TODAY.
EVER THINK THAT SOME OF US LIKE THE *INTERSTATE* THE WAY IT IS?
FOOLISH HEROES! WHAT KIND OF SCIENTIST WOULD I BE--
ARGGGH!
--IF I DIDN'T HAVE *MICRO-EMITTERS* IN THE FLOOR?

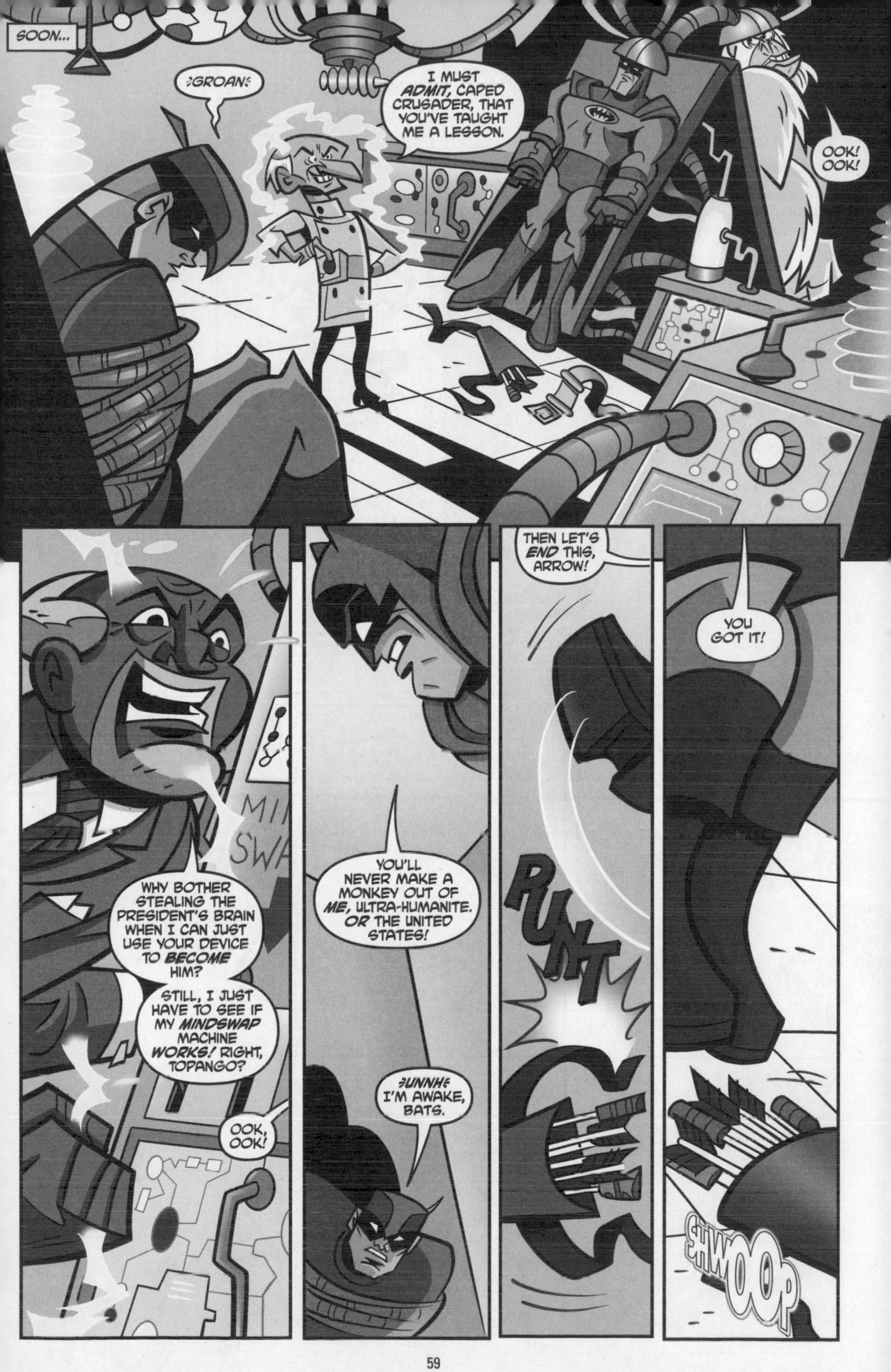
SOON...
GROAN
I MUST ADMIT, CAPED CRUSADER, THAT YOU'VE TAUGHT ME A LESSON.
OOK! OOK!
WHY BOTHER STEALING THE PRESIDENT'S BRAIN WHEN I CAN JUST USE YOUR DEVICE TO BECOME HIM?
STILL, I JUST HAVE TO SEE IF MY MINDSWAP MACHINE WORKS! RIGHT, TOPANGO?
OOK, OOK!
YOU'LL NEVER MAKE A MONKEY OUT OF ME, ULTRA-HUMANITE. OR THE UNITED STATES!
UNNH I'M AWAKE, BATS.
THEN LET'S END THIS, ARROW!
PUNT
YOU GOT IT!
SHWOOP

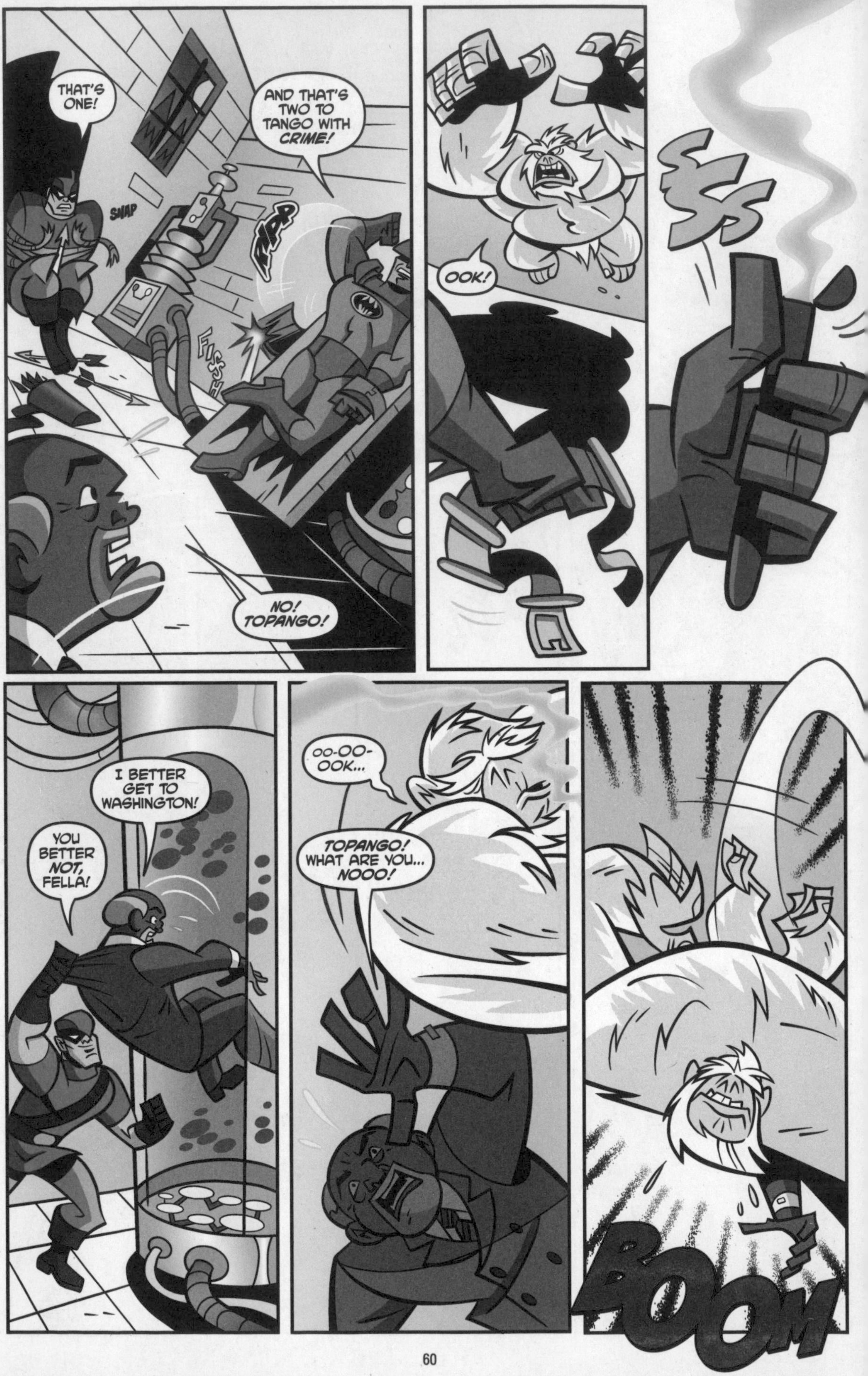
THAT'S ONE!
SNAP
AND THAT'S TWO TO TANGO WITH CRIME!
FISSH
NO! TOPANGO!
OOK!
I BETTER GET TO WASHINGTON!
YOU BETTER NOT, FELLA!
OO-OO-OOK...
TOPANGO! WHAT ARE YOU... NOOO!
BOOM

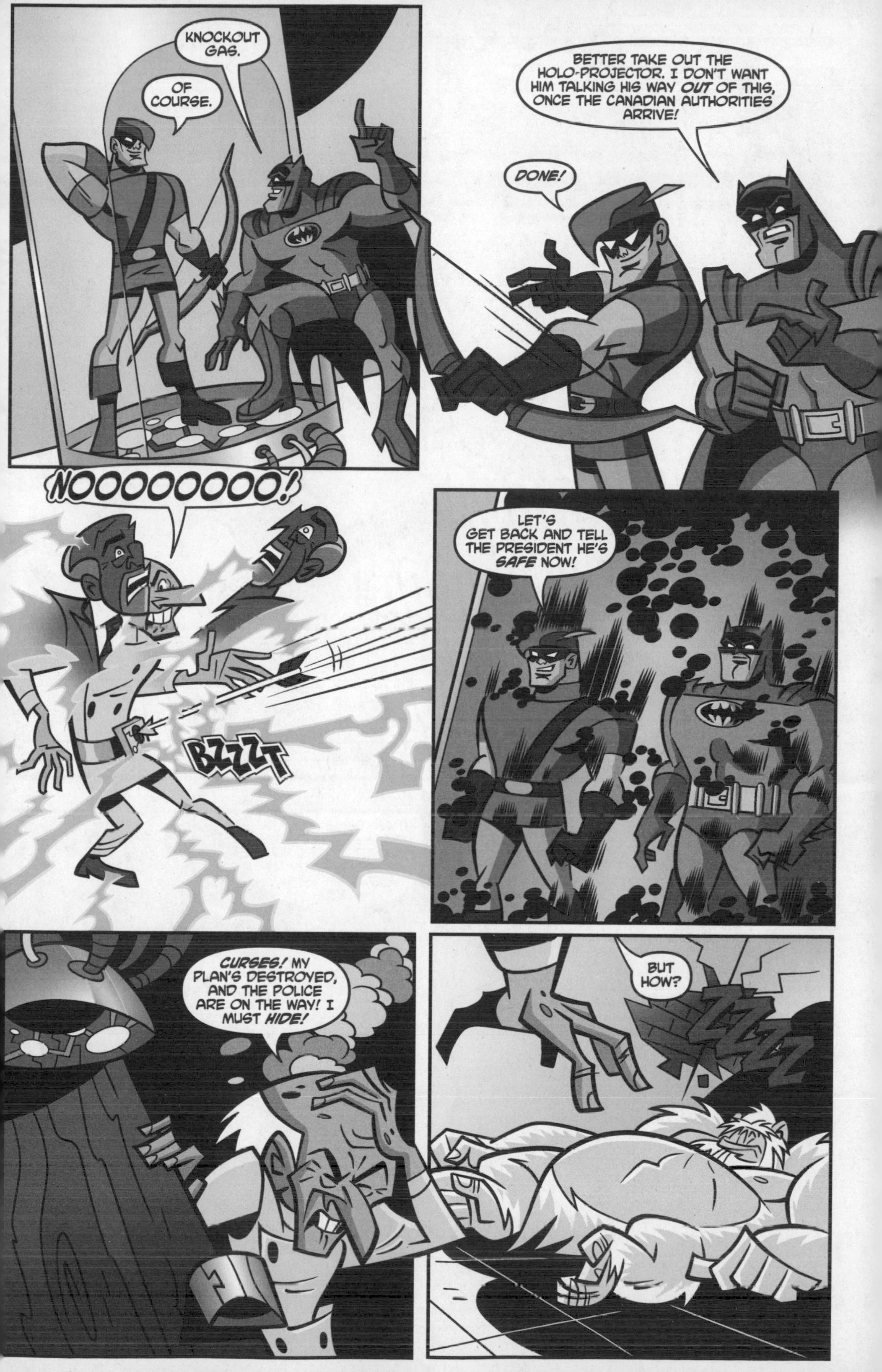
KNOCKOUT GAS.
OF COURSE.
BETTER TAKE OUT THE HOLO-PROJECTOR. I DON'T WANT HIM TALKING HIS WAY *OUT* OF THIS, ONCE THE CANADIAN AUTHORITIES ARRIVE!
DONE!
NOOOOOOOO!
BZZZT
LET'S GET BACK AND TELL THE PRESIDENT HE'S *SAFE* NOW!
CURSES! MY PLAN'S DESTROYED, AND THE POLICE ARE ON THE WAY! I MUST *HIDE!*
BUT HOW?
ZZZZ

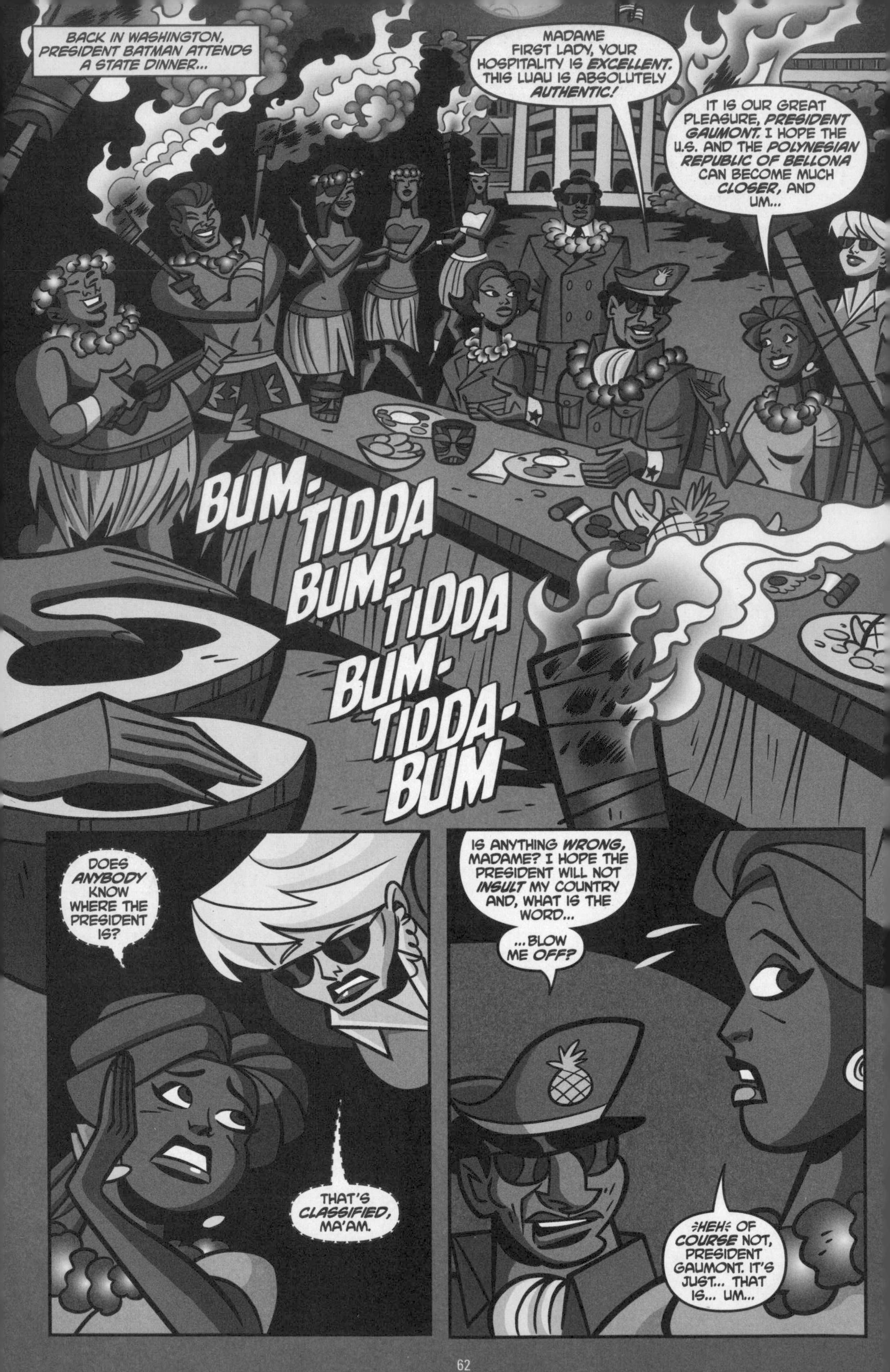
BACK IN WASHINGTON, PRESIDENT BATMAN ATTENDS A STATE DINNER...
MADAME FIRST LADY, YOUR HOSPITALITY IS EXCELLENT. THIS LUAU IS ABSOLUTELY AUTHENTIC!
IT IS OUR GREAT PLEASURE, PRESIDENT GAUMONT. I HOPE THE U.S. AND THE POLYNESIAN REPUBLIC OF BELLONA CAN BECOME MUCH CLOSER, AND UM...
BUM-TIDDA BUM-TIDDA BUM-TIDDA-BUM
DOES ANYBODY KNOW WHERE THE PRESIDENT IS?
THAT'S CLASSIFIED, MA'AM.
IS ANYTHING WRONG, MADAME? I HOPE THE PRESIDENT WILL NOT INSULT MY COUNTRY AND, WHAT IS THE WORD...
...BLOW ME OFF?
HEH OF COURSE NOT, PRESIDENT GAUMONT. IT'S JUST... THAT IS... UM...

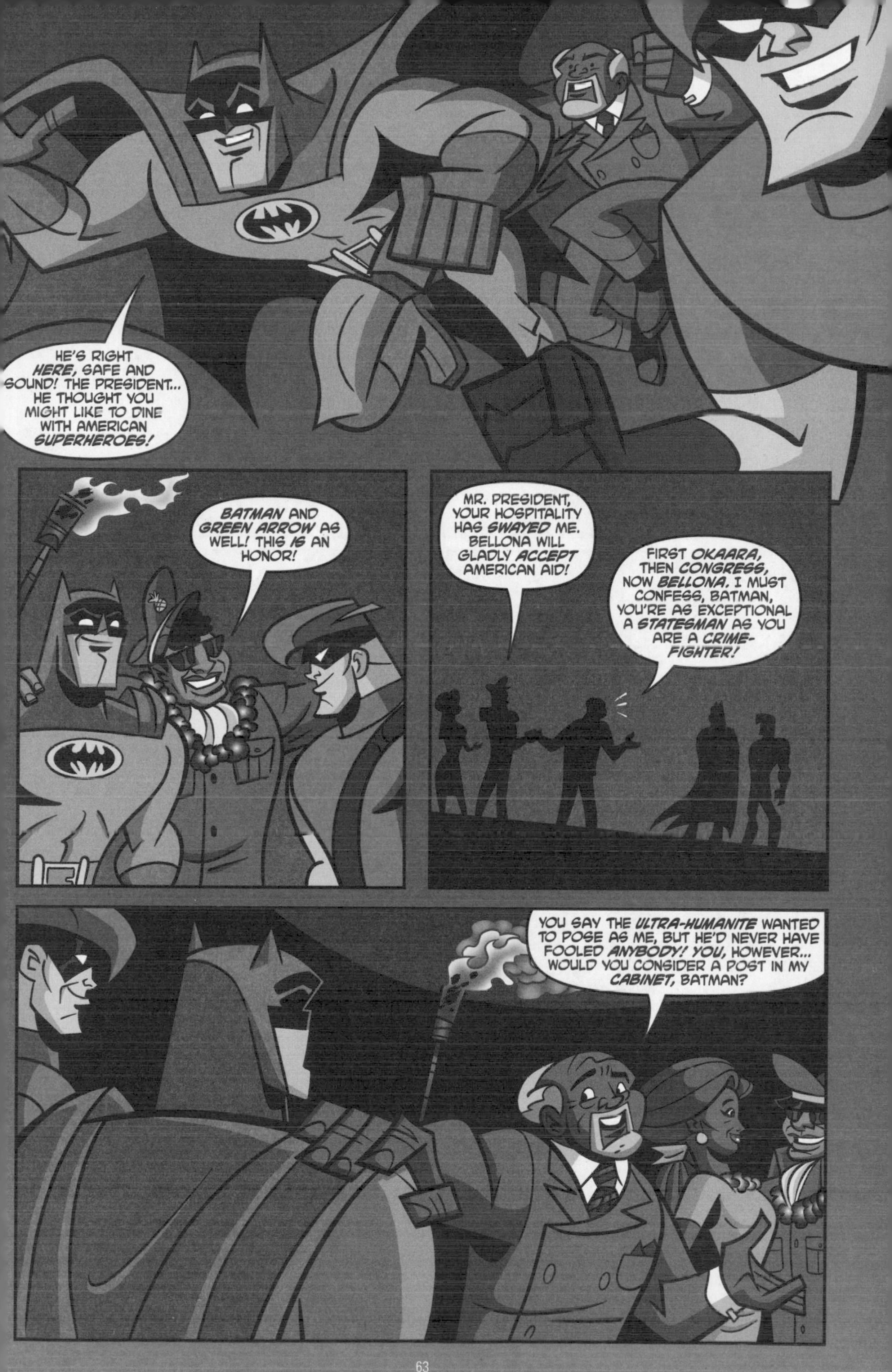
HE'S RIGHT HERE, SAFE AND SOUND! THE PRESIDENT... HE THOUGHT YOU MIGHT LIKE TO DINE WITH AMERICAN SUPERHEROES!
BATMAN AND GREEN ARROW AS WELL! THIS IS AN HONOR!
MR. PRESIDENT, YOUR HOSPITALITY HAS SWAYED ME. BELLONA WILL GLADLY ACCEPT AMERICAN AID!
FIRST OKAARA, THEN CONGRESS, NOW BELLONA. I MUST CONFESS, BATMAN, YOU'RE AS EXCEPTIONAL A STATESMAN AS YOU ARE A CRIME-FIGHTER!
YOU SAY THE ULTRA-HUMANITE WANTED TO POSE AS ME, BUT HE'D NEVER HAVE FOOLED ANYBODY! YOU, HOWEVER... WOULD YOU CONSIDER A POST IN MY CABINET, BATMAN?

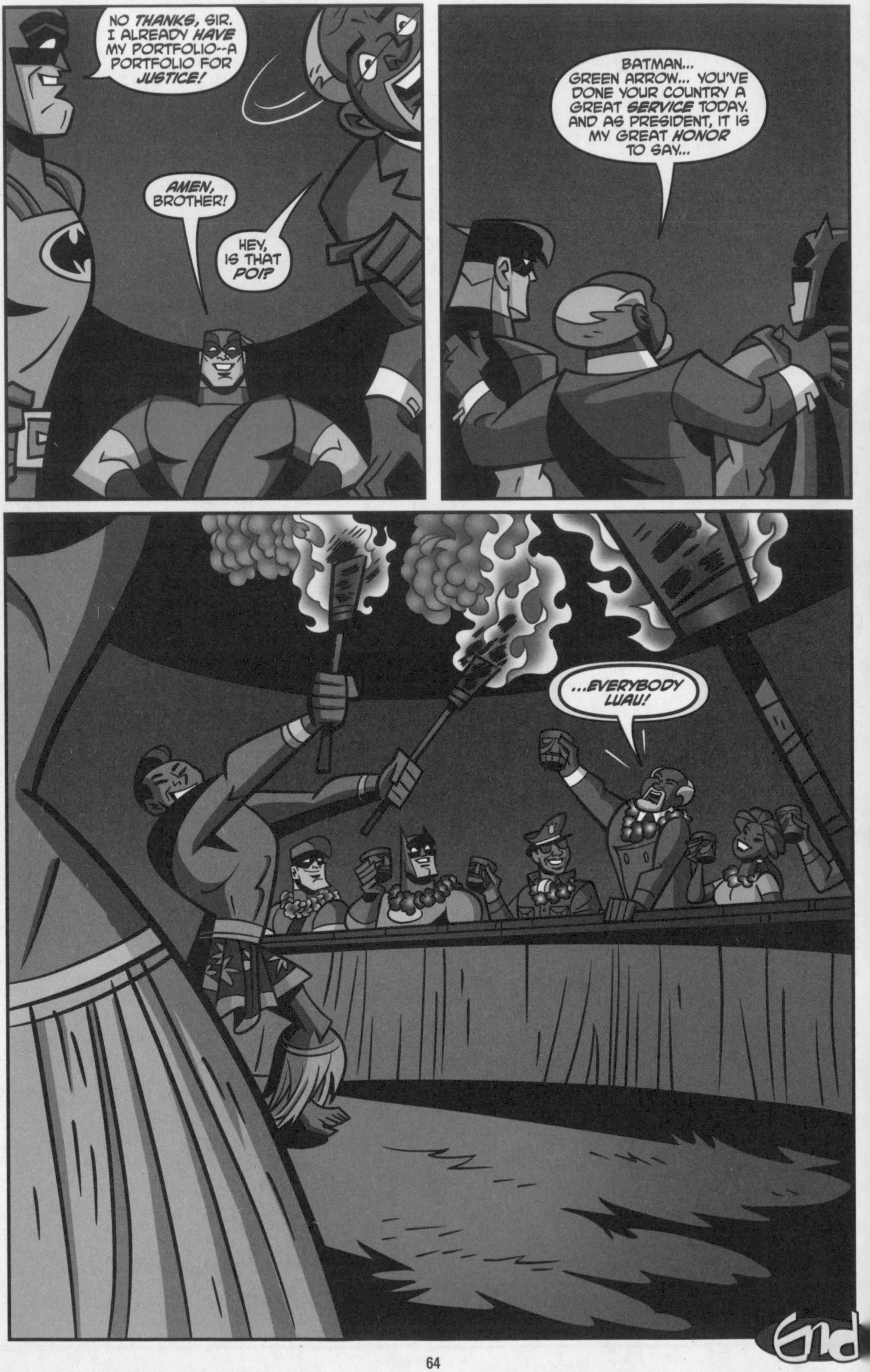
NO THANKS, SIR. I ALREADY HAVE MY PORTFOLIO--A PORTFOLIO FOR JUSTICE!
AMEN, BROTHER!
HEY, IS THAT POI?
BATMAN... GREEN ARROW... YOU'VE DONE YOUR COUNTRY A GREAT SERVICE TODAY. AND AS PRESIDENT, IT IS MY GREAT HONOR TO SAY...
...EVERYBODY LUAU!
End

THE ULTRA-HUMANITE:

THE ULTRA-HUMANITE considers his criminal mind to be the most evolved in the universe. After developing a "hot-swappable" brain case in a failed scheme to take over the United States, the Ultra-Humanite settled for putting his brain into the body of a powerful gorilla.

TOP SECRET:
The real reason Ultra-Humanite put his brain in a gorilla's body: To stop people from confusing him with that other mad scientist, LUTHOR.

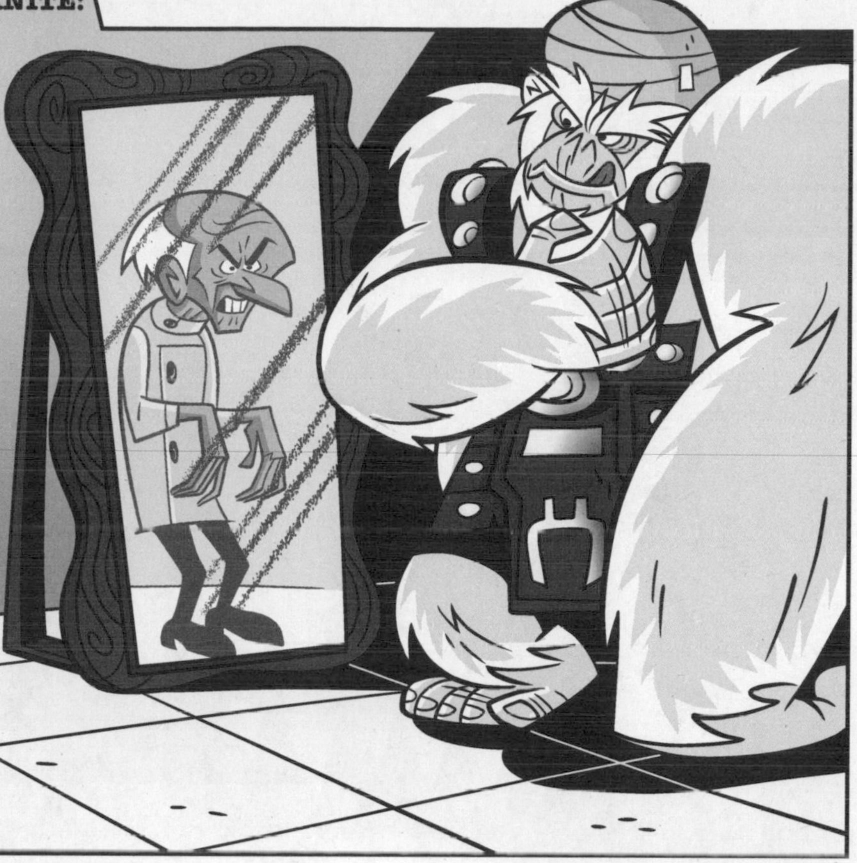

SECRET BAT-FILES

GREEN ARROW:

A wealthy businessman turned hero, expert archer OLIVER QUEEN fights crime as straight-shooting GREEN ARROW. His quiver contains dozens of "trick" arrows. Some cleverly dispense explosives, acid and sleep gas, while others are more whimsical, such as the infamously effective boxing-glove arrow.

TOP SECRET:
Ollie was fighting crime for months before he realized he'd unconsciously copied Robin Hood's costume.

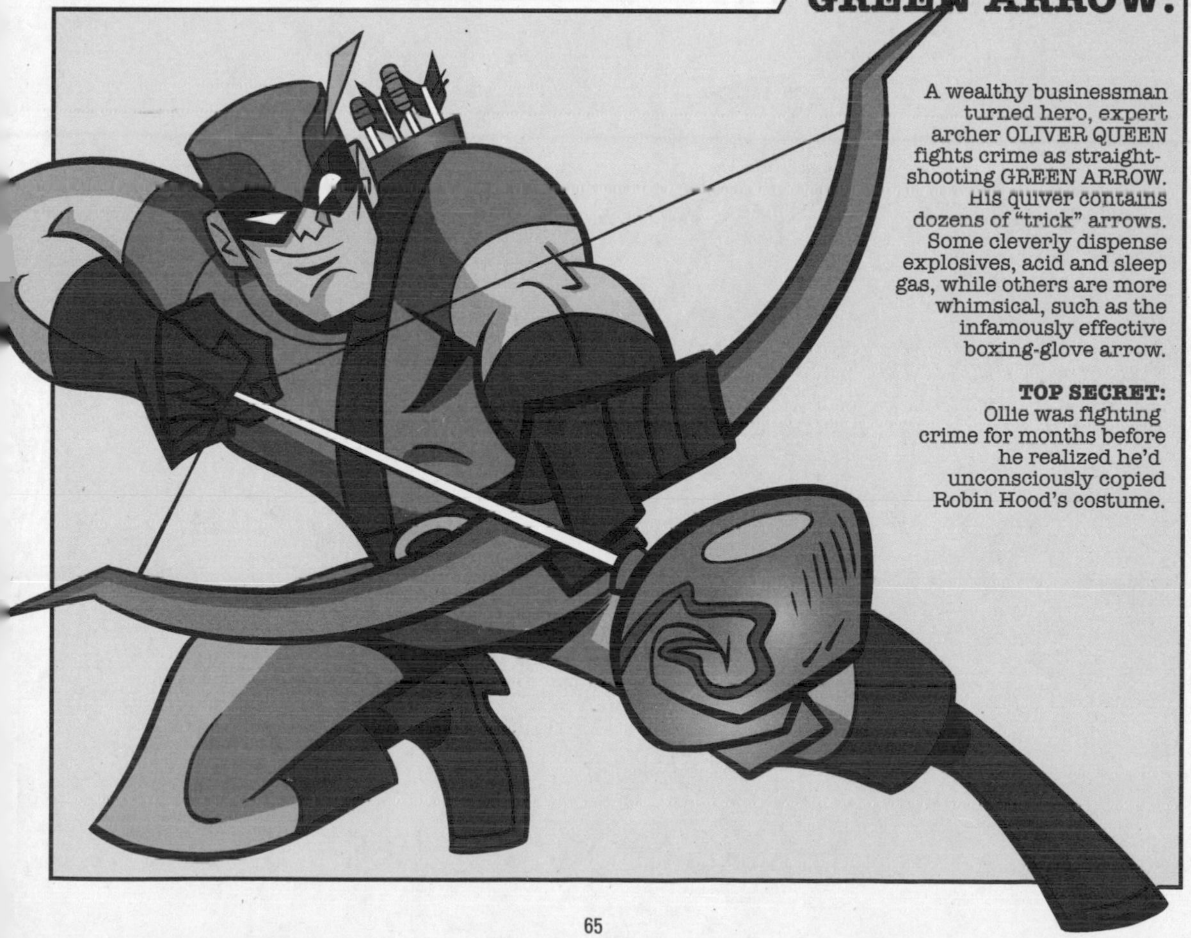

BATMAN: THE BRAVE AND THE BOLD #4
Cover by Scott Jeralds with Hi-Fi

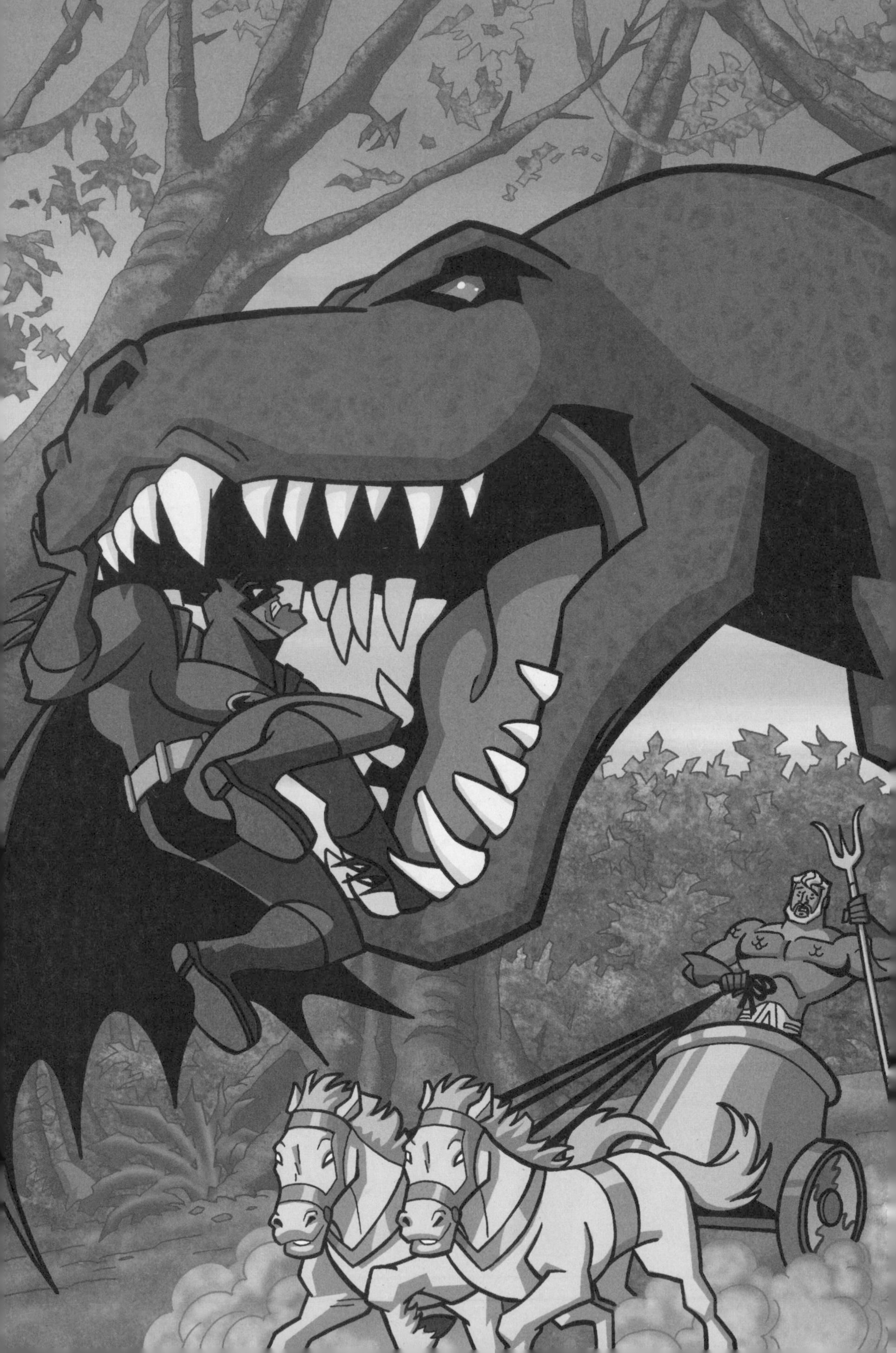

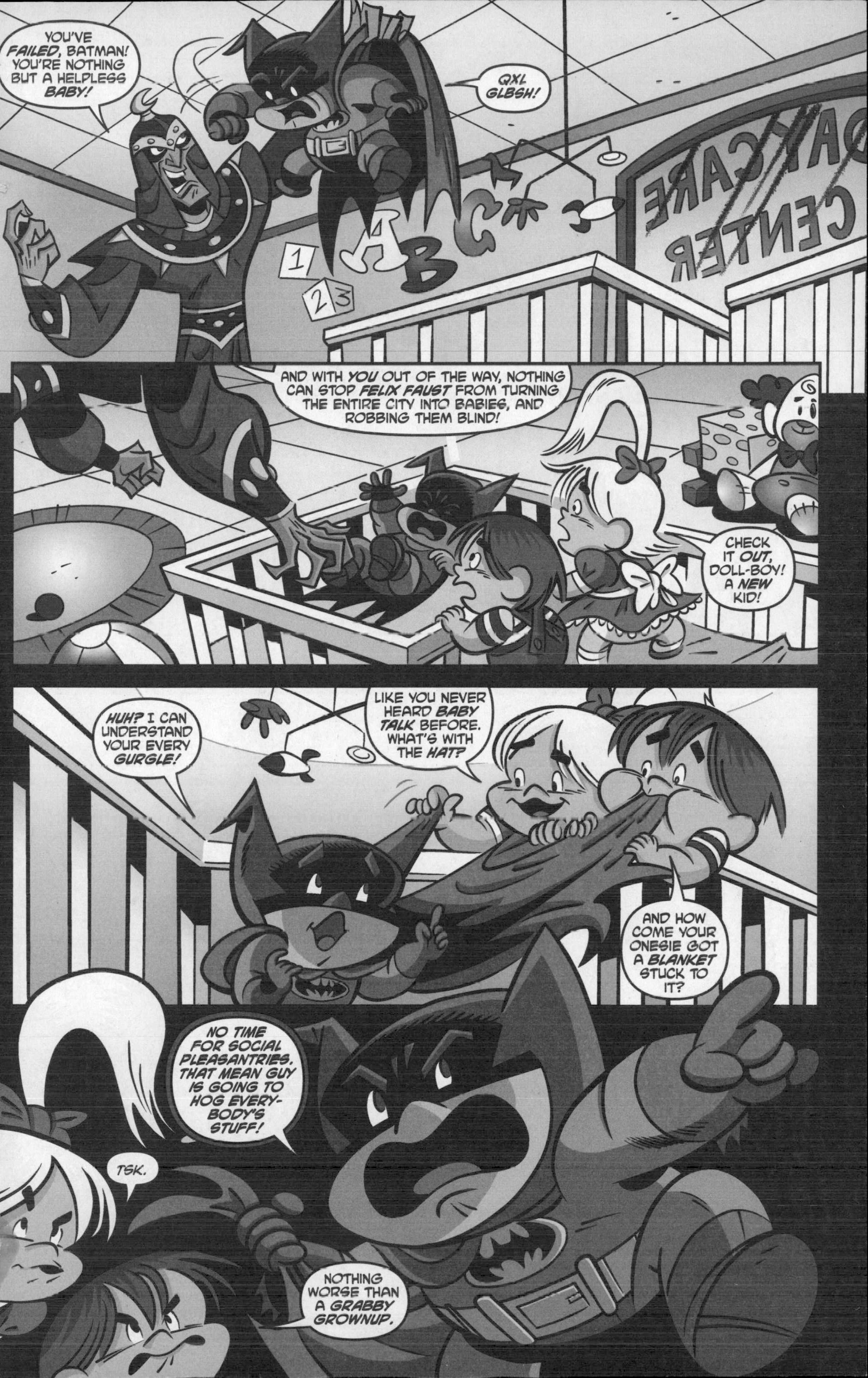
YOU'VE *FAILED*, BATMAN! YOU'RE NOTHING BUT A HELPLESS *BABY!*
QXL GLBSH!
DAYCARE CENTER
AND WITH *YOU* OUT OF THE WAY, NOTHING CAN STOP *FELIX FAUST* FROM TURNING THE ENTIRE CITY INTO BABIES, AND ROBBING THEM BLIND!
CHECK IT *OUT*, DOLL-BOY! A *NEW* KID!
HUH? I CAN UNDERSTAND YOUR EVERY *GURGLE!*
LIKE YOU NEVER HEARD *BABY TALK* BEFORE. WHAT'S WITH THE *HAT?*
AND HOW COME YOUR ONESIE GOT A *BLANKET* STUCK TO IT?
NO TIME FOR SOCIAL PLEASANTRIES. THAT MEAN GUY IS GOING TO HOG EVERY-BODY'S STUFF!
TSK.
NOTHING WORSE THAN A *GRABBY GROWNUP.*

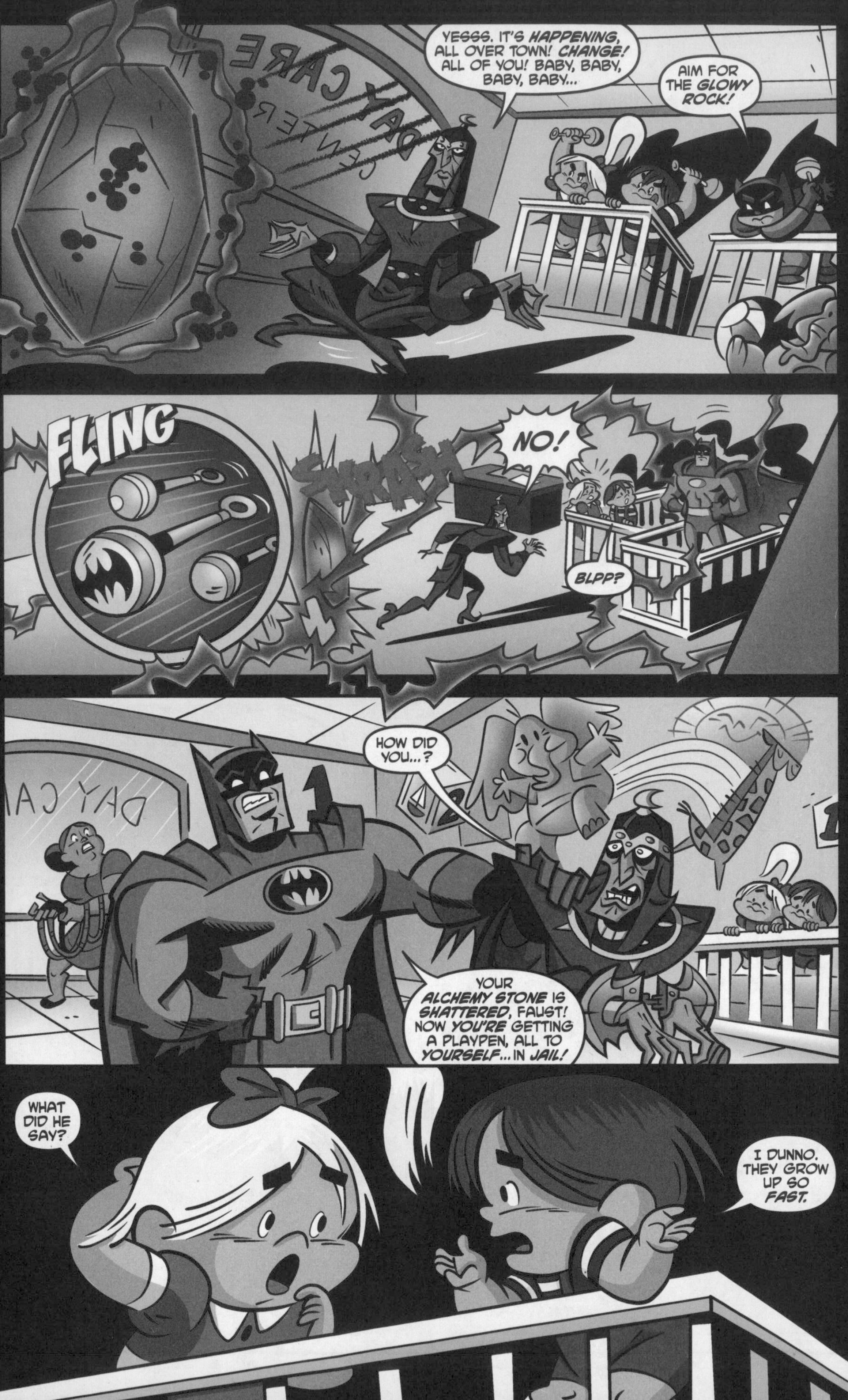

DAY CARE CENTER
YESSS. IT'S HAPPENING, ALL OVER TOWN! CHANGE! ALL OF YOU! BABY, BABY, BABY, BABY...
AIM FOR THE GLOWY ROCK!
FLING
SMASH
NO!
BLPP?
HOW DID YOU...?
YOUR ALCHEMY STONE IS SHATTERED, FAUST! NOW YOU'RE GETTING A PLAYPEN, ALL TO YOURSELF...IN JAIL!
WHAT DID HE SAY?
I DUNNO. THEY GROW UP SO FAST.

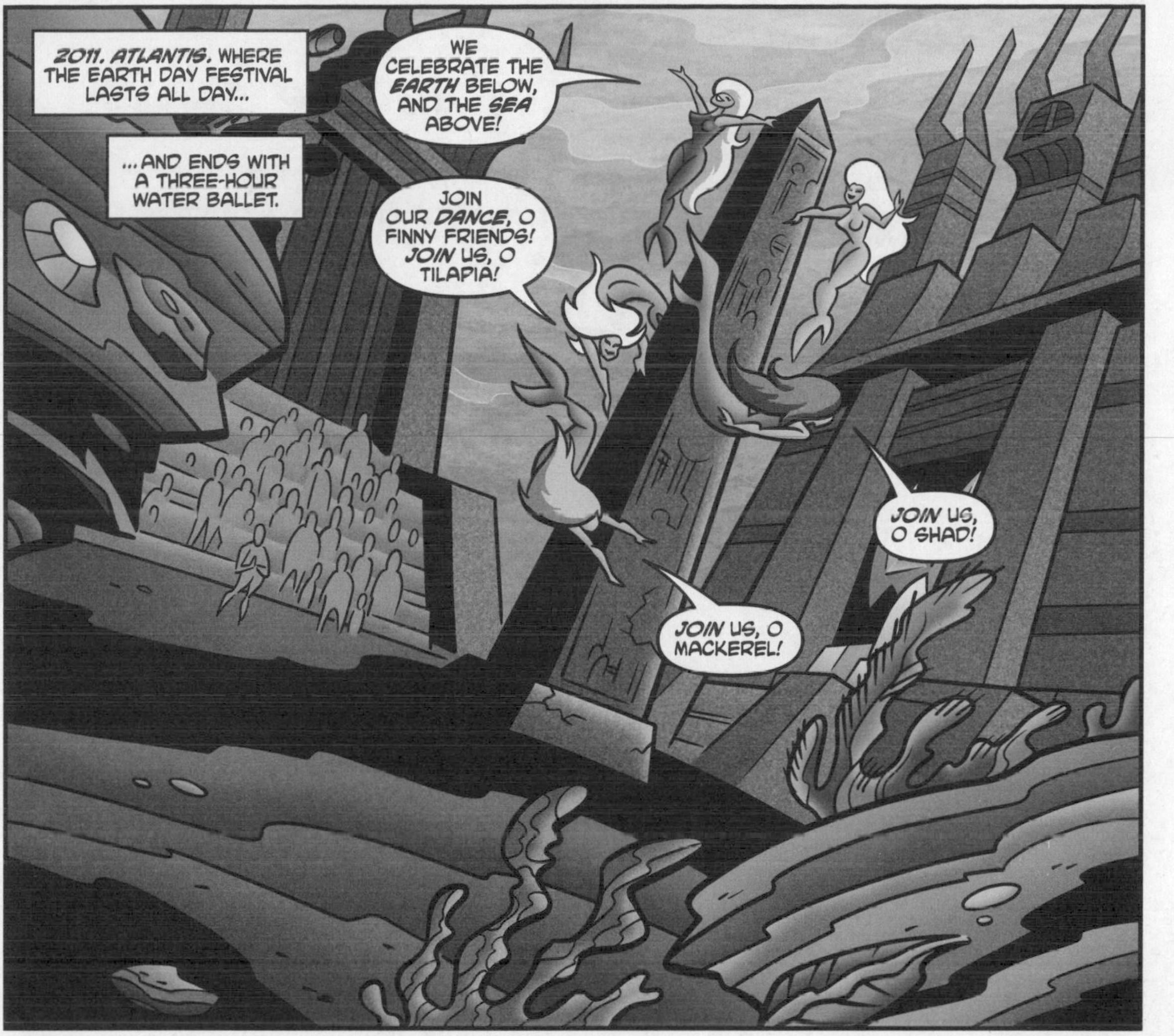
2011. ATLANTIS. WHERE THE EARTH DAY FESTIVAL LASTS ALL DAY...
...AND ENDS WITH A THREE-HOUR WATER BALLET.
WE CELEBRATE THE EARTH BELOW, AND THE SEA ABOVE!
JOIN OUR DANCE, O FINNY FRIENDS! JOIN US, O TILAPIA!
JOIN US, O SHAD!
JOIN US, O MACKEREL!

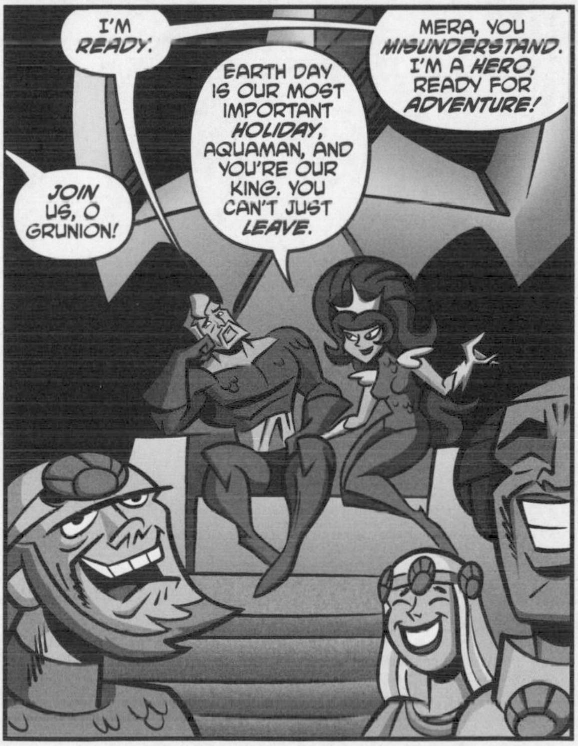
I'M READY.
MERA, YOU MISUNDERSTAND. I'M A HERO, READY FOR ADVENTURE!
EARTH DAY IS OUR MOST IMPORTANT HOLIDAY, AQUAMAN, AND YOU'RE OUR KING. YOU CAN'T JUST LEAVE.
JOIN US, O GRUNION!

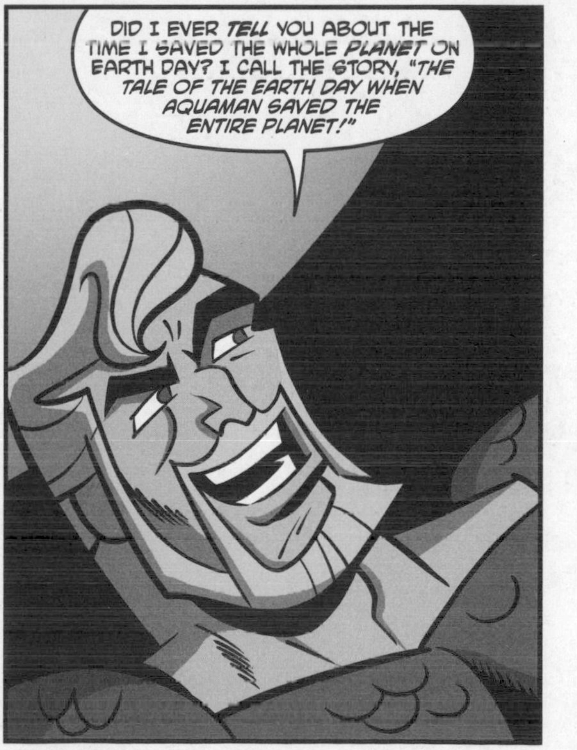
DID I EVER TELL YOU ABOUT THE TIME I SAVED THE WHOLE PLANET ON EARTH DAY? I CALL THE STORY, "THE TALE OF THE EARTH DAY WHEN AQUAMAN SAVED THE ENTIRE PLANET!"

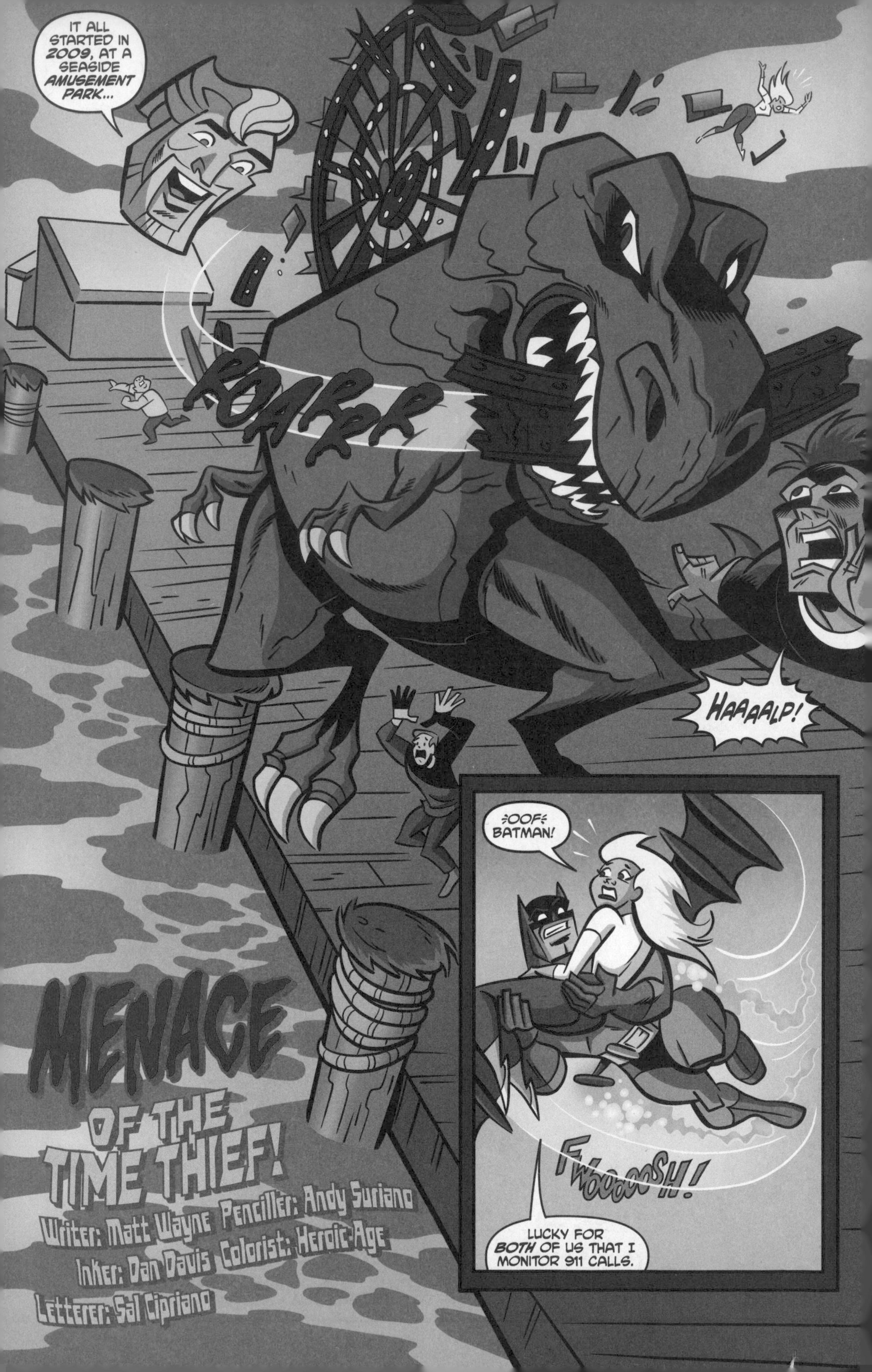
IT ALL STARTED IN 2009, AT A SEASIDE AMUSEMENT PARK...
ROARRR
HAAAALP!
OOF BATMAN!
FWOOOOOSH!
LUCKY FOR BOTH OF US THAT I MONITOR 911 CALLS.
MENACE OF THE TIME THIEF!
Writer: Matt Wayne Penciller: Andy Suriano
Inker: Dan Davis Colorist: Heroic Age
Letterer: Sal Cipriano

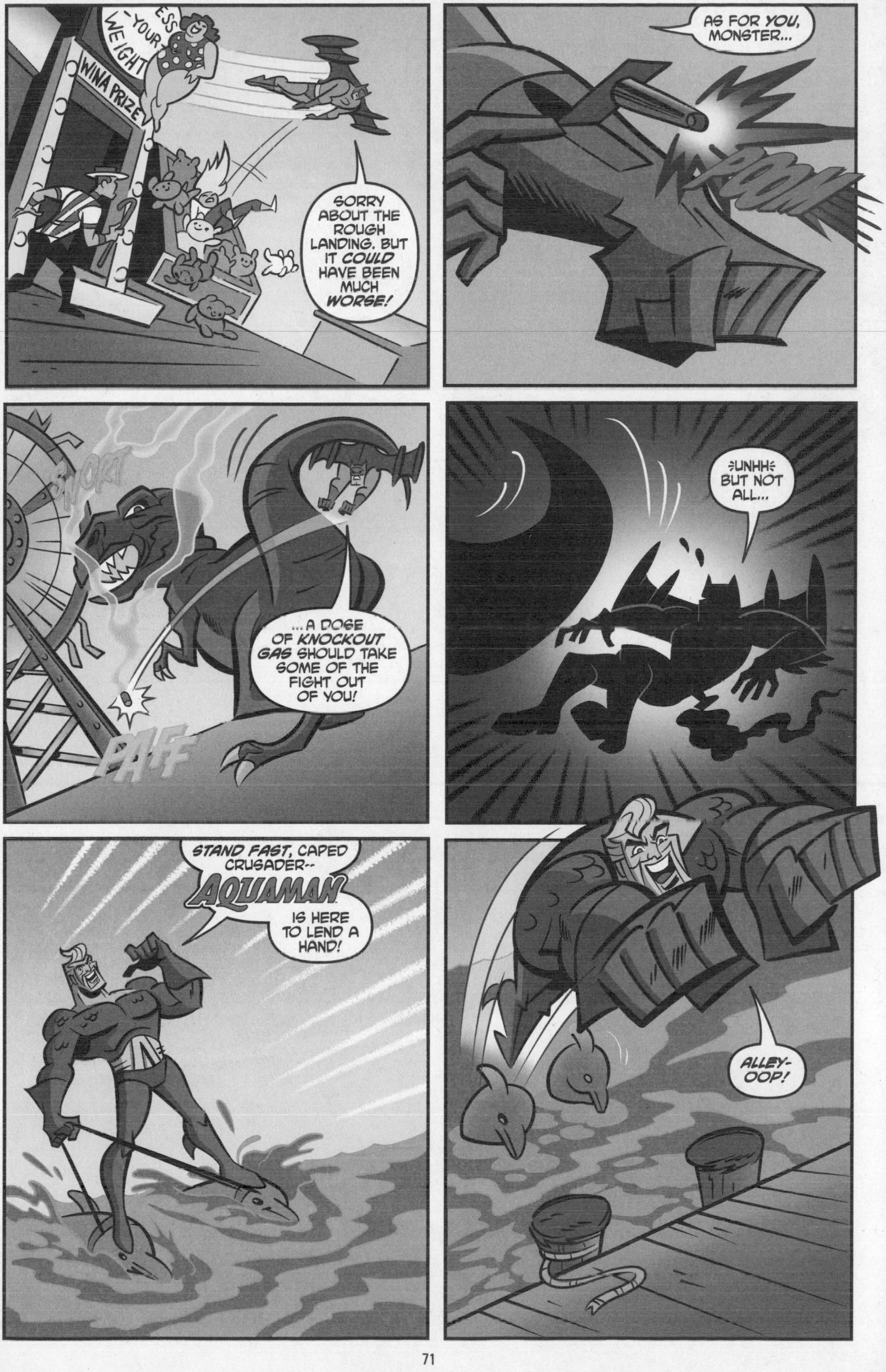
ESS
-YOUR-
WEIGHT
WIN A PRIZE
SORRY ABOUT THE ROUGH LANDING. BUT IT *COULD* HAVE BEEN MUCH *WORSE!*
AS FOR *YOU,* MONSTER...
WPOOM
SNORT
...A DOSE OF *KNOCKOUT GAS* SHOULD TAKE SOME OF THE FIGHT OUT OF YOU!
PAFF
UNHH BUT NOT ALL...
STAND FAST, CAPED CRUSADER--
AQUAMAN
IS HERE TO LEND A HAND!
ALLEY-OOP!

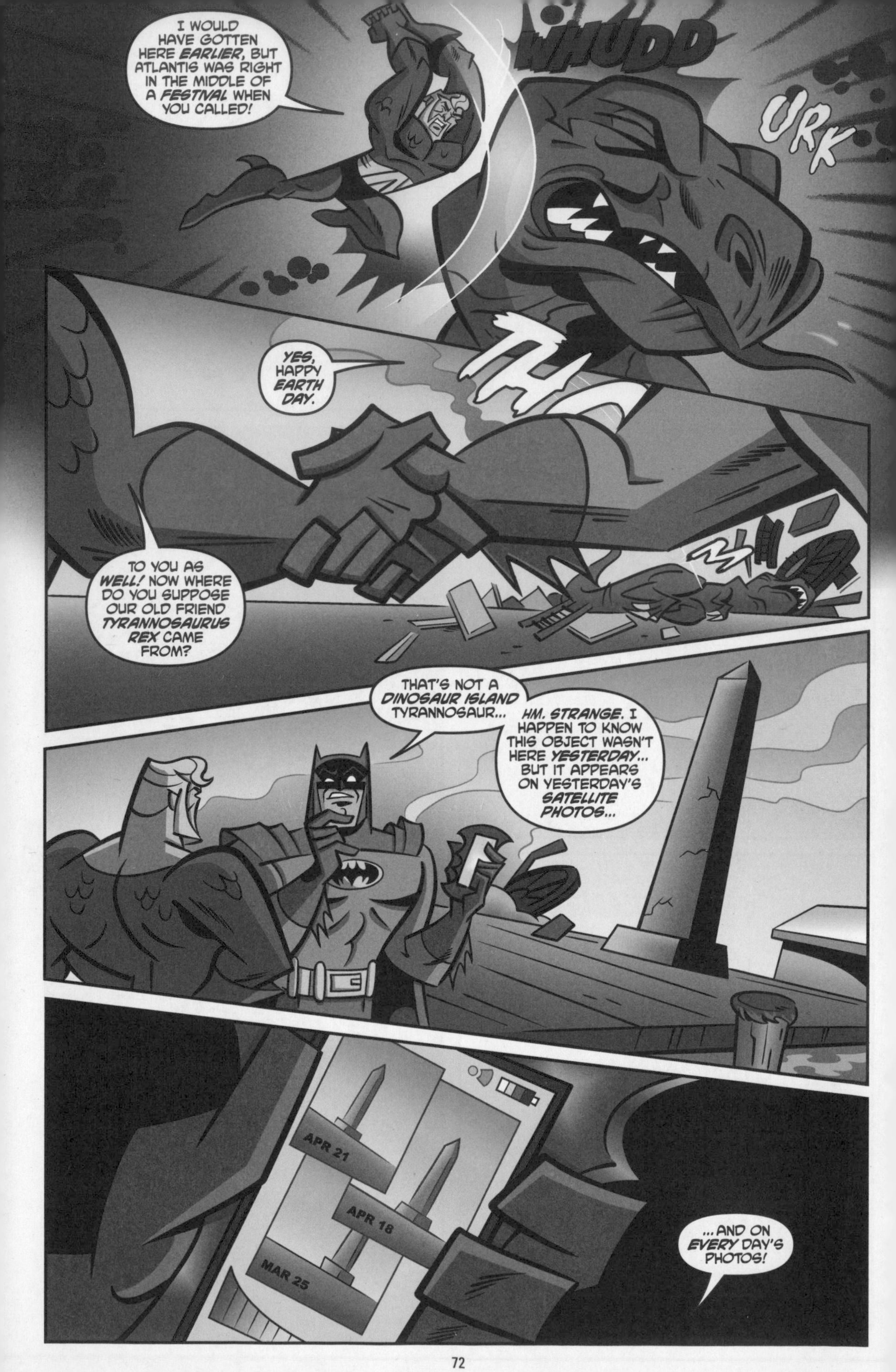
I WOULD HAVE GOTTEN HERE EARLIER, BUT ATLANTIS WAS RIGHT IN THE MIDDLE OF A FESTIVAL WHEN YOU CALLED!
WHUDD
URK
YES, HAPPY EARTH DAY.
TO YOU AS WELL! NOW WHERE DO YOU SUPPOSE OUR OLD FRIEND TYRANNOSAURUS REX CAME FROM?
THAT'S NOT A DINOSAUR ISLAND TYRANNOSAUR...
HM. STRANGE. I HAPPEN TO KNOW THIS OBJECT WASN'T HERE YESTERDAY... BUT IT APPEARS ON YESTERDAY'S SATELLITE PHOTOS...
APR 21
APR 18
MAR 25
...AND ON EVERY DAY'S PHOTOS!

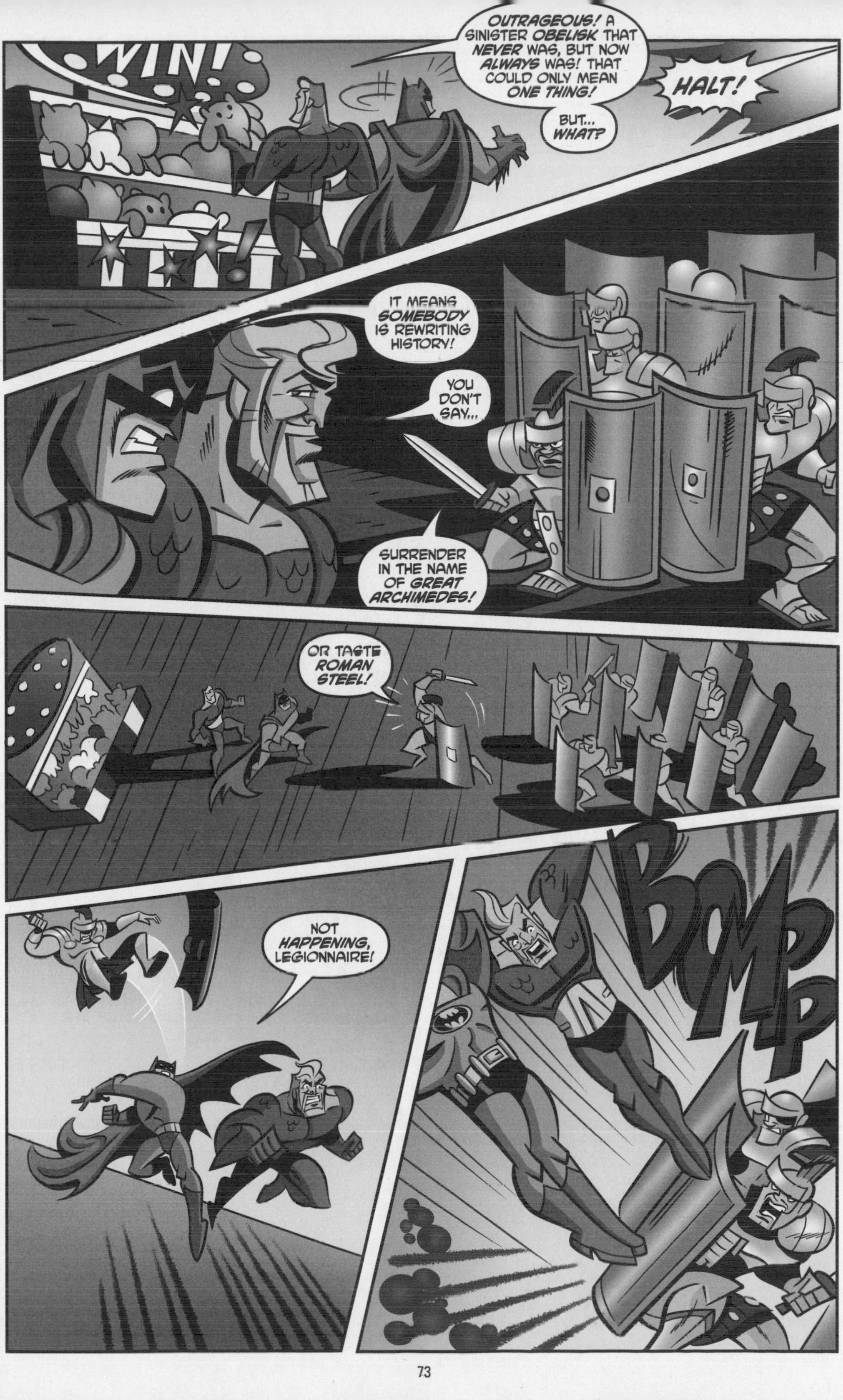
WIN!
OUTRAGEOUS! A SINISTER OBELISK THAT NEVER WAS, BUT NOW ALWAYS WAS! THAT COULD ONLY MEAN ONE THING!
BUT... WHAT?
HALT!
IT MEANS SOMEBODY IS REWRITING HISTORY!
YOU DON'T SAY...
SURRENDER IN THE NAME OF GREAT ARCHIMEDES!
OR TASTE ROMAN STEEL!
NOT HAPPENING, LEGIONNAIRE!
BOMP

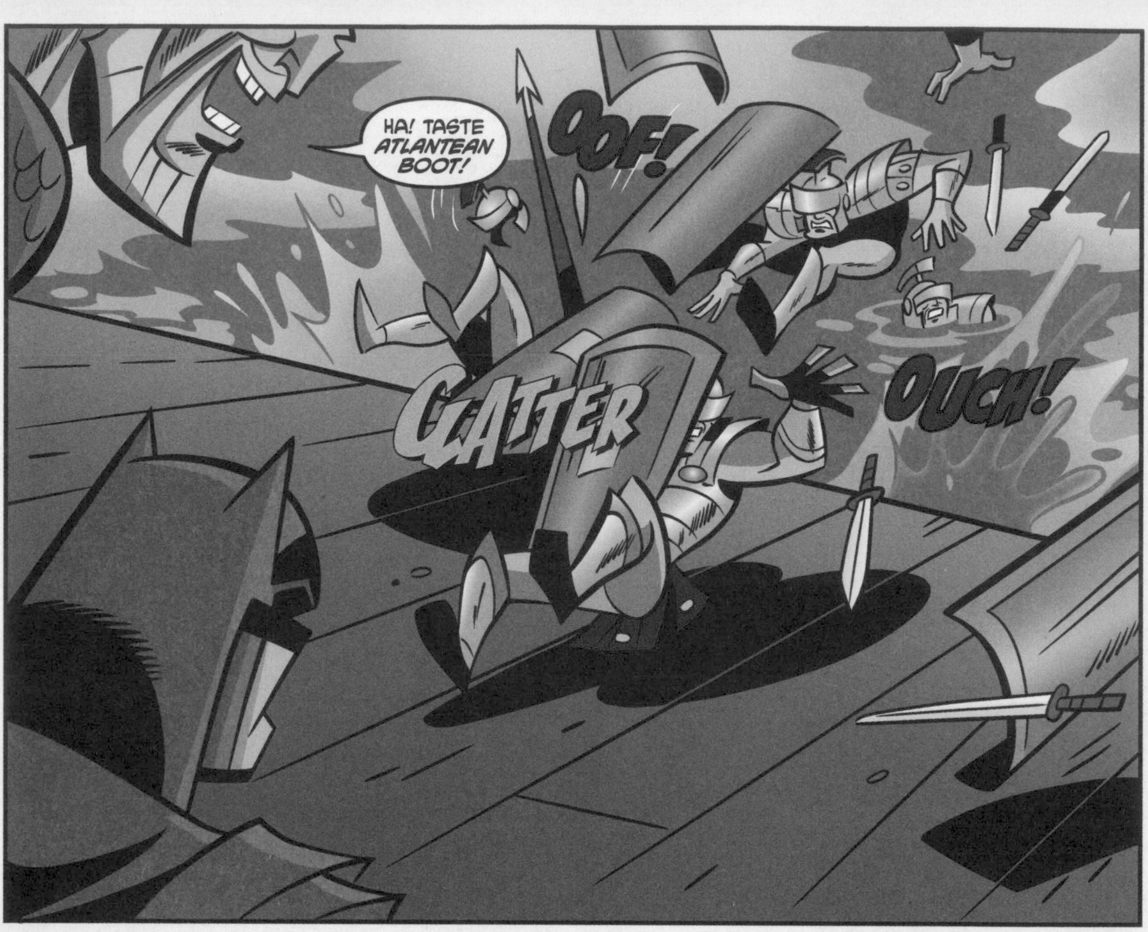
HA! TASTE ATLANTEAN BOOT!
OOF!
CLATTER
OUCH!

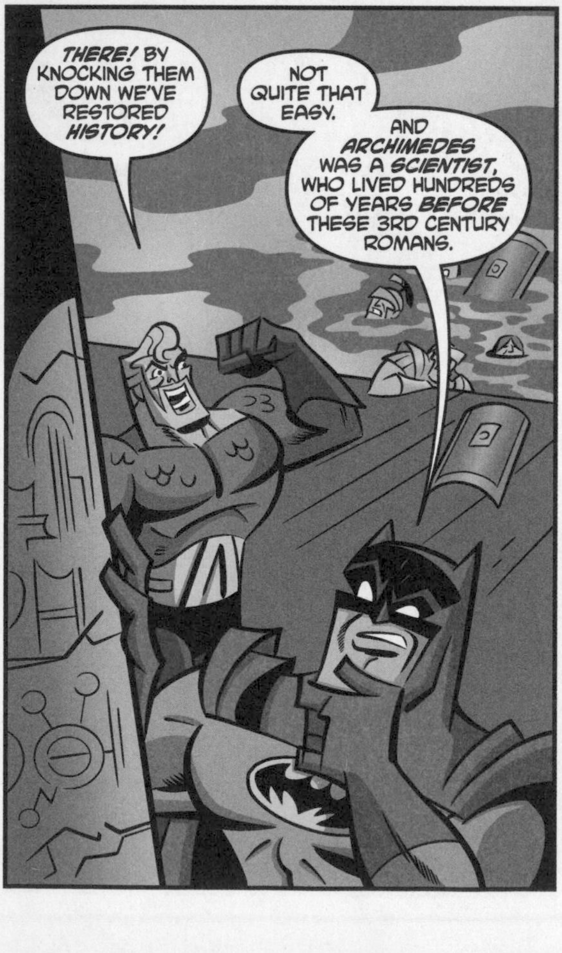
THERE! BY KNOCKING THEM DOWN WE'VE RESTORED HISTORY!
NOT QUITE THAT EASY.
AND ARCHIMEDES WAS A SCIENTIST, WHO LIVED HUNDREDS OF YEARS BEFORE THESE 3RD CENTURY ROMANS.

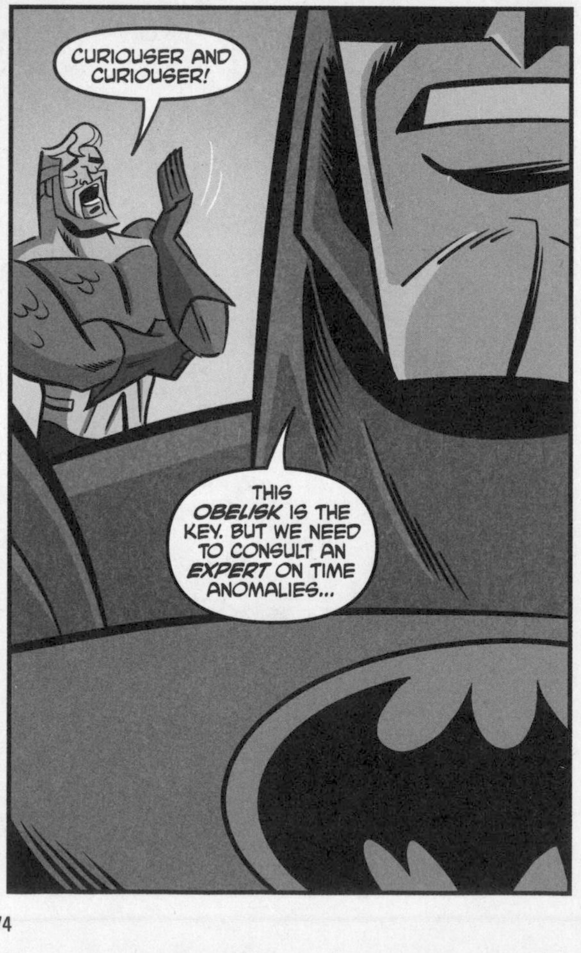
CURIOUSER AND CURIOUSER!
THIS OBELISK IS THE KEY. BUT WE NEED TO CONSULT AN EXPERT ON TIME ANOMALIES...

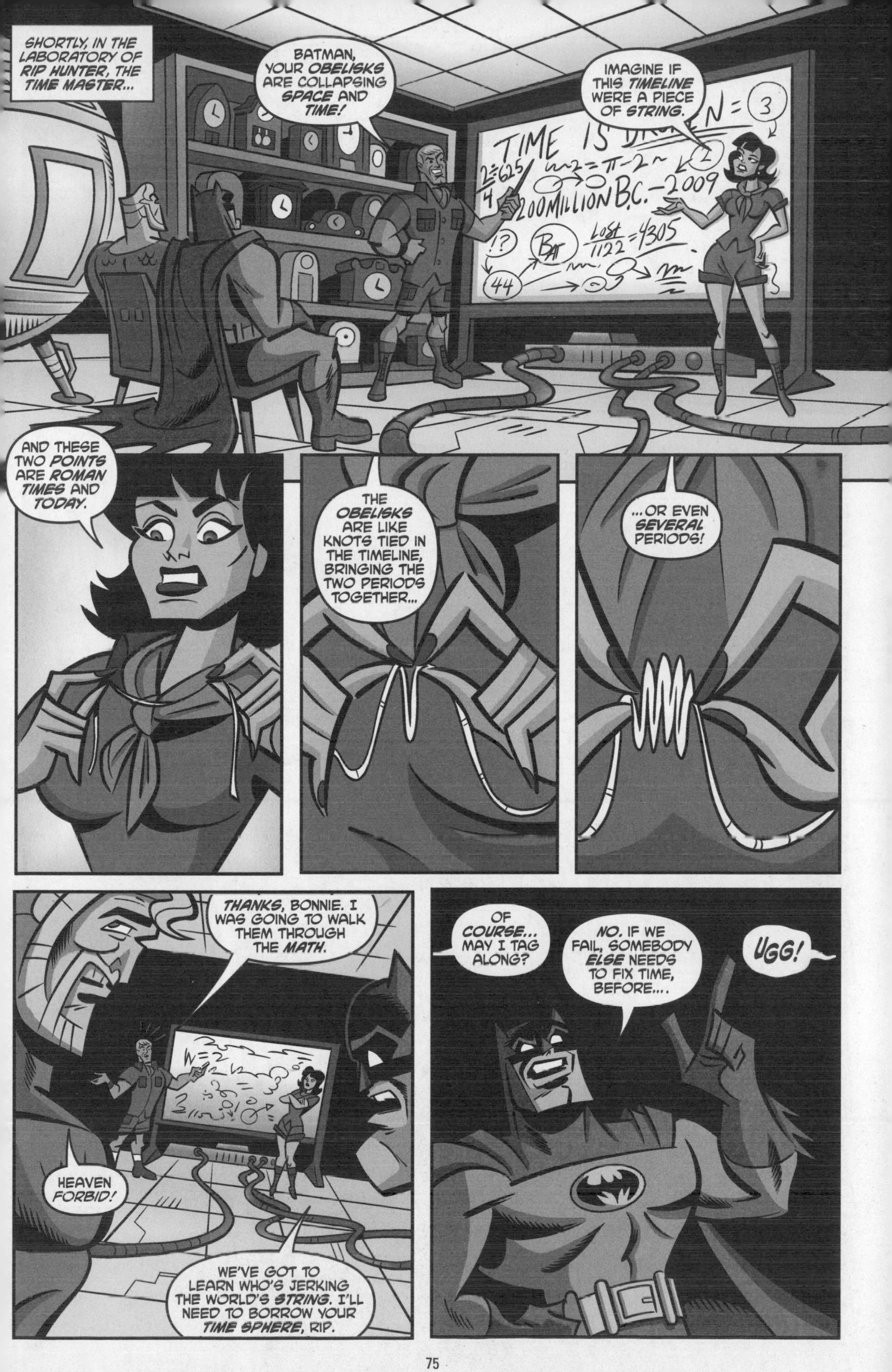
SHORTLY, IN THE LABORATORY OF RIP HUNTER, THE TIME MASTER...
BATMAN, YOUR OBELISKS ARE COLLAPSING SPACE AND TIME!
IMAGINE IF THIS TIMELINE WERE A PIECE OF STRING.
TIME IS
200 MILLION B.C. - 2009
AND THESE TWO POINTS ARE ROMAN TIMES AND TODAY.
THE OBELISKS ARE LIKE KNOTS TIED IN THE TIMELINE, BRINGING THE TWO PERIODS TOGETHER...
...OR EVEN SEVERAL PERIODS!
THANKS, BONNIE. I WAS GOING TO WALK THEM THROUGH THE MATH.
HEAVEN FORBID!
WE'VE GOT TO LEARN WHO'S JERKING THE WORLD'S STRING. I'LL NEED TO BORROW YOUR TIME SPHERE, RIP.
OF COURSE... MAY I TAG ALONG?
NO. IF WE FAIL, SOMEBODY ELSE NEEDS TO FIX TIME, BEFORE....
UGG!

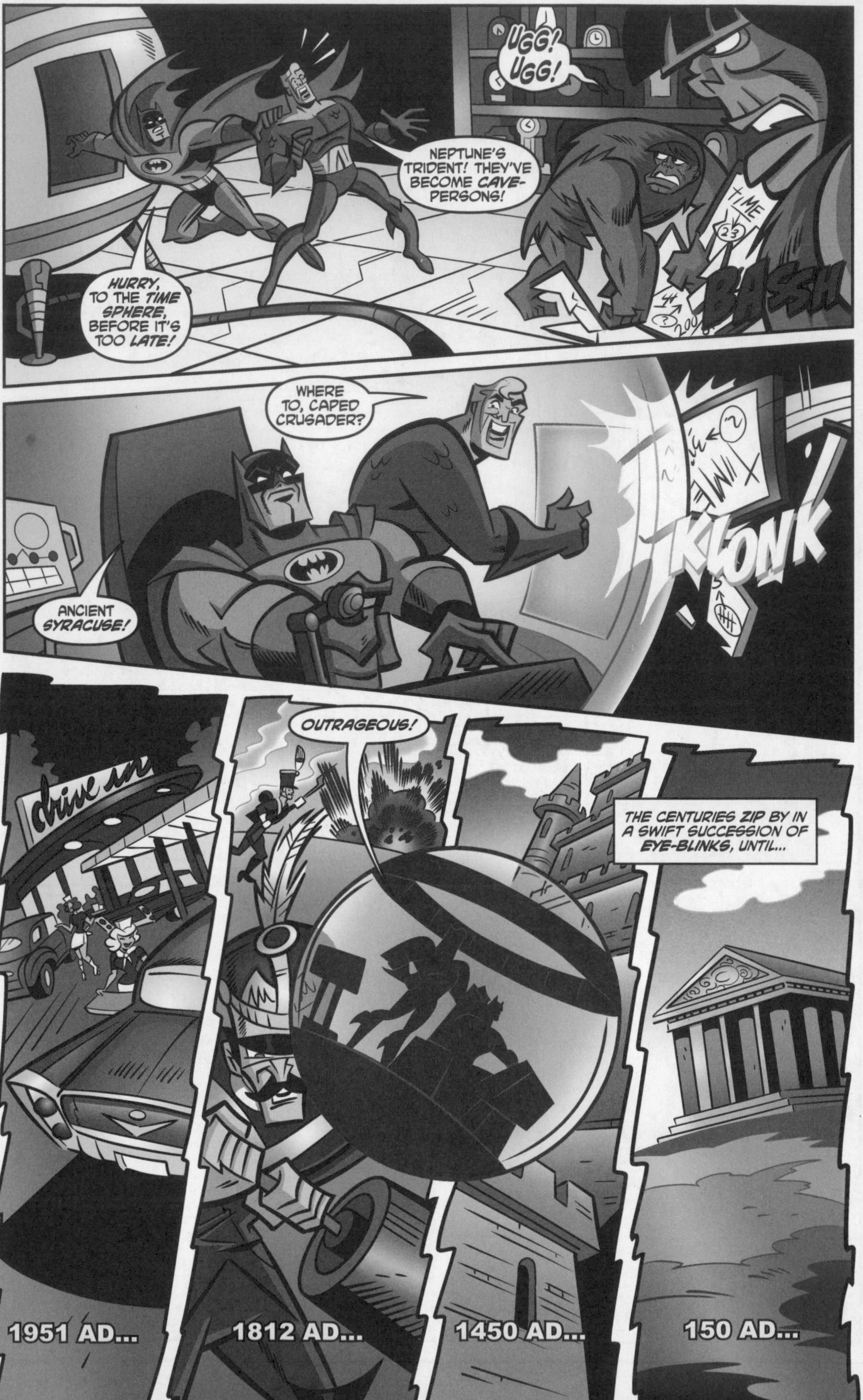

UGG! UGG!
NEPTUNE'S TRIDENT! THEY'VE BECOME CAVE-PERSONS!
HURRY, TO THE TIME SPHERE, BEFORE IT'S TOO LATE!
BASH
WHERE TO, CAPED CRUSADER?
ANCIENT SYRACUSE!
KLONK
drive in
OUTRAGEOUS!
THE CENTURIES ZIP BY IN A SWIFT SUCCESSION OF EYE-BLINKS, UNTIL...
1951 AD...
1812 AD...
1450 AD...
150 AD...

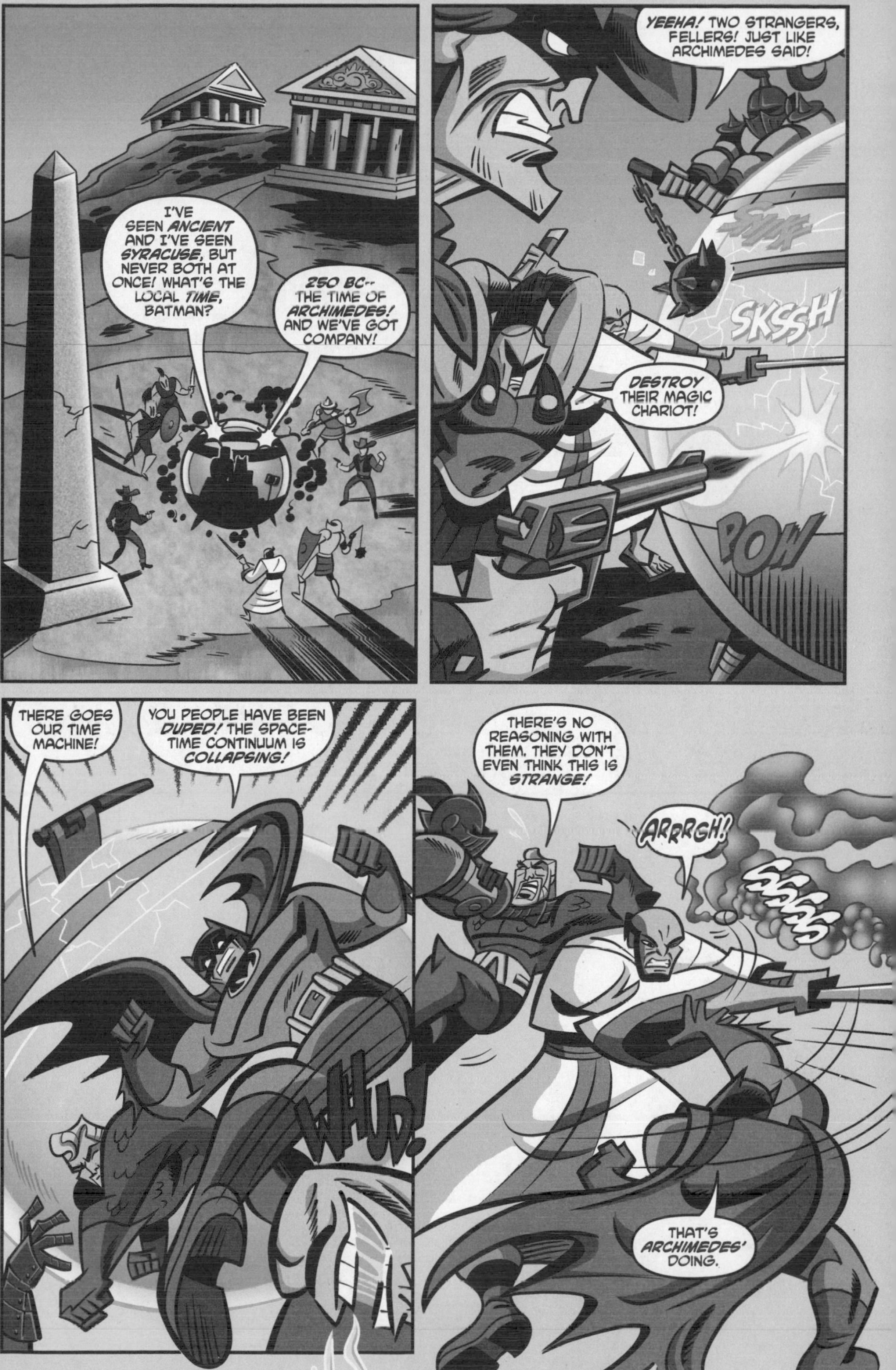
I'VE SEEN ANCIENT AND I'VE SEEN SYRACUSE, BUT NEVER BOTH AT ONCE! WHAT'S THE LOCAL TIME, BATMAN?
250 BC-- THE TIME OF ARCHIMEDES! AND WE'VE GOT COMPANY!
YEEHA! TWO STRANGERS, FELLERS! JUST LIKE ARCHIMEDES SAID!
SKSSH
DESTROY THEIR MAGIC CHARIOT!
POW
THERE GOES OUR TIME MACHINE!
YOU PEOPLE HAVE BEEN DUPED! THE SPACE-TIME CONTINUUM IS COLLAPSING!
WHUD!
THERE'S NO REASONING WITH THEM. THEY DON'T EVEN THINK THIS IS STRANGE!
ARRRGH!
THAT'S ARCHIMEDES' DOING.

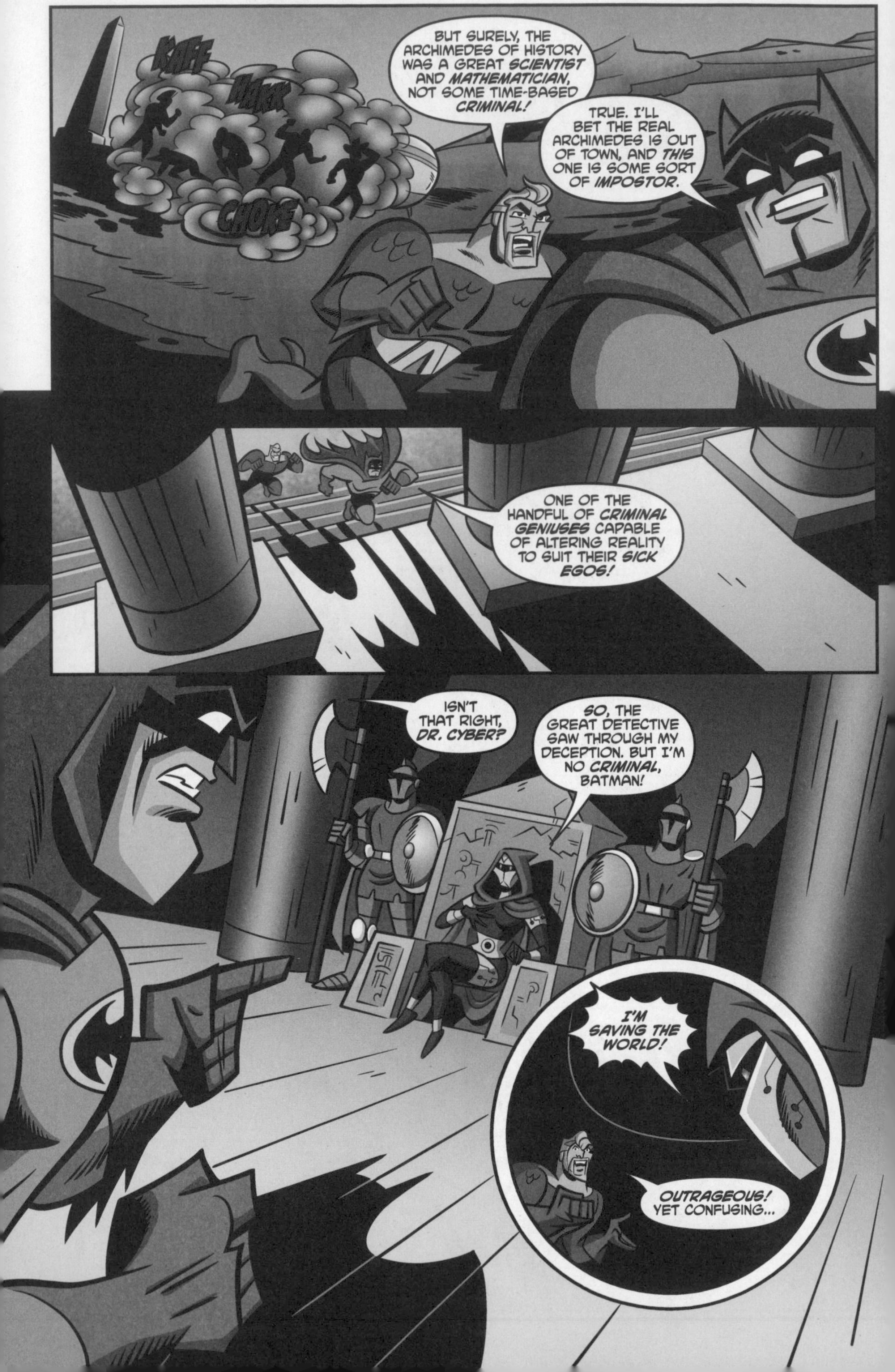

KAFF
HARK
CHOKE
BUT SURELY, THE ARCHIMEDES OF HISTORY WAS A GREAT SCIENTIST AND MATHEMATICIAN, NOT SOME TIME-BASED CRIMINAL!
TRUE. I'LL BET THE REAL ARCHIMEDES IS OUT OF TOWN, AND THIS ONE IS SOME SORT OF IMPOSTOR.
ONE OF THE HANDFUL OF CRIMINAL GENIUSES CAPABLE OF ALTERING REALITY TO SUIT THEIR SICK EGOS!
ISN'T THAT RIGHT, DR. CYBER?
SO, THE GREAT DETECTIVE SAW THROUGH MY DECEPTION. BUT I'M NO CRIMINAL, BATMAN!
I'M SAVING THE WORLD!
OUTRAGEOUS! YET CONFUSING...

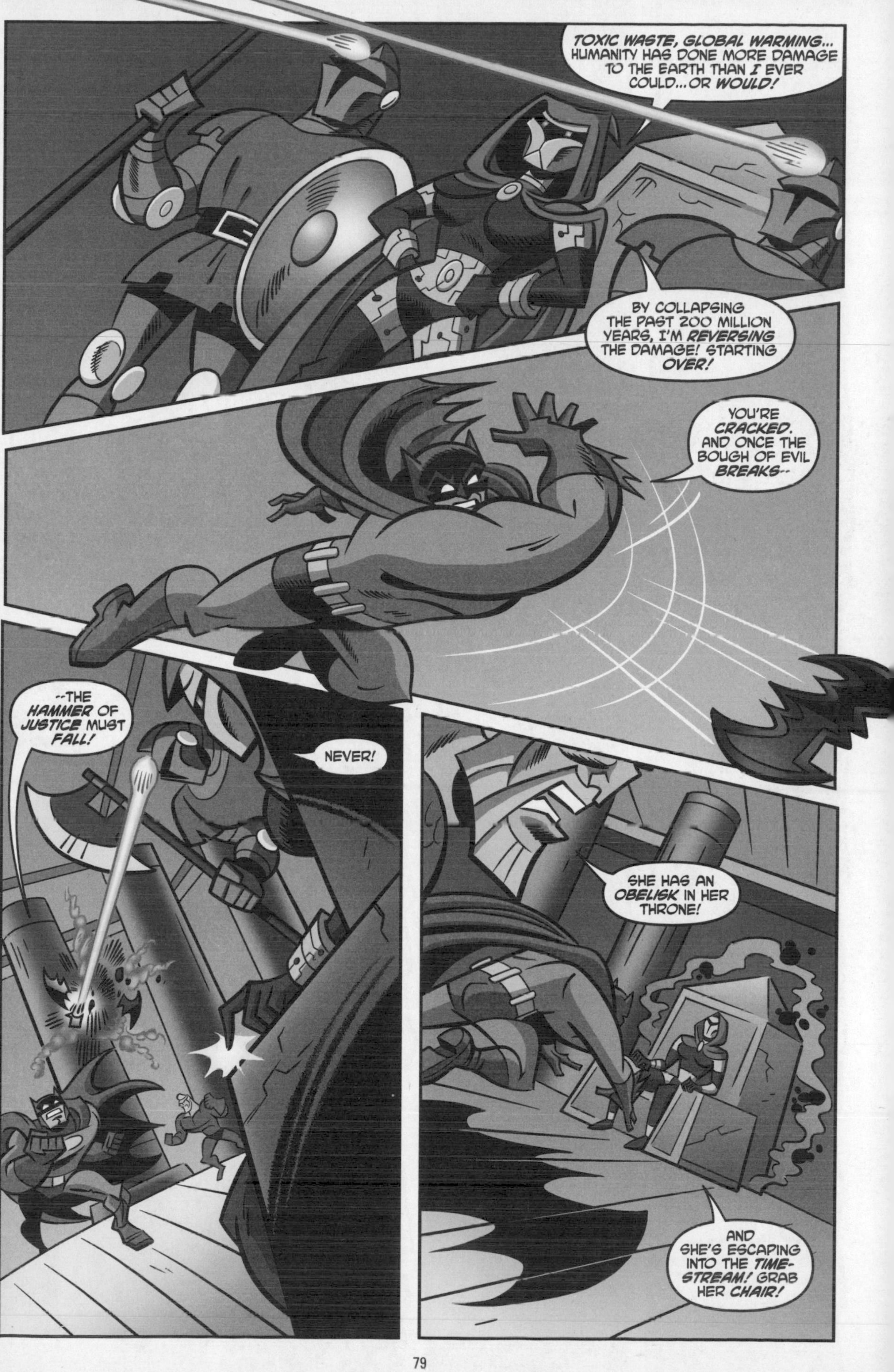
TOXIC WASTE, GLOBAL WARMING... HUMANITY HAS DONE MORE DAMAGE TO THE EARTH THAN I EVER COULD...OR WOULD!
BY COLLAPSING THE PAST 200 MILLION YEARS, I'M REVERSING THE DAMAGE! STARTING OVER!
YOU'RE CRACKED. AND ONCE THE BOUGH OF EVIL BREAKS--
--THE HAMMER OF JUSTICE MUST FALL!
NEVER!
SHE HAS AN OBELISK IN HER THRONE!
AND SHE'S ESCAPING INTO THE TIME-STREAM! GRAB HER CHAIR!

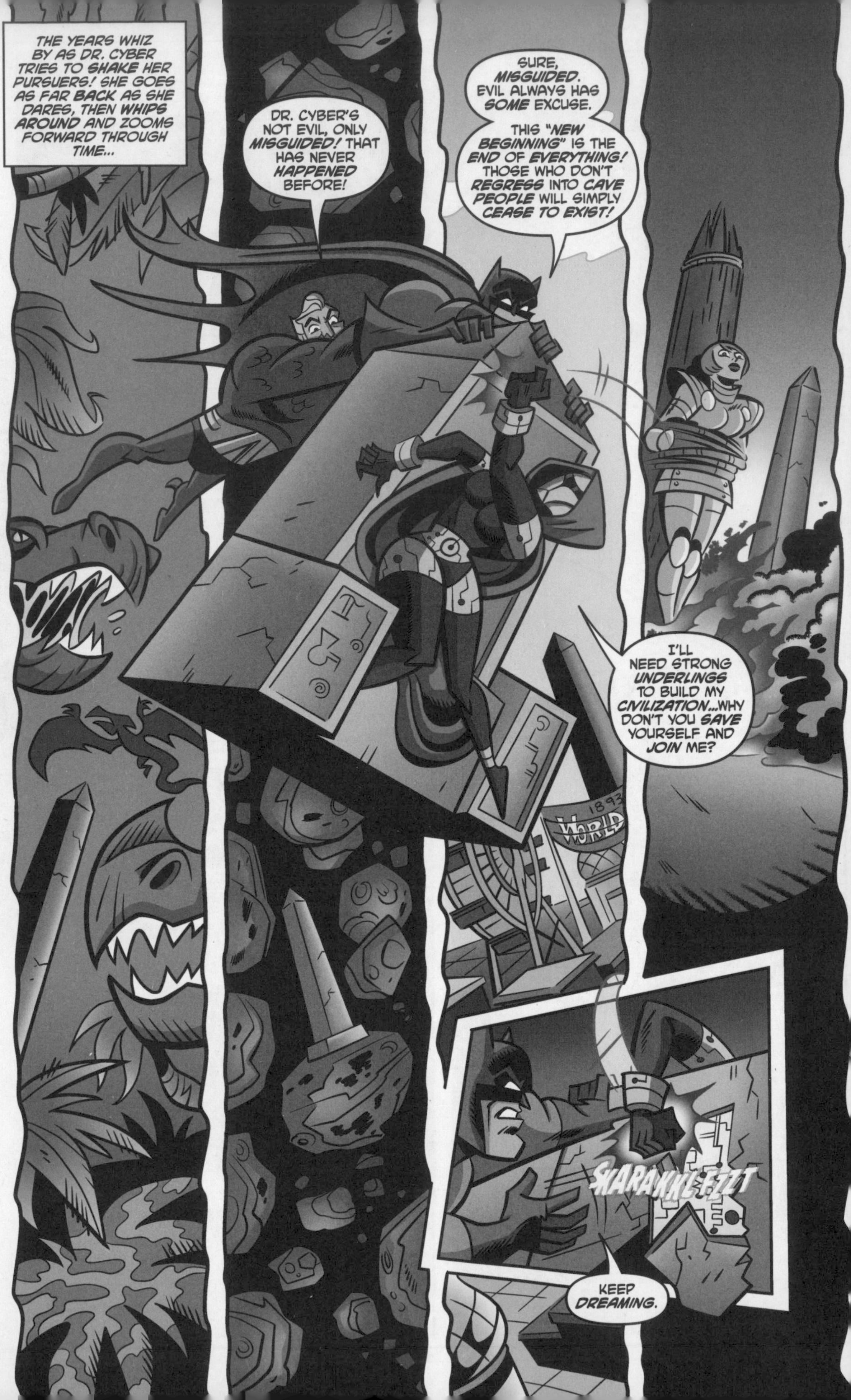
THE YEARS WHIZ BY AS DR. CYBER TRIES TO SHAKE HER PURSUERS! SHE GOES AS FAR BACK AS SHE DARES, THEN WHIPS AROUND AND ZOOMS FORWARD THROUGH TIME...
DR. CYBER'S NOT EVIL, ONLY MISGUIDED! THAT HAS NEVER HAPPENED BEFORE!
SURE, MISGUIDED. EVIL ALWAYS HAS SOME EXCUSE.
THIS "NEW BEGINNING" IS THE END OF EVERYTHING! THOSE WHO DON'T REGRESS INTO CAVE PEOPLE WILL SIMPLY CEASE TO EXIST!
I'LL NEED STRONG UNDERLINGS TO BUILD MY CIVILIZATION...WHY DON'T YOU SAVE YOURSELF AND JOIN ME?
1893
WORLD
SKARAKKLEZZT
KEEP DREAMING.

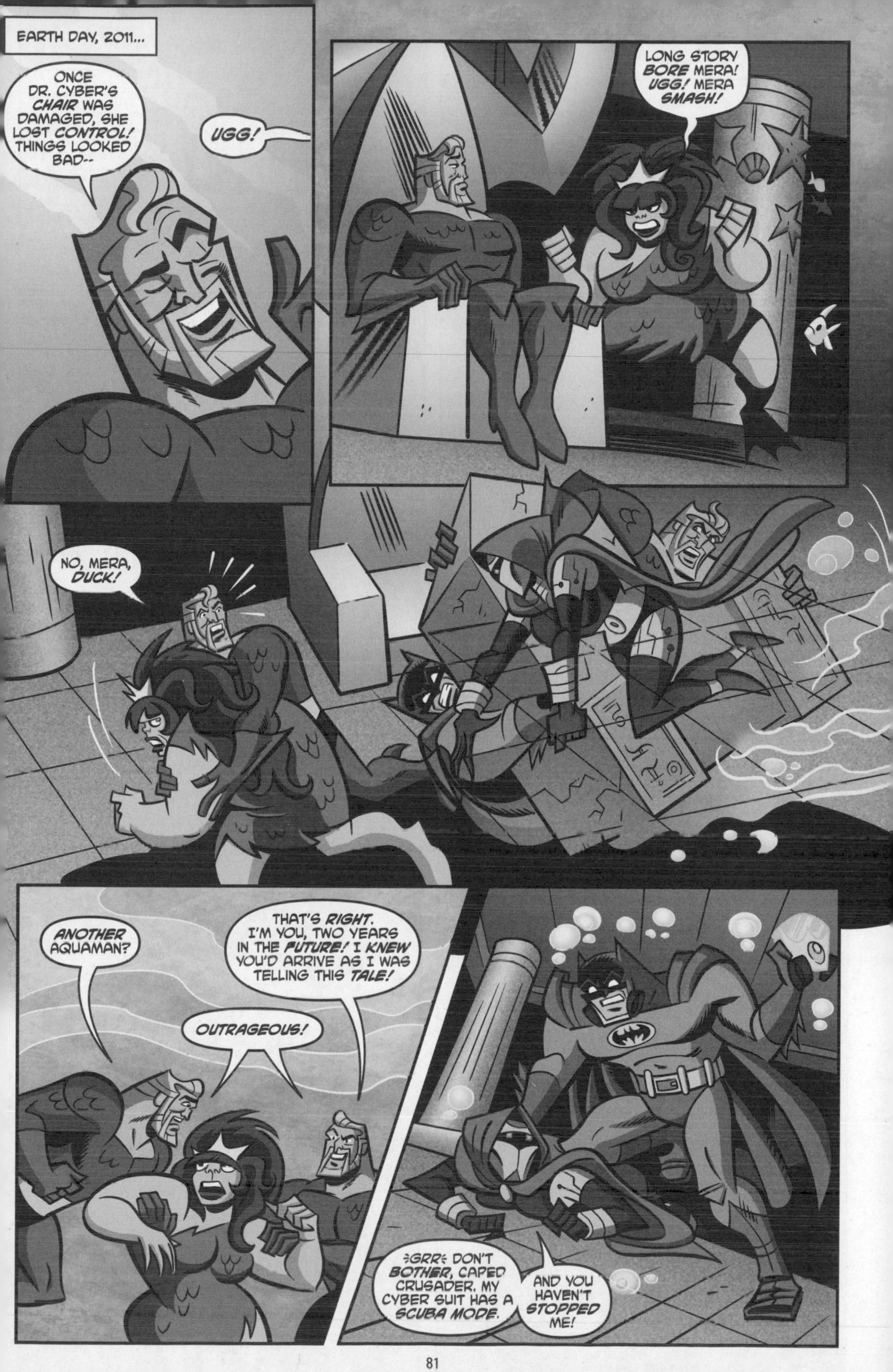
EARTH DAY, 2011...
ONCE DR. CYBER'S CHAIR WAS DAMAGED, SHE LOST CONTROL! THINGS LOOKED BAD--
UGG!
LONG STORY BORE MERA! UGG! MERA SMASH!
NO, MERA, DUCK!
ANOTHER AQUAMAN?
THAT'S RIGHT. I'M YOU, TWO YEARS IN THE FUTURE! I KNEW YOU'D ARRIVE AS I WAS TELLING THIS TALE!
OUTRAGEOUS!
GRR DON'T BOTHER, CAPED CRUSADER. MY CYBER SUIT HAS A SCUBA MODE.
AND YOU HAVEN'T STOPPED ME!

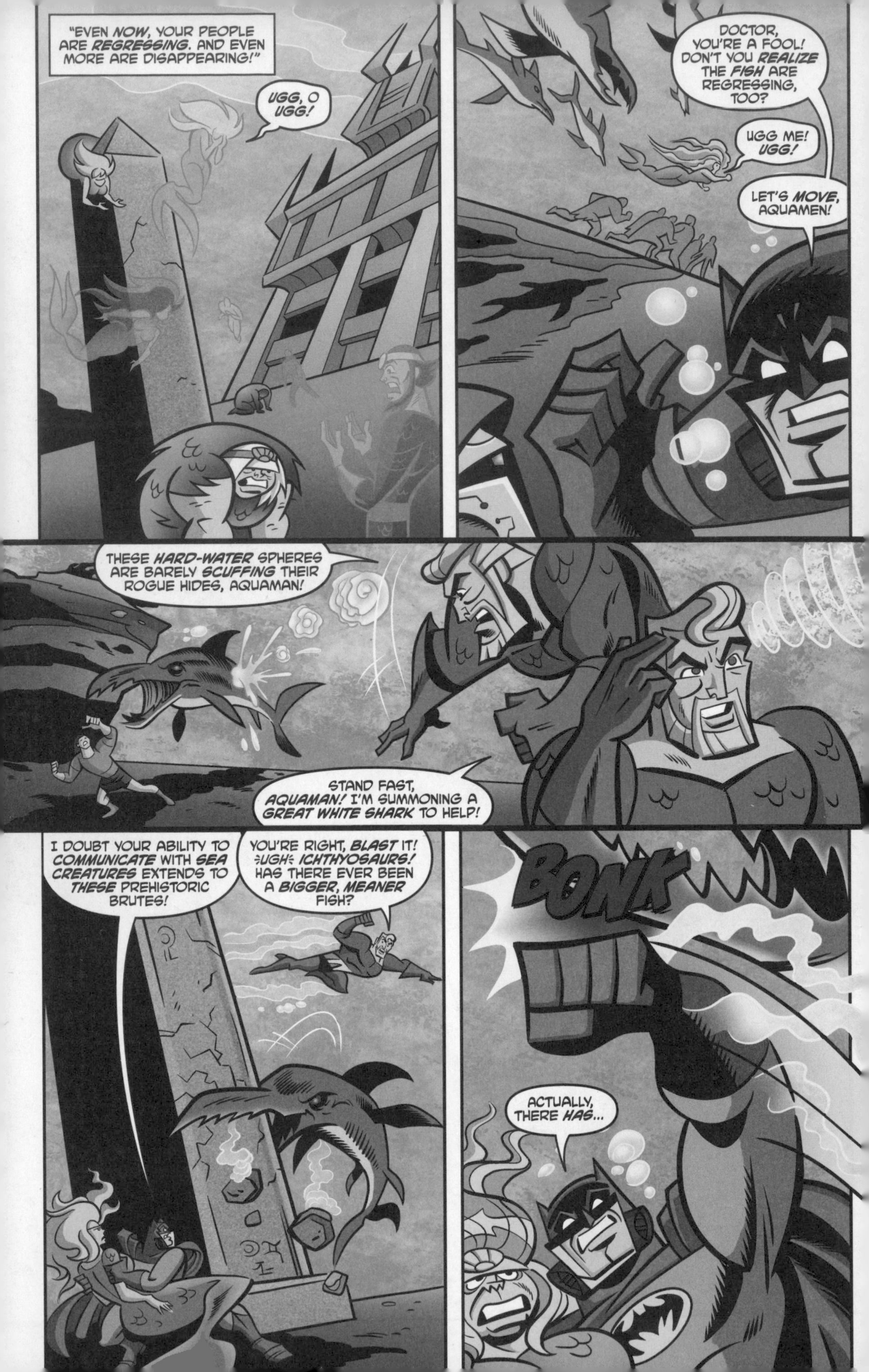
"EVEN NOW, YOUR PEOPLE ARE REGRESSING. AND EVEN MORE ARE DISAPPEARING!"
UGG, O UGG!
DOCTOR, YOU'RE A FOOL! DON'T YOU REALIZE THE FISH ARE REGRESSING, TOO?
UGG ME! UGG!
LET'S MOVE, AQUAMEN!
THESE HARD-WATER SPHERES ARE BARELY SCUFFING THEIR ROGUE HIDES, AQUAMAN!
STAND FAST, AQUAMAN! I'M SUMMONING A GREAT WHITE SHARK TO HELP!
I DOUBT YOUR ABILITY TO COMMUNICATE WITH SEA CREATURES EXTENDS TO THESE PREHISTORIC BRUTES!
YOU'RE RIGHT, BLAST IT! UGH ICHTHYOSAURS! HAS THERE EVER BEEN A BIGGER, MEANER FISH?
BONK
ACTUALLY, THERE HAS...

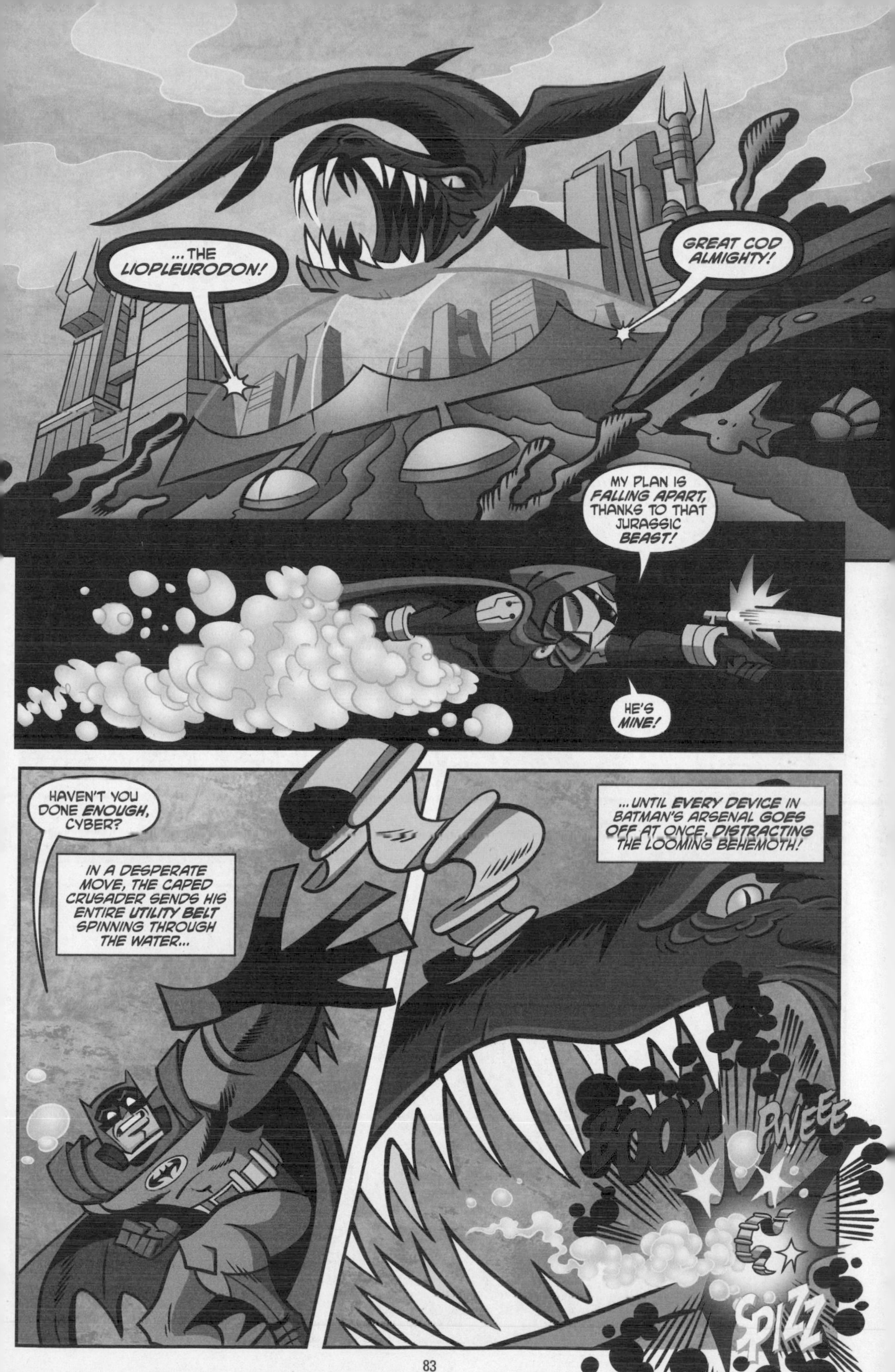
...THE LIOPLEURODON!
GREAT COD ALMIGHTY!
MY PLAN IS FALLING APART, THANKS TO THAT JURASSIC BEAST!
HE'S MINE!
HAVEN'T YOU DONE ENOUGH, CYBER?
IN A DESPERATE MOVE, THE CAPED CRUSADER SENDS HIS ENTIRE UTILITY BELT SPINNING THROUGH THE WATER...
...UNTIL EVERY DEVICE IN BATMAN'S ARSENAL GOES OFF AT ONCE, DISTRACTING THE LOOMING BEHEMOTH!
BOOM
PWEEE
SPIZZ

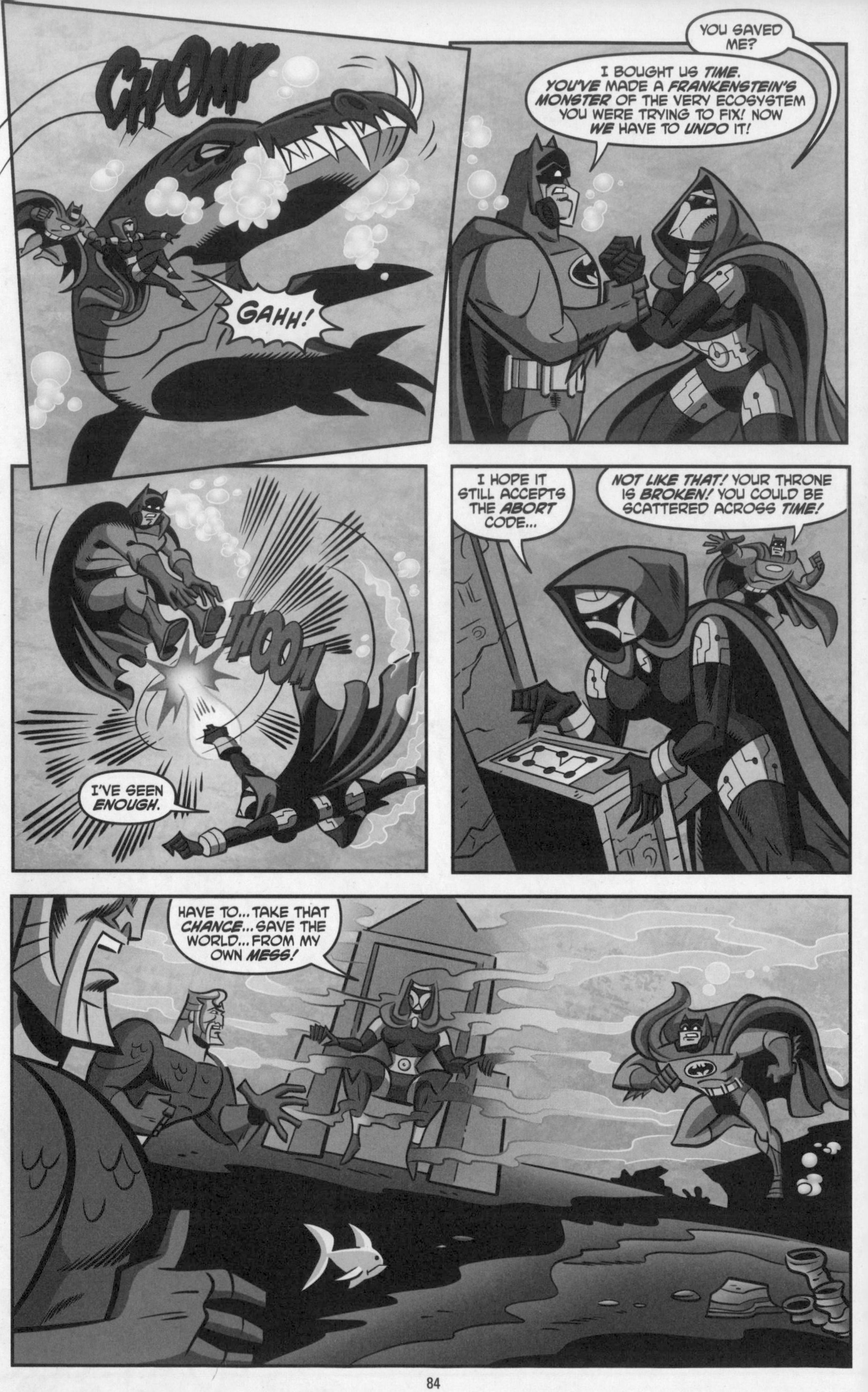
CHOMP
GAHH!
YOU SAVED ME?
I BOUGHT US TIME. YOU'VE MADE A FRANKENSTEIN'S MONSTER OF THE VERY ECOSYSTEM YOU WERE TRYING TO FIX! NOW WE HAVE TO UNDO IT!
THOOM
I'VE SEEN ENOUGH.
I HOPE IT STILL ACCEPTS THE ABORT CODE...
NOT LIKE THAT! YOUR THRONE IS BROKEN! YOU COULD BE SCATTERED ACROSS TIME!
HAVE TO... TAKE THAT CHANCE... SAVE THE WORLD... FROM MY OWN MESS!

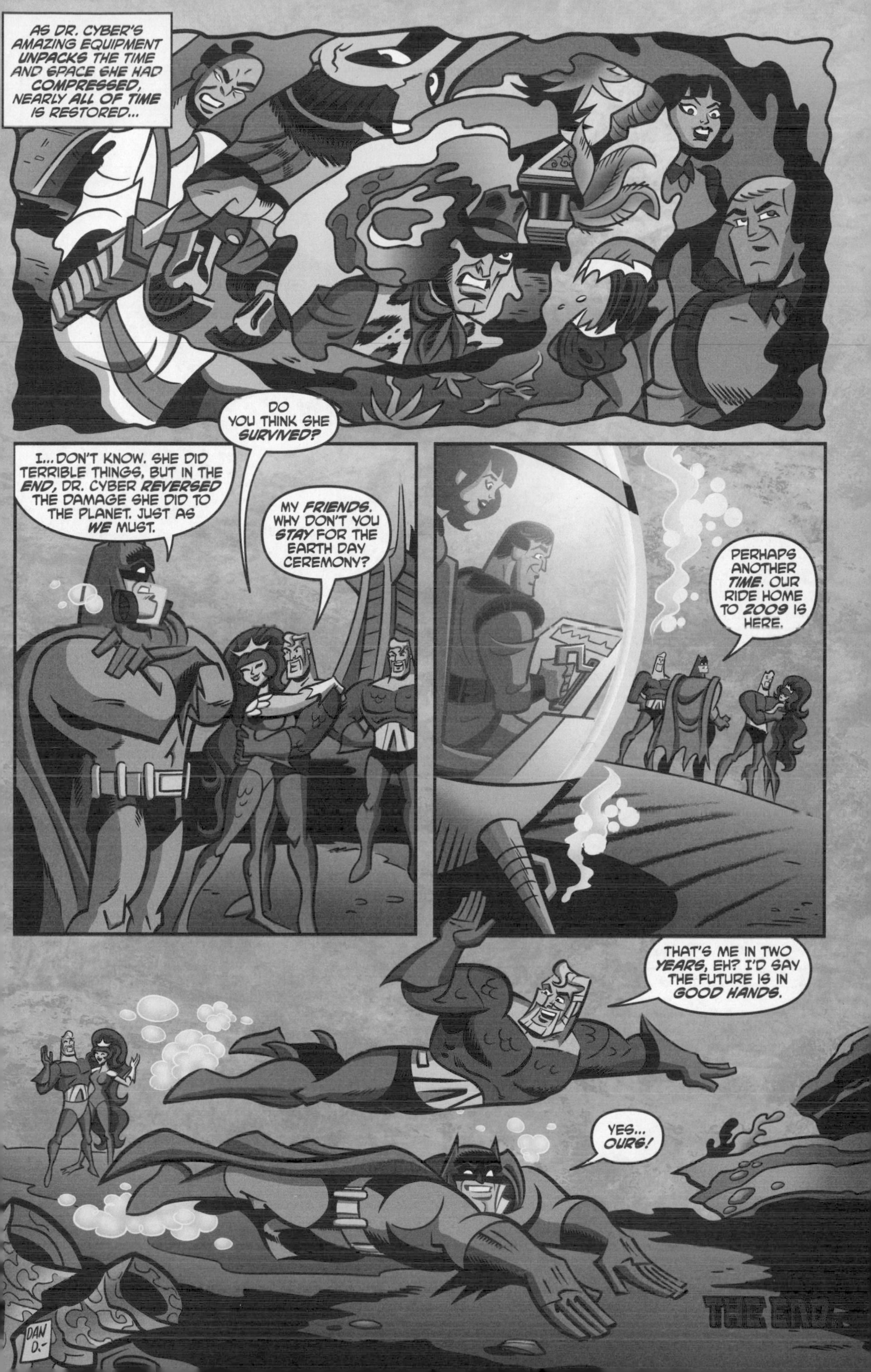
AS DR. CYBER'S AMAZING EQUIPMENT UNPACKS THE TIME AND SPACE SHE HAD COMPRESSED, NEARLY ALL OF TIME IS RESTORED...
DO YOU THINK SHE SURVIVED?
I... DON'T KNOW. SHE DID TERRIBLE THINGS, BUT IN THE END, DR. CYBER REVERSED THE DAMAGE SHE DID TO THE PLANET. JUST AS WE MUST.
MY FRIENDS. WHY DON'T YOU STAY FOR THE EARTH DAY CEREMONY?
PERHAPS ANOTHER TIME. OUR RIDE HOME TO 2009 IS HERE.
THAT'S ME IN TWO YEARS, EH? I'D SAY THE FUTURE IS IN GOOD HANDS.
YES... OURS!
THE END.
DAN D.-

DR. CYBER

Brilliant **Dr. CYBER** longs to rule a technological utopia. Using an incredibly advanced cyber suit of her own design, her amazing micro-circuitry can create any number of trans-spatial, dimensional and temporal effects. Never one to make the same mistake twice, her failed attempts to take over the world always leave her more powerful than before.

TOP SECRET:
For all her technical genius, **Dr. Cyber** isn't a doctor of science. She holds multiple advanced degrees in literature.

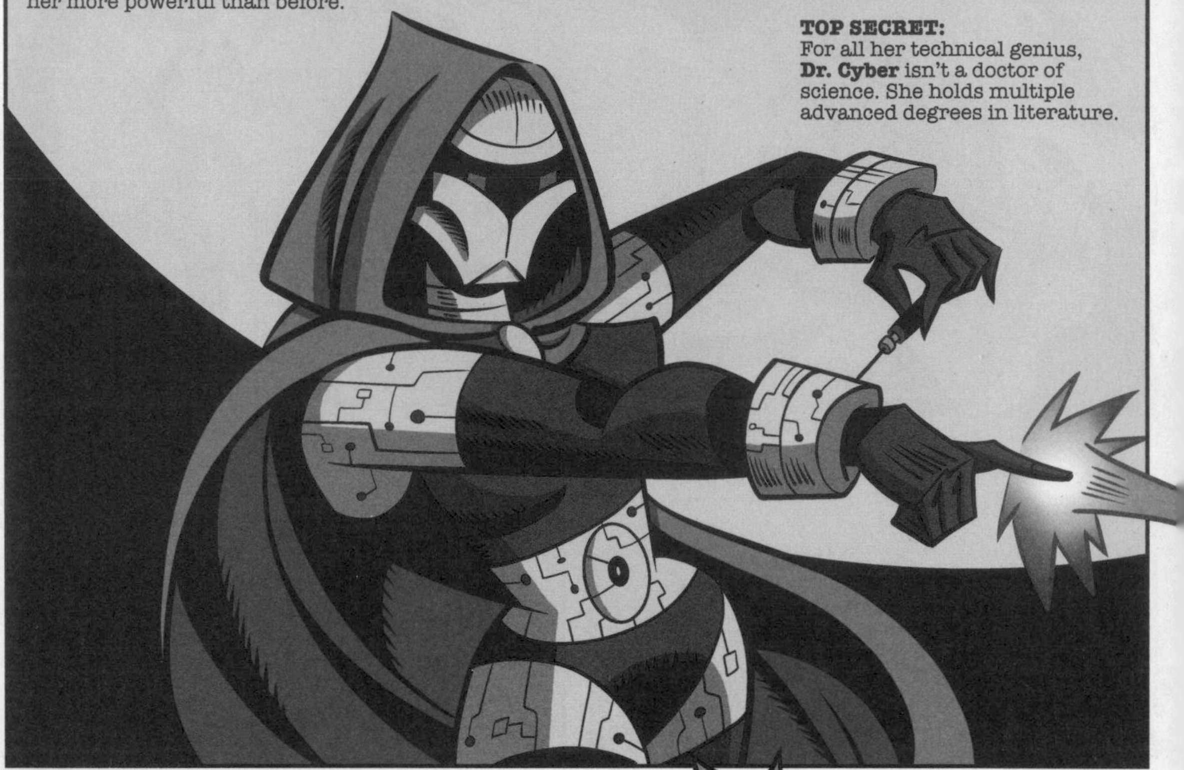

SECRET BAT-FILES

AQUAMAN

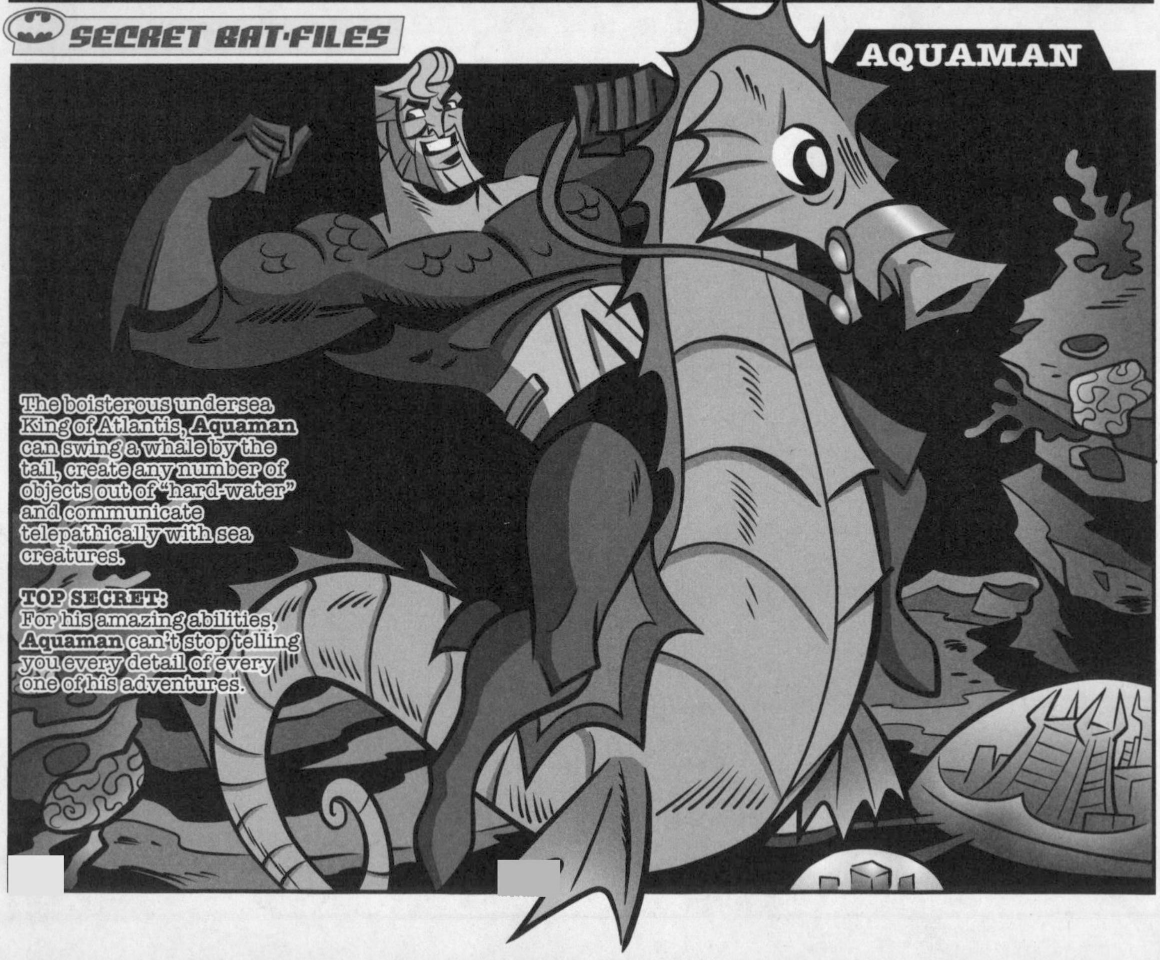

The boisterous undersea King of Atlantis, **Aquaman** can swing a whale by the tail, create any number of objects out of "hard-water" and communicate telepathically with sea creatures.

TOP SECRET:
For his amazing abilities, **Aquaman** can't stop telling you every detail of every one of his adventures.

BATMAN: THE BRAVE AND THE BOLD #5
Cover by Scott Jeralds with Hi-Fi

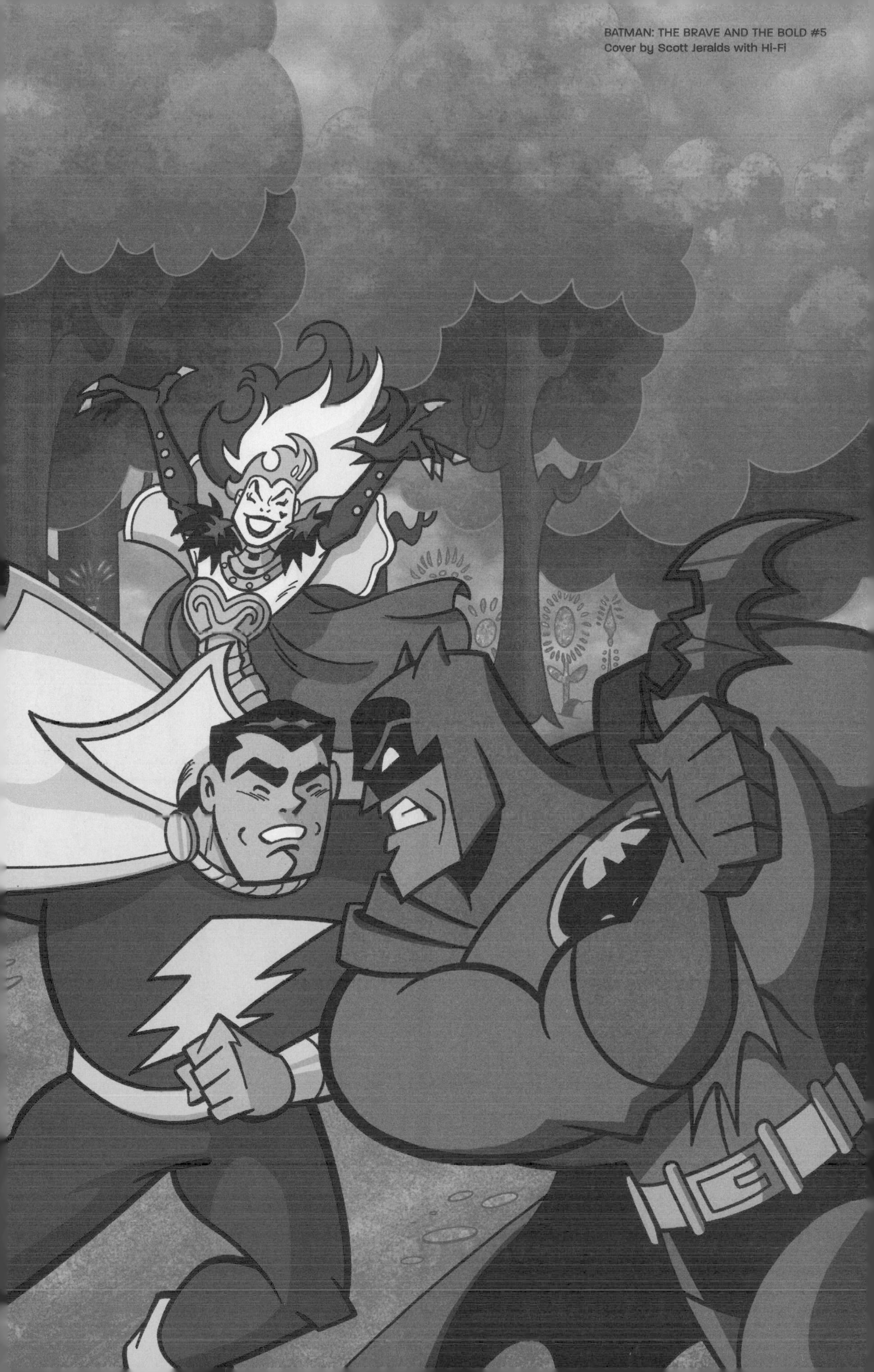

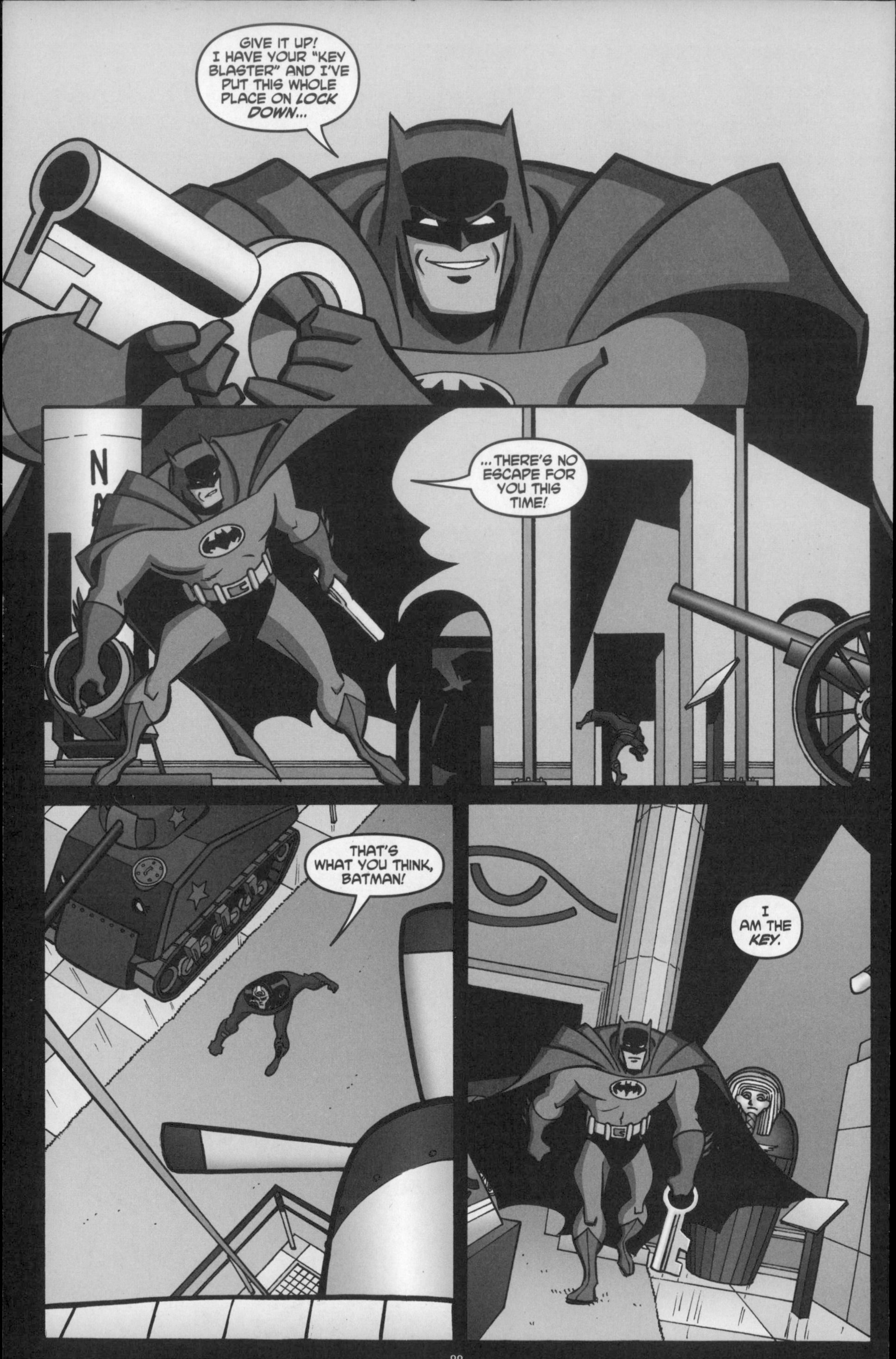
GIVE IT UP! I HAVE YOUR "KEY BLASTER" AND I'VE PUT THIS WHOLE PLACE ON LOCK DOWN...
...THERE'S NO ESCAPE FOR YOU THIS TIME!
THAT'S WHAT YOU THINK, BATMAN!
I AM THE KEY.

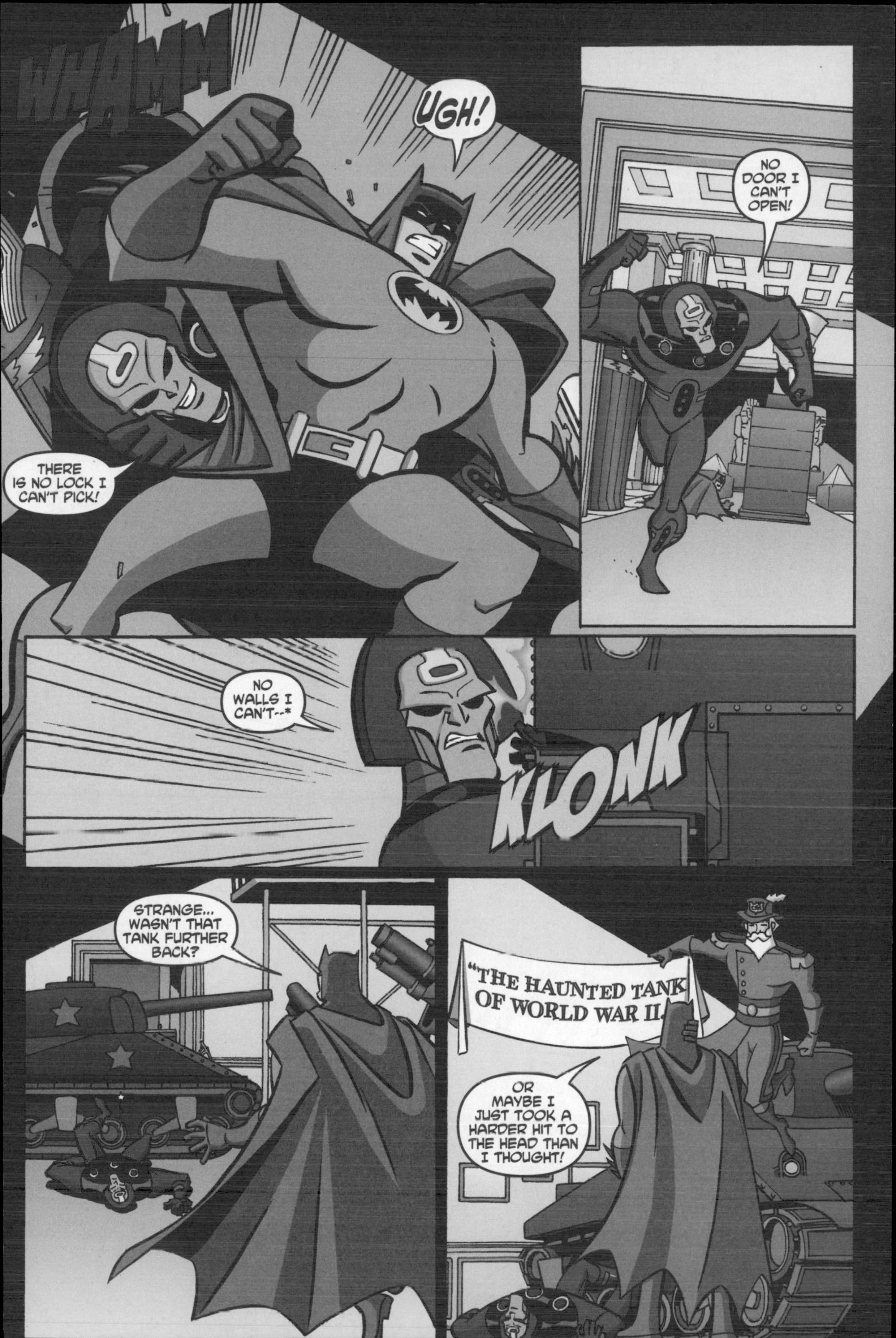
WHAMM
UGH!
THERE IS NO LOCK I CAN'T PICK!
NO DOOR I CAN'T OPEN!
NO WALLS I CAN'T--*
KLONK
STRANGE... WASN'T THAT TANK FURTHER BACK?
"THE HAUNTED TANK OF WORLD WAR II."
OR MAYBE I JUST TOOK A HARDER HIT TO THE HEAD THAN I THOUGHT!

THE CASE OF THE FRACTURED FAIRY TALE!

WRITER: J. TORRES PENCILS: CARLO BARBERI INKS: TERRY BEATTY
COLORIST: HEROIC AGE LETTERER: SAL CIPRIANO

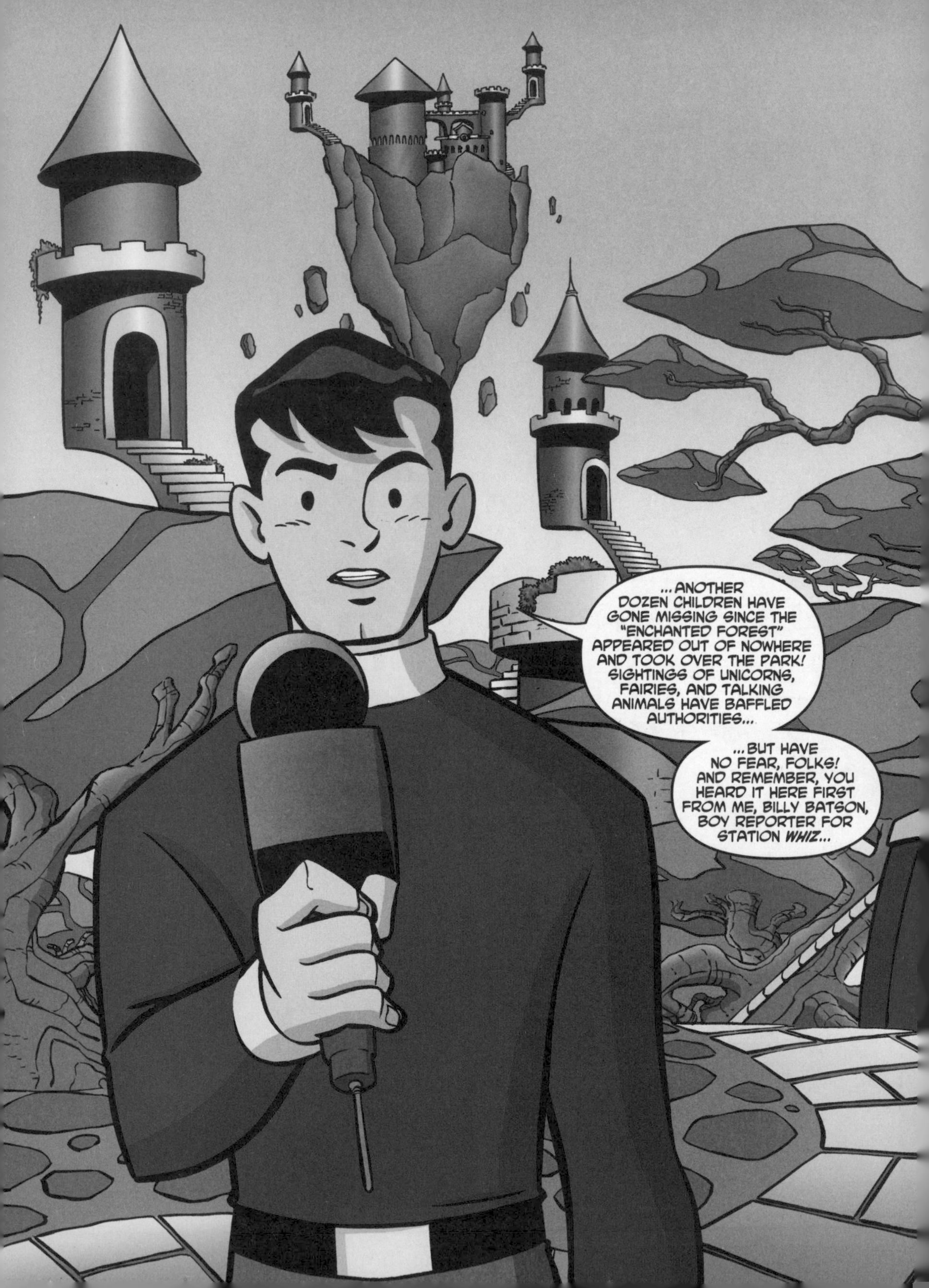
...ANOTHER DOZEN CHILDREN HAVE GONE MISSING SINCE THE "ENCHANTED FOREST" APPEARED OUT OF NOWHERE AND TOOK OVER THE PARK! SIGHTINGS OF UNICORNS, FAIRIES, AND TALKING ANIMALS HAVE BAFFLED AUTHORITIES...
...BUT HAVE NO FEAR, FOLKS! AND REMEMBER, YOU HEARD IT HERE FIRST FROM ME, BILLY BATSON, BOY REPORTER FOR STATION *WHIZ*...

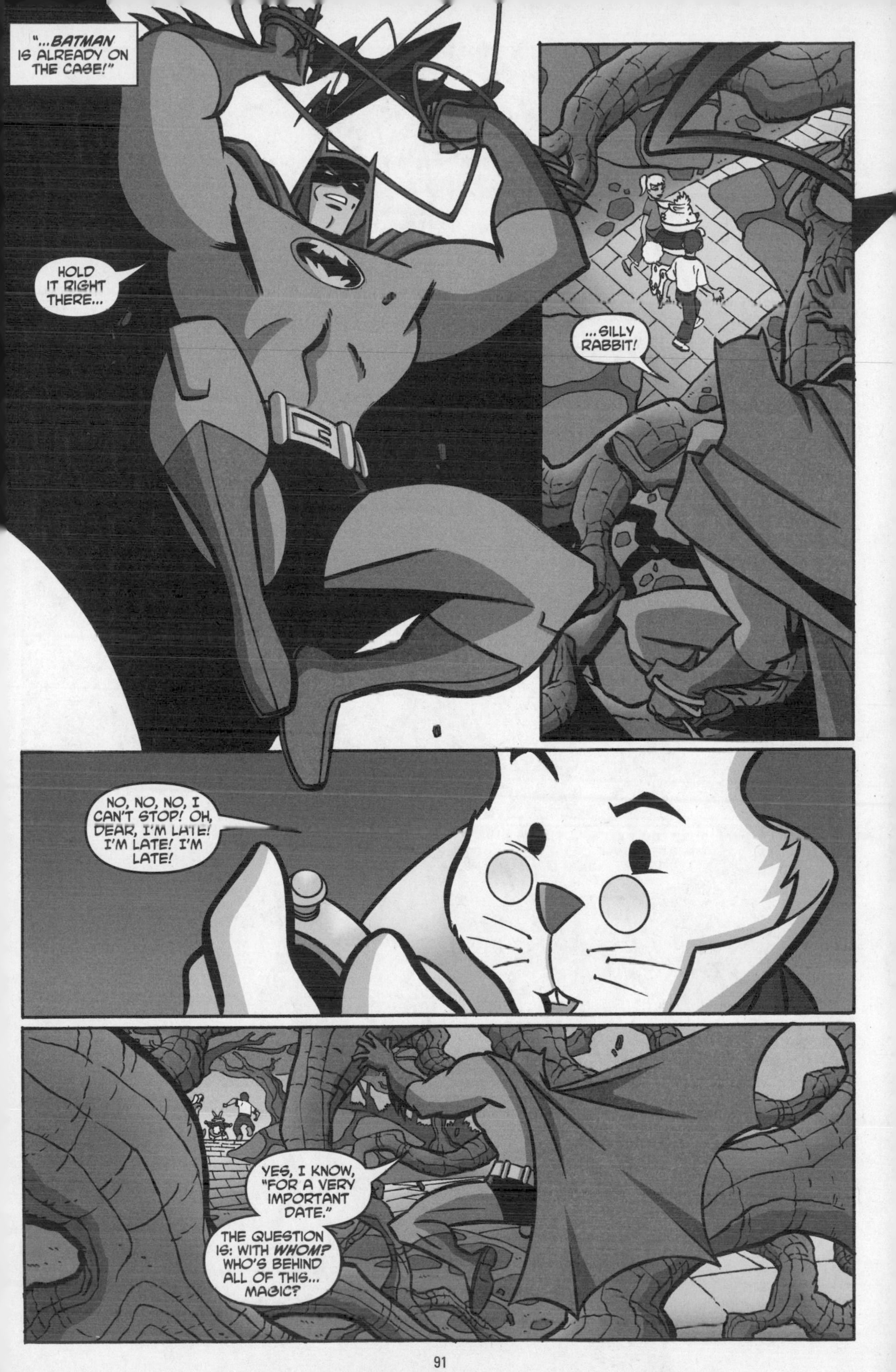
"...BATMAN IS ALREADY ON THE CASE!"
HOLD IT RIGHT THERE...
...SILLY RABBIT!
NO, NO, NO, I CAN'T STOP! OH, DEAR, I'M LATE! I'M LATE! I'M LATE!
YES, I KNOW, "FOR A VERY IMPORTANT DATE."
THE QUESTION IS: WITH WHOM? WHO'S BEHIND ALL OF THIS... MAGIC?

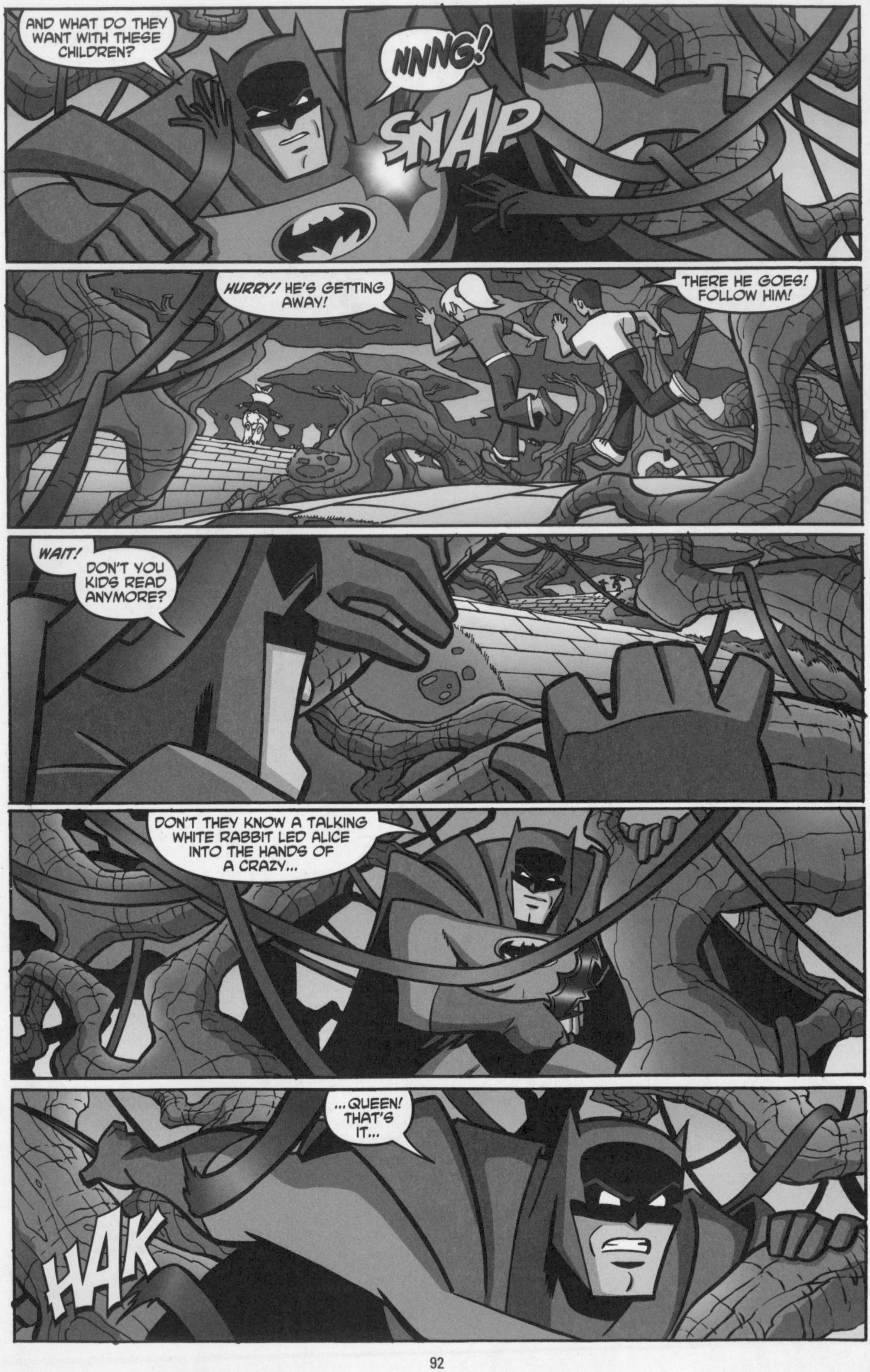
AND WHAT DO THEY WANT WITH THESE CHILDREN?
NNNG!
SNAP
HURRY! HE'S GETTING AWAY!
THERE HE GOES! FOLLOW HIM!
WAIT!
DON'T YOU KIDS READ ANYMORE?
DON'T THEY KNOW A TALKING WHITE RABBIT LED ALICE INTO THE HANDS OF A CRAZY...
...QUEEN! THAT'S IT...
HAK

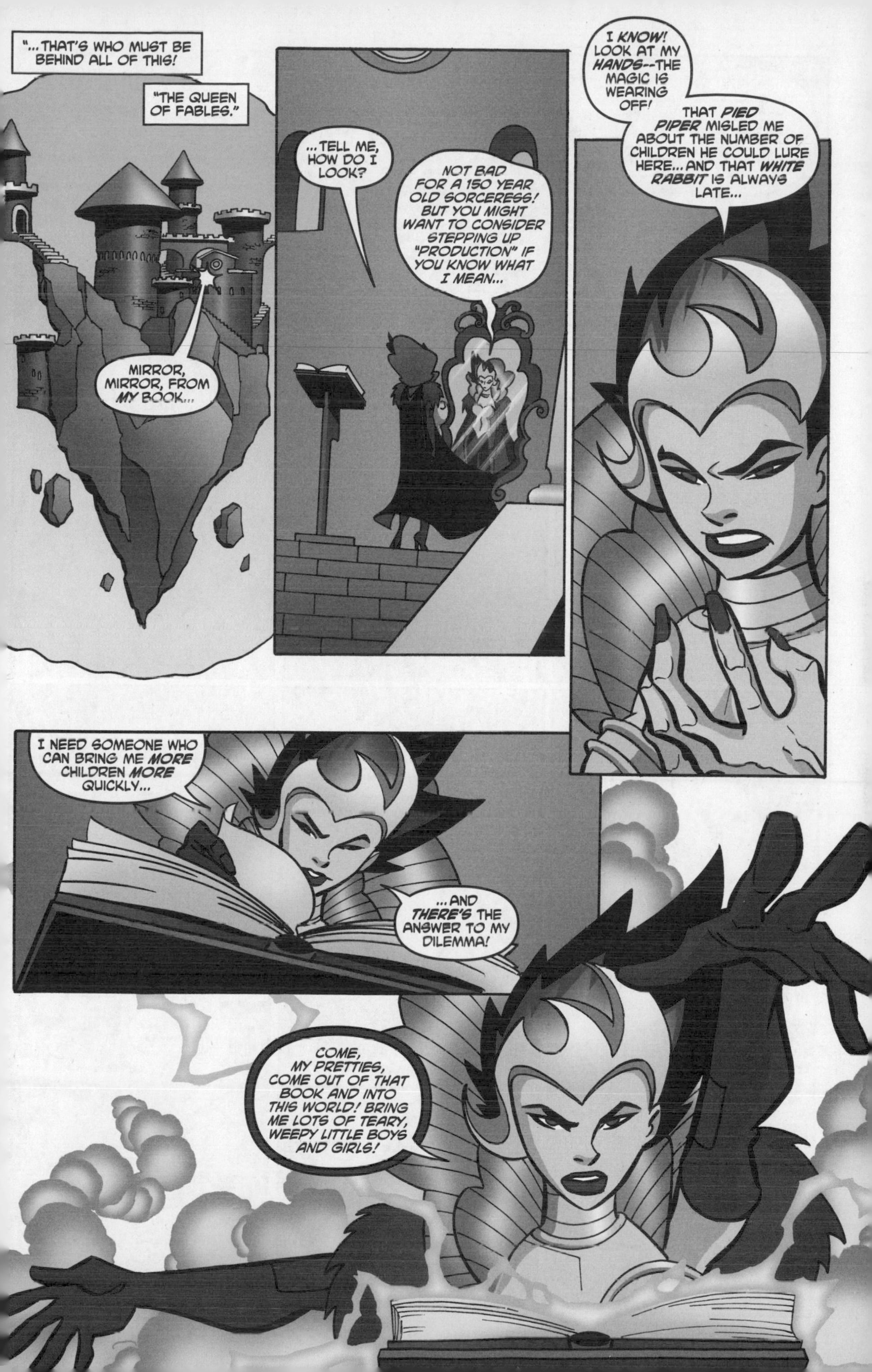

"...THAT'S WHO MUST BE BEHIND ALL OF THIS!
"THE QUEEN OF FABLES."
MIRROR, MIRROR, FROM *MY* BOOK...
...TELL ME, HOW DO I LOOK?
NOT BAD FOR A 150 YEAR OLD SORCERESS! BUT YOU MIGHT WANT TO CONSIDER STEPPING UP "PRODUCTION" IF YOU KNOW WHAT I MEAN...
I *KNOW*! LOOK AT MY *HANDS*--THE MAGIC IS WEARING OFF!
THAT *PIED PIPER* MISLED ME ABOUT THE NUMBER OF CHILDREN HE COULD LURE HERE...AND THAT *WHITE RABBIT* IS ALWAYS LATE...
I NEED SOMEONE WHO CAN BRING ME *MORE* CHILDREN *MORE* QUICKLY...
...AND *THERE'S* THE ANSWER TO MY DILEMMA!
COME, MY PRETTIES, COME OUT OF THAT BOOK AND INTO THIS WORLD! BRING ME LOTS OF TEARY, WEEPY LITTLE BOYS AND GIRLS!

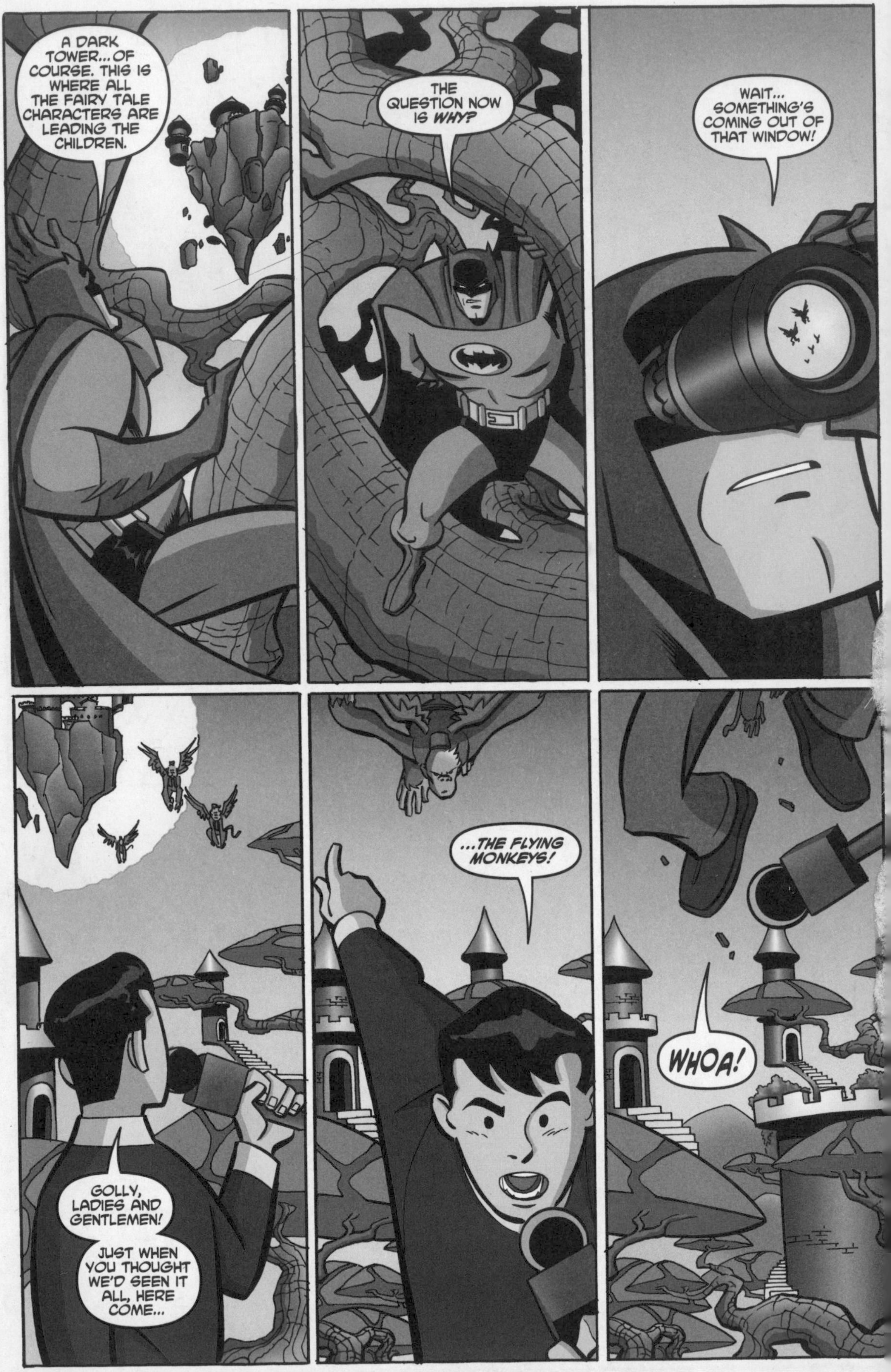
A DARK TOWER...OF COURSE. THIS IS WHERE ALL THE FAIRY TALE CHARACTERS ARE LEADING THE CHILDREN.
THE QUESTION NOW IS WHY?
WAIT... SOMETHING'S COMING OUT OF THAT WINDOW!
GOLLY, LADIES AND GENTLEMEN!
JUST WHEN YOU THOUGHT WE'D SEEN IT ALL, HERE COME...
...THE FLYING MONKEYS!
WHOA!

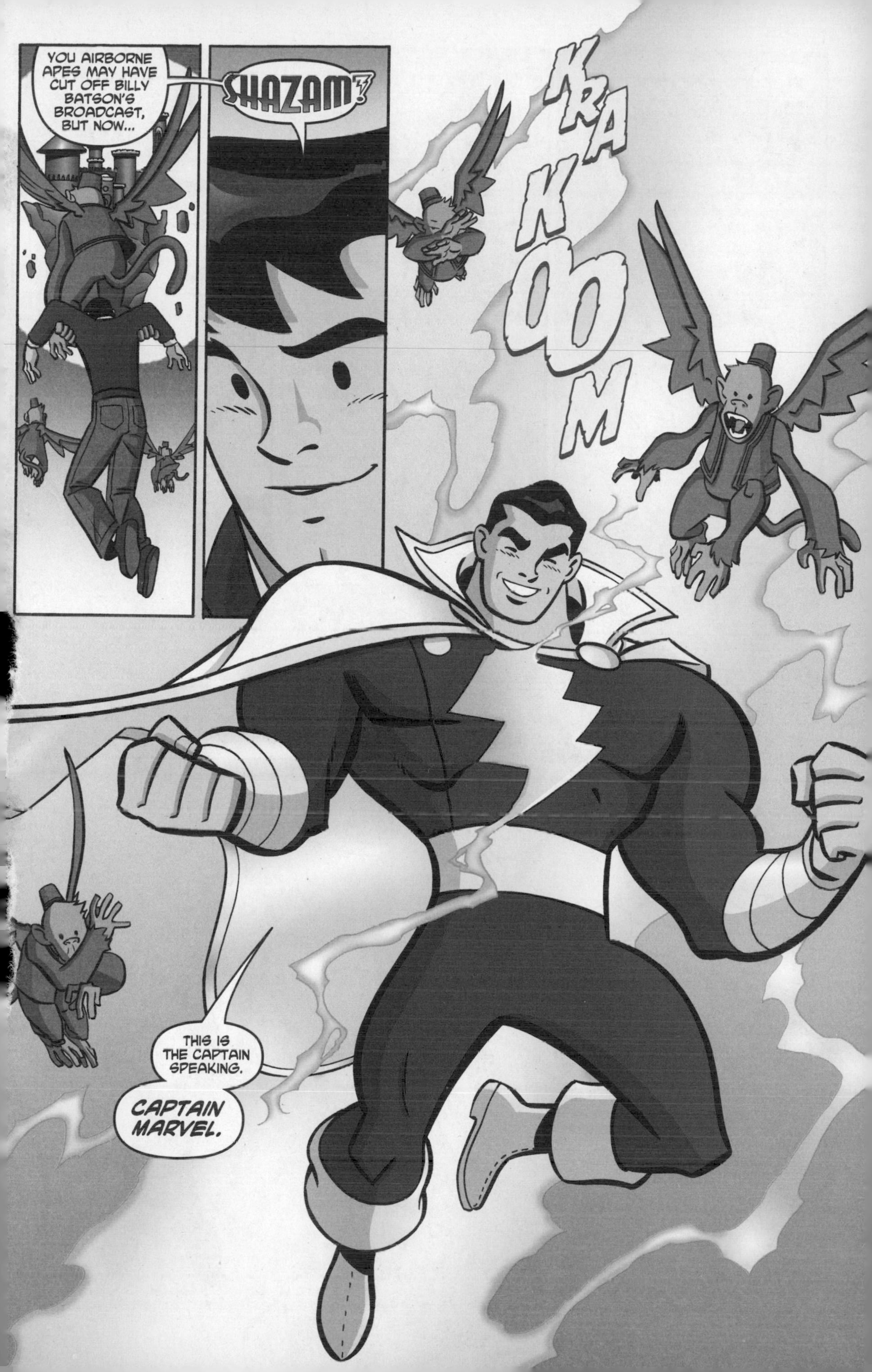
YOU AIRBORNE APES MAY HAVE CUT OFF BILLY BATSON'S BROADCAST, BUT NOW...
SHAZAM!
KRAKOOM
THIS IS THE CAPTAIN SPEAKING.
CAPTAIN MARVEL.

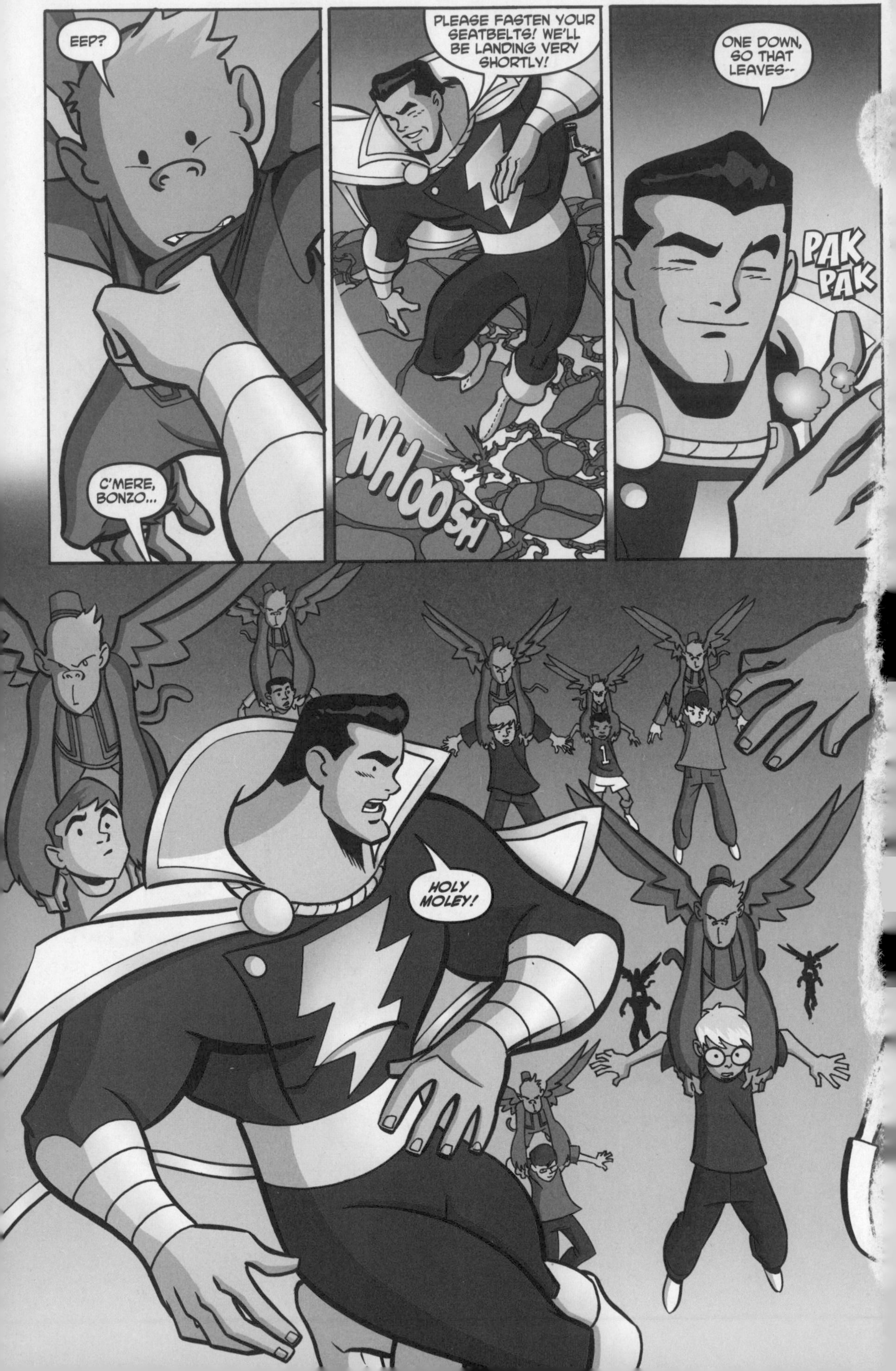
EEP?
C'MERE, BONZO...
PLEASE FASTEN YOUR SEATBELTS! WE'LL BE LANDING VERY SHORTLY!
WHOOSH
ONE DOWN, SO THAT LEAVES--
PAK PAK
HOLY MOLEY!

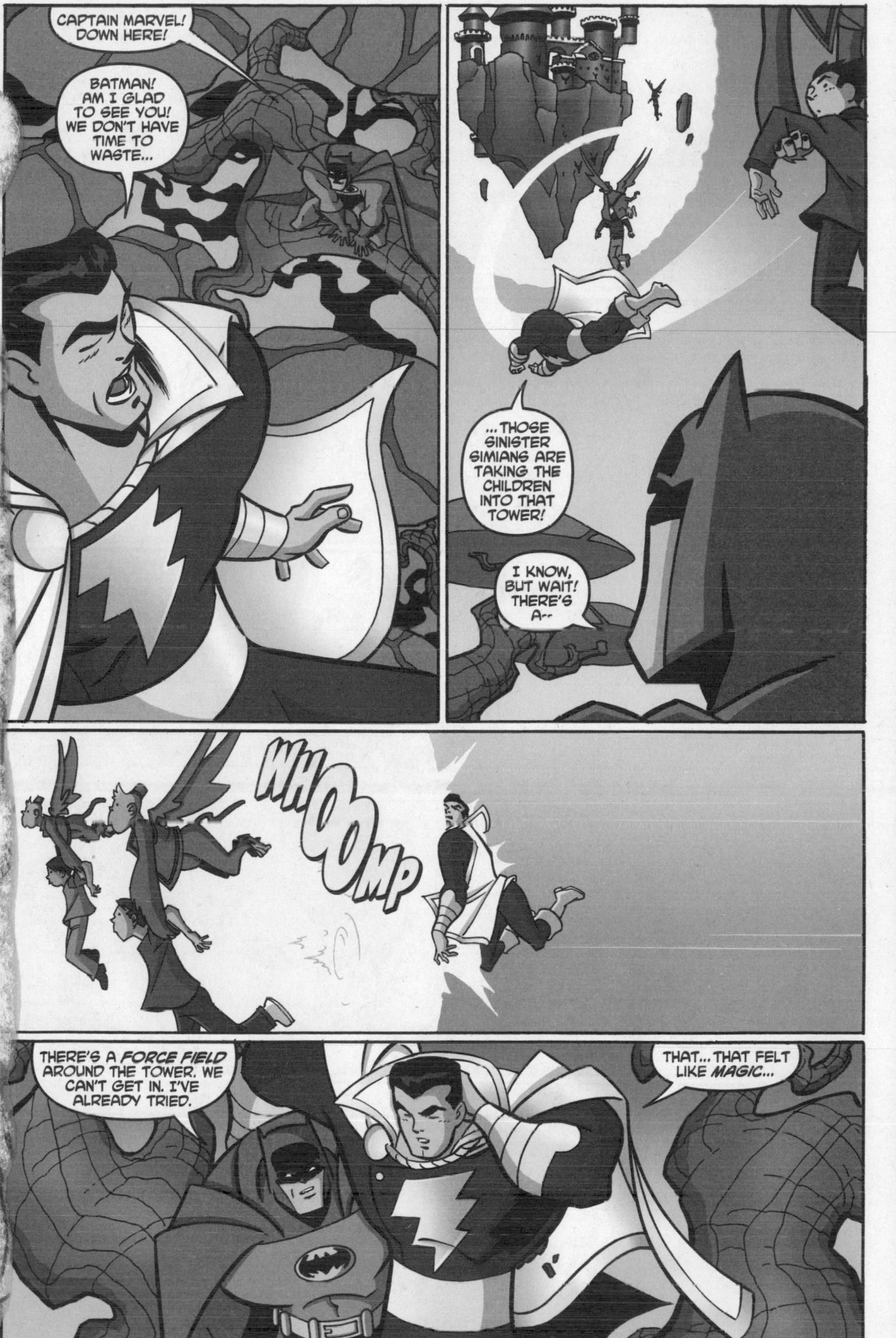
CAPTAIN MARVEL! DOWN HERE!
BATMAN! AM I GLAD TO SEE YOU! WE DON'T HAVE TIME TO WASTE...
...THOSE SINISTER SIMIANS ARE TAKING THE CHILDREN INTO THAT TOWER!
I KNOW, BUT WAIT! THERE'S A--
WHOOOMP
THERE'S A *FORCE FIELD* AROUND THE TOWER. WE CAN'T GET IN. I'VE ALREADY TRIED.
THAT... THAT FELT LIKE *MAGIC*...

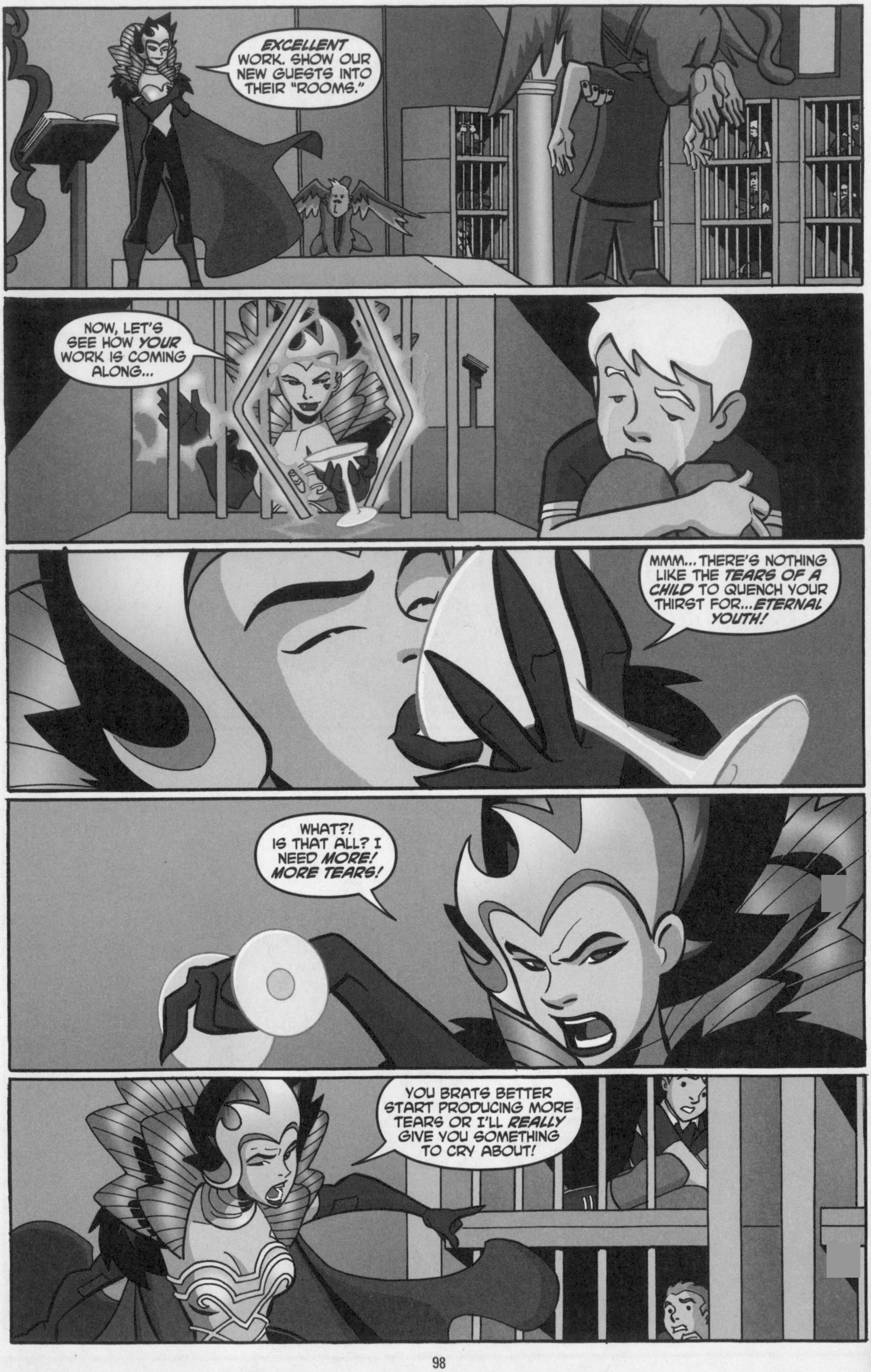
EXCELLENT WORK. SHOW OUR NEW GUESTS INTO THEIR "ROOMS."
NOW, LET'S SEE HOW YOUR WORK IS COMING ALONG...
MMM... THERE'S NOTHING LIKE THE TEARS OF A CHILD TO QUENCH YOUR THIRST FOR... ETERNAL YOUTH!
WHAT?! IS THAT ALL? I NEED MORE! MORE TEARS!
YOU BRATS BETTER START PRODUCING MORE TEARS OR I'LL REALLY GIVE YOU SOMETHING TO CRY ABOUT!

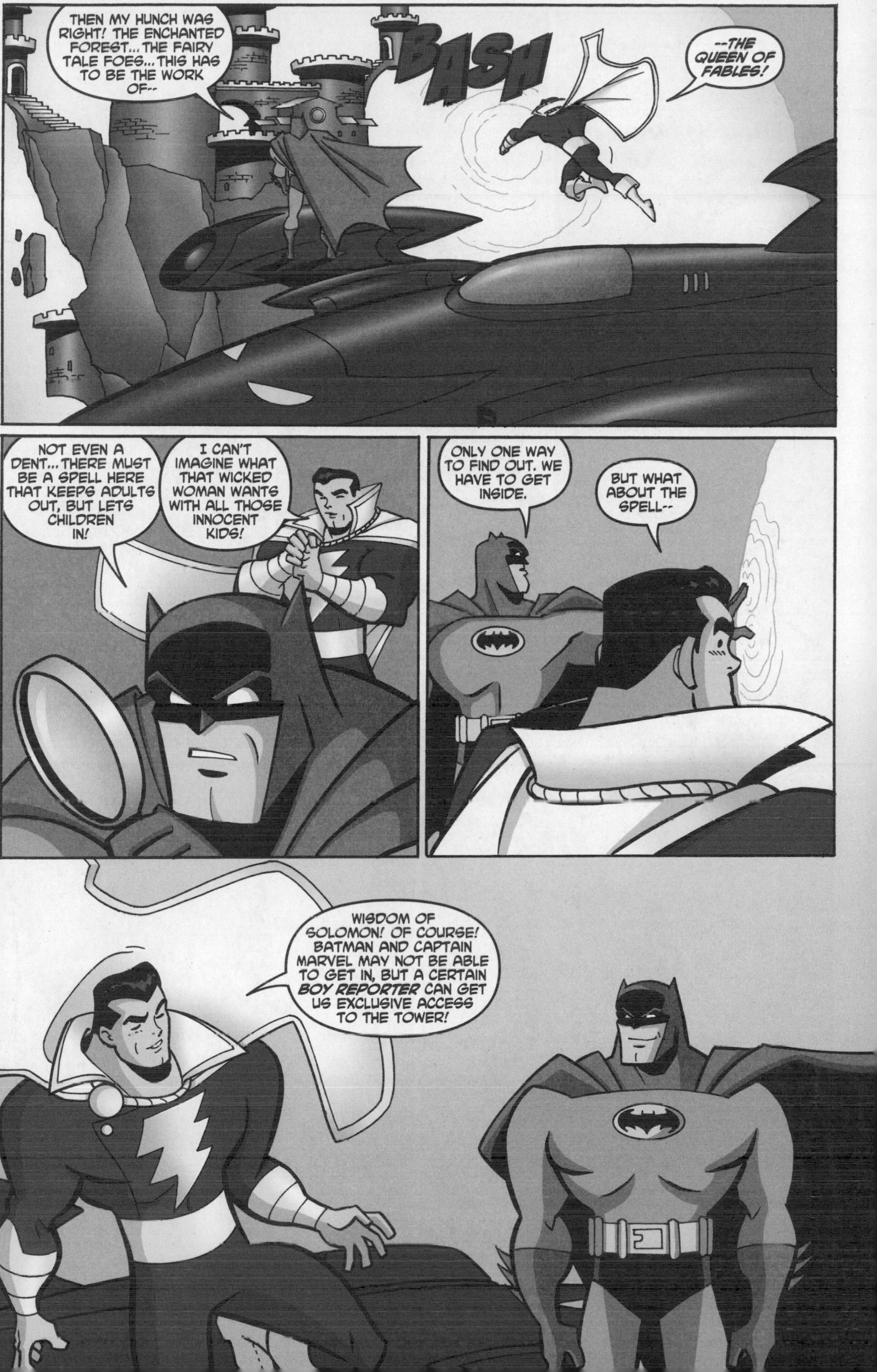
THEN MY HUNCH WAS RIGHT! THE ENCHANTED FOREST... THE FAIRY TALE FOES... THIS HAS TO BE THE WORK OF--
BASH
--THE QUEEN OF FABLES!
NOT EVEN A DENT... THERE MUST BE A SPELL HERE THAT KEEPS ADULTS OUT, BUT LETS CHILDREN IN!
I CAN'T IMAGINE WHAT THAT WICKED WOMAN WANTS WITH ALL THOSE INNOCENT KIDS!
ONLY ONE WAY TO FIND OUT. WE HAVE TO GET INSIDE.
BUT WHAT ABOUT THE SPELL--
WISDOM OF SOLOMON! OF COURSE! BATMAN AND CAPTAIN MARVEL MAY NOT BE ABLE TO GET IN, BUT A CERTAIN BOY REPORTER CAN GET US EXCLUSIVE ACCESS TO THE TOWER!

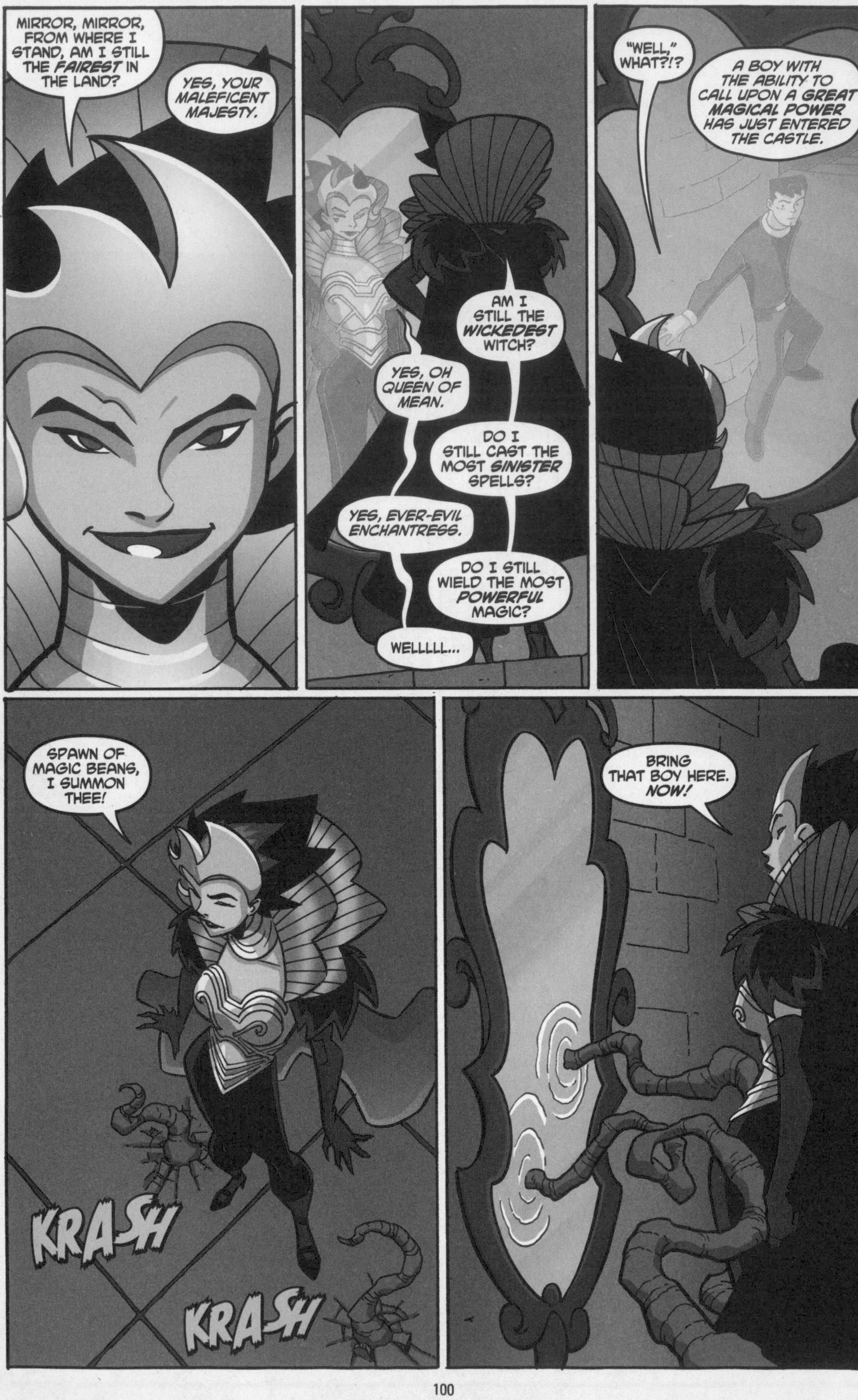
MIRROR, MIRROR, FROM WHERE I STAND, AM I STILL THE *FAIREST* IN THE LAND?
YES, YOUR MALEFICENT MAJESTY.
AM I STILL THE *WICKEDEST* WITCH?
YES, OH QUEEN OF MEAN.
DO I STILL CAST THE MOST *SINISTER* SPELLS?
YES, EVER-EVIL ENCHANTRESS.
DO I STILL WIELD THE MOST *POWERFUL* MAGIC?
WELLLLL...
"WELL," WHAT?!?
A BOY WITH THE ABILITY TO CALL UPON A GREAT MAGICAL POWER HAS JUST ENTERED THE CASTLE.
SPAWN OF MAGIC BEANS, I SUMMON THEE!
KRASH
KRASH
BRING THAT BOY HERE. *NOW!*

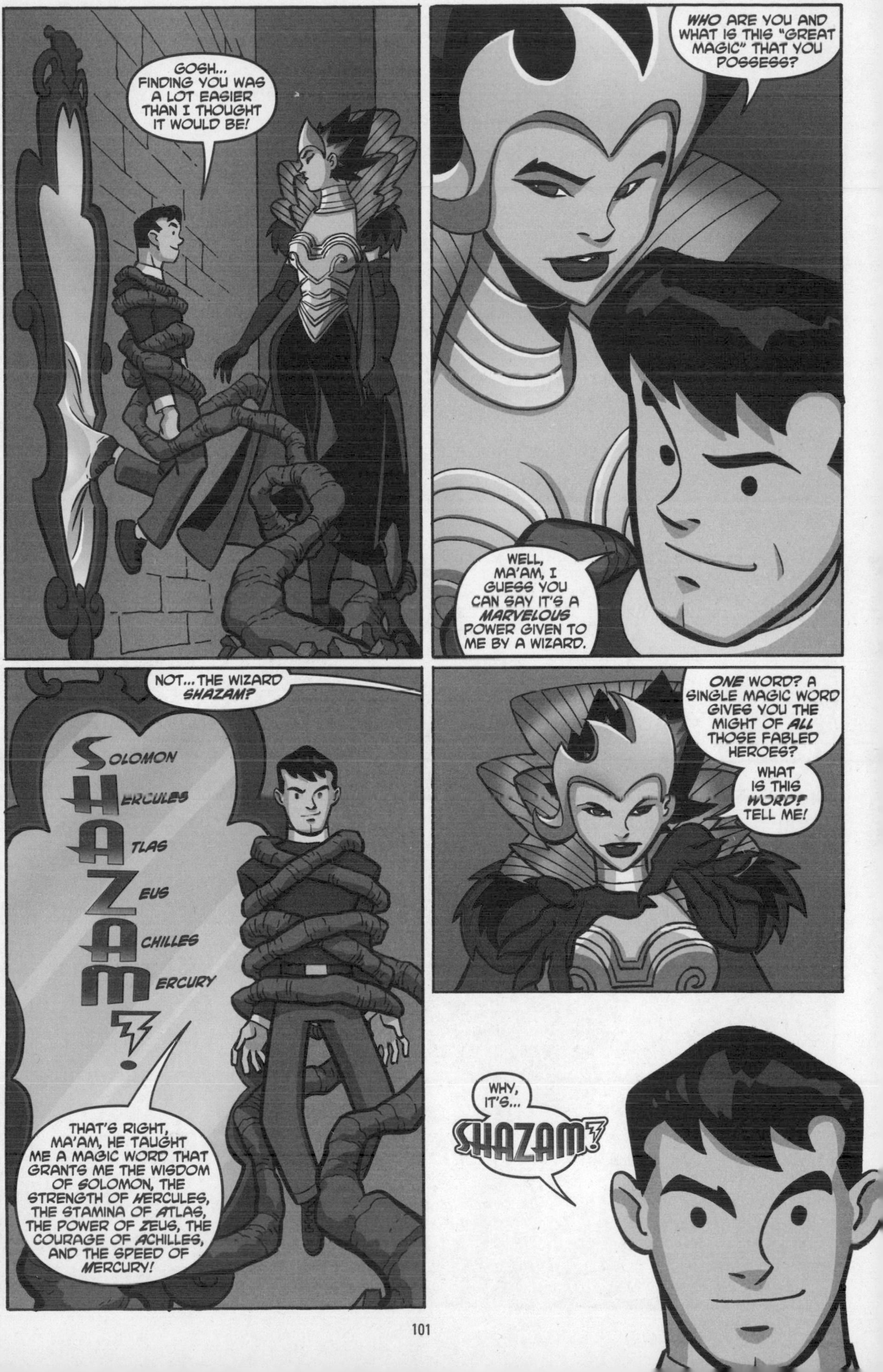
GOSH... FINDING YOU WAS A LOT EASIER THAN I THOUGHT IT WOULD BE!
WHO ARE YOU AND WHAT IS THIS "GREAT MAGIC" THAT YOU POSSESS?
WELL, MA'AM, I GUESS YOU CAN SAY IT'S A MARVELOUS POWER GIVEN TO ME BY A WIZARD.
NOT... THE WIZARD SHAZAM?
THAT'S RIGHT, MA'AM, HE TAUGHT ME A MAGIC WORD THAT GRANTS ME THE WISDOM OF SOLOMON, THE STRENGTH OF HERCULES, THE STAMINA OF ATLAS, THE POWER OF ZEUS, THE COURAGE OF ACHILLES, AND THE SPEED OF MERCURY!
SOLOMON
HERCULES
ATLAS
ZEUS
ACHILLES
MERCURY
SHAZAM!
ONE WORD? A SINGLE MAGIC WORD GIVES YOU THE MIGHT OF ALL THOSE FABLED HEROES?
WHAT IS THIS WORD? TELL ME!
WHY, IT'S...
SHAZAM!

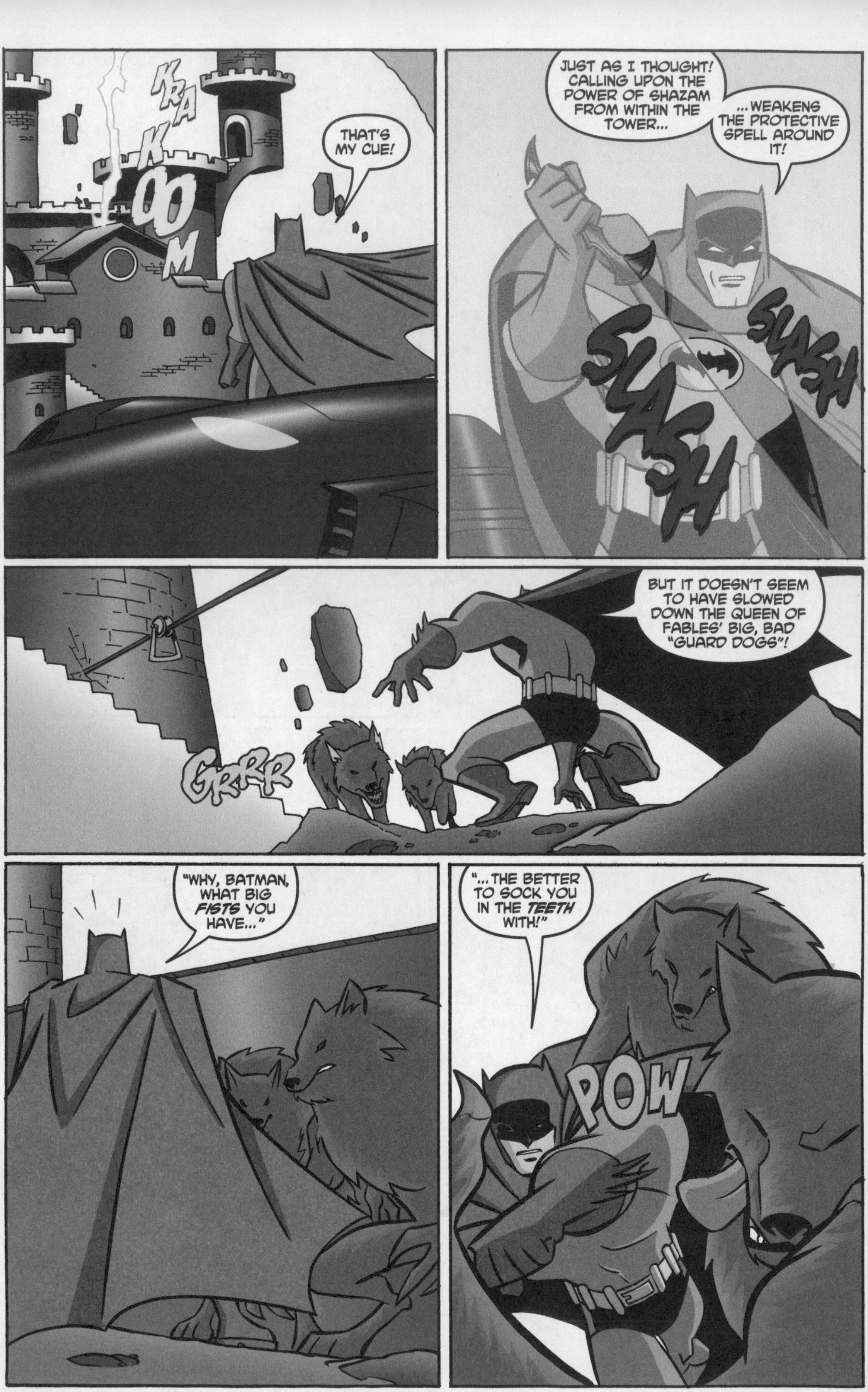
KRAKKOOM
THAT'S MY CUE!
JUST AS I THOUGHT! CALLING UPON THE POWER OF SHAZAM FROM WITHIN THE TOWER...
...WEAKENS THE PROTECTIVE SPELL AROUND IT!
SLASH
SLASH
BUT IT DOESN'T SEEM TO HAVE SLOWED DOWN THE QUEEN OF FABLES' BIG, BAD "GUARD DOGS"!
GRRR
"WHY, BATMAN, WHAT BIG *FISTS* YOU HAVE..."
"...THE BETTER TO SOCK YOU IN THE *TEETH* WITH!"
POW

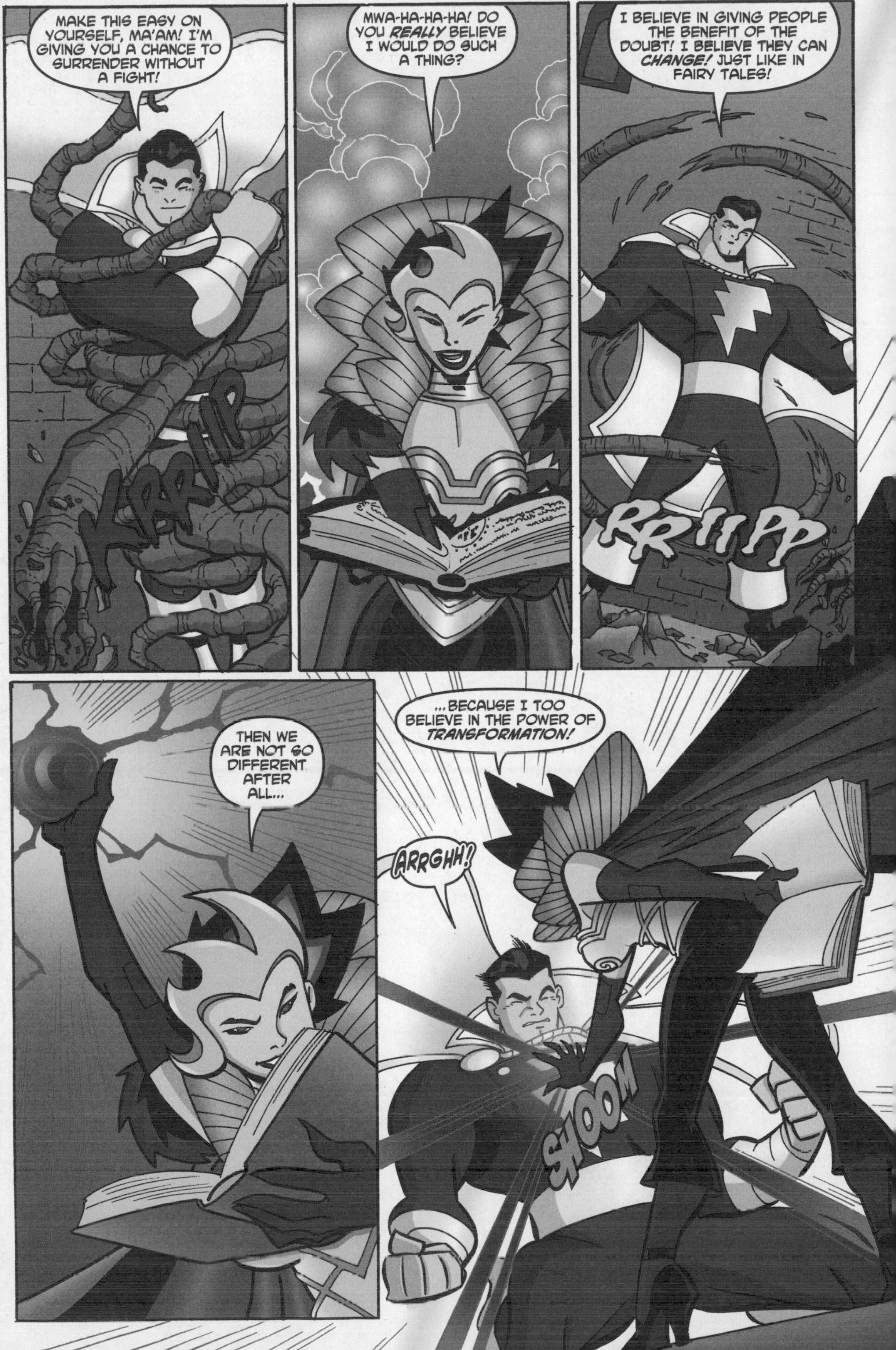
MAKE THIS EASY ON YOURSELF, MA'AM! I'M GIVING YOU A CHANCE TO SURRENDER WITHOUT A FIGHT!
KRRIIP
MWA-HA-HA-HA! DO YOU REALLY BELIEVE I WOULD DO SUCH A THING?
I BELIEVE IN GIVING PEOPLE THE BENEFIT OF THE DOUBT! I BELIEVE THEY CAN CHANGE! JUST LIKE IN FAIRY TALES!
RRIIPP
THEN WE ARE NOT SO DIFFERENT AFTER ALL...
...BECAUSE I TOO BELIEVE IN THE POWER OF TRANSFORMATION!
ARRGHH!
SHOOM

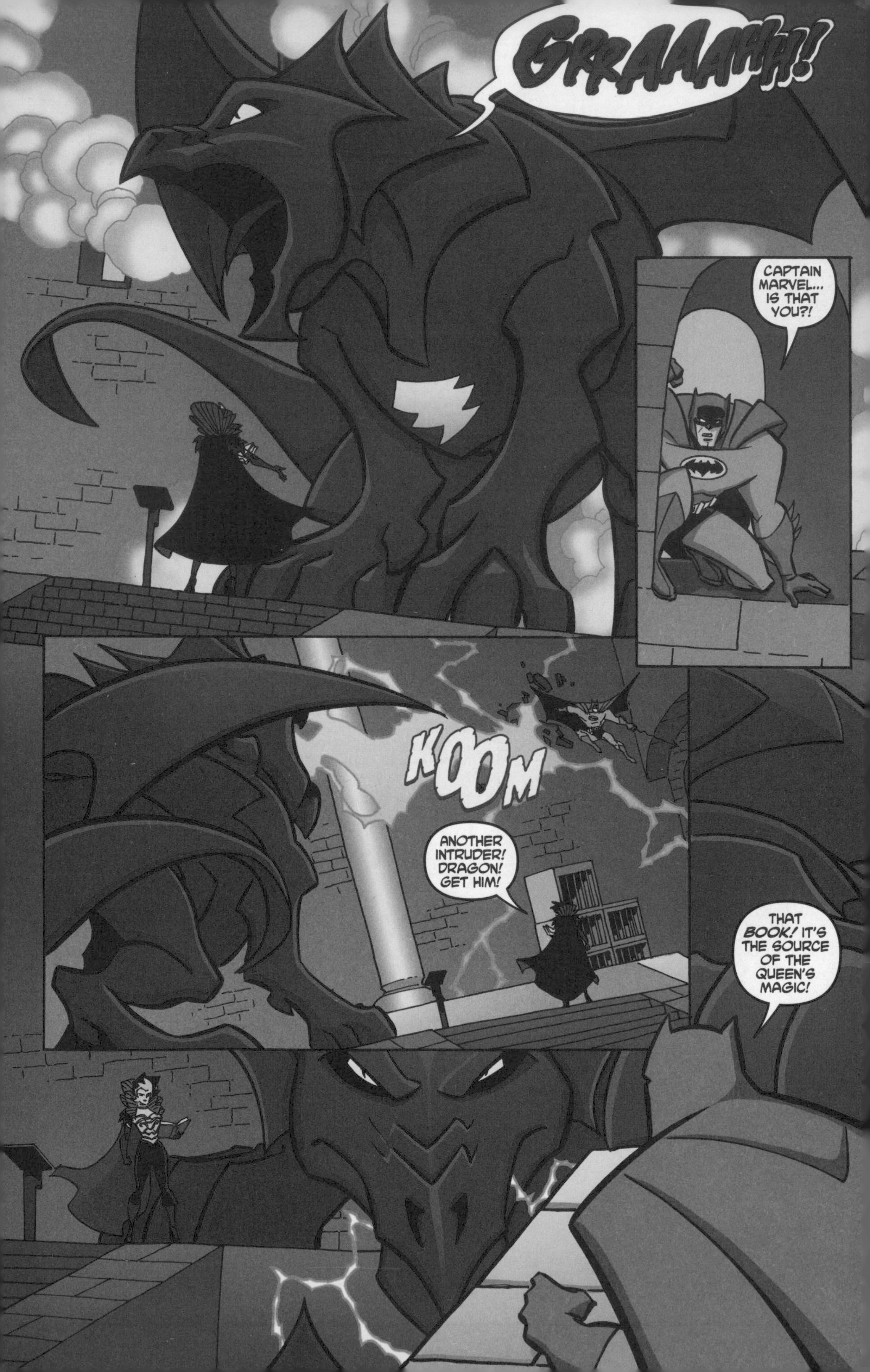
GRRAAAHHH!
CAPTAIN MARVEL... IS THAT YOU?!
KOOM
ANOTHER INTRUDER! DRAGON! GET HIM!
THAT BOOK! IT'S THE SOURCE OF THE QUEEN'S MAGIC!

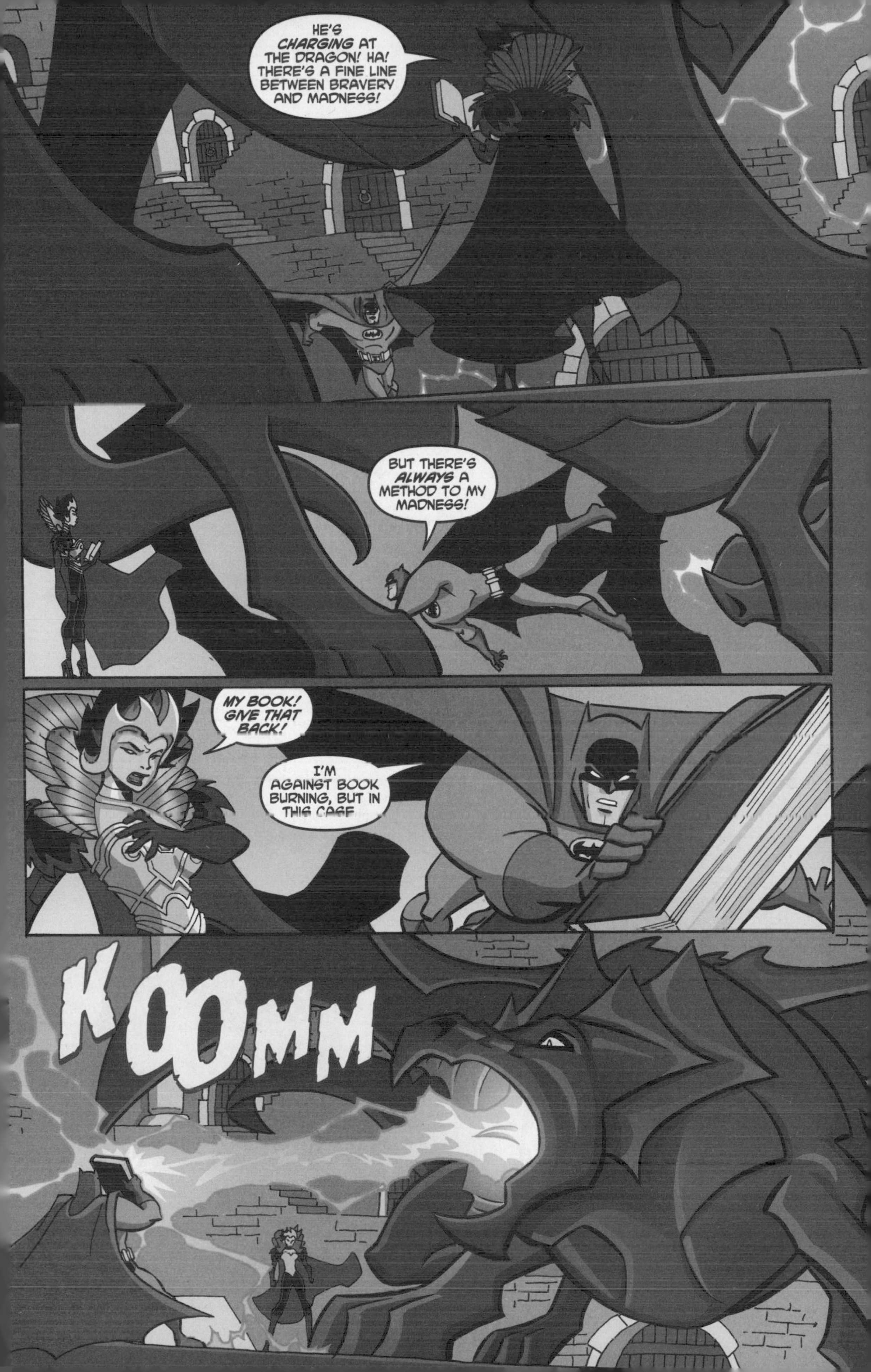
HE'S *CHARGING* AT THE DRAGON! HA! THERE'S A FINE LINE BETWEEN BRAVERY AND MADNESS!
BUT THERE'S *ALWAYS* A METHOD TO MY MADNESS!
MY BOOK! GIVE THAT BACK!
I'M AGAINST BOOK BURNING, BUT IN THIS CASE
KOOMM

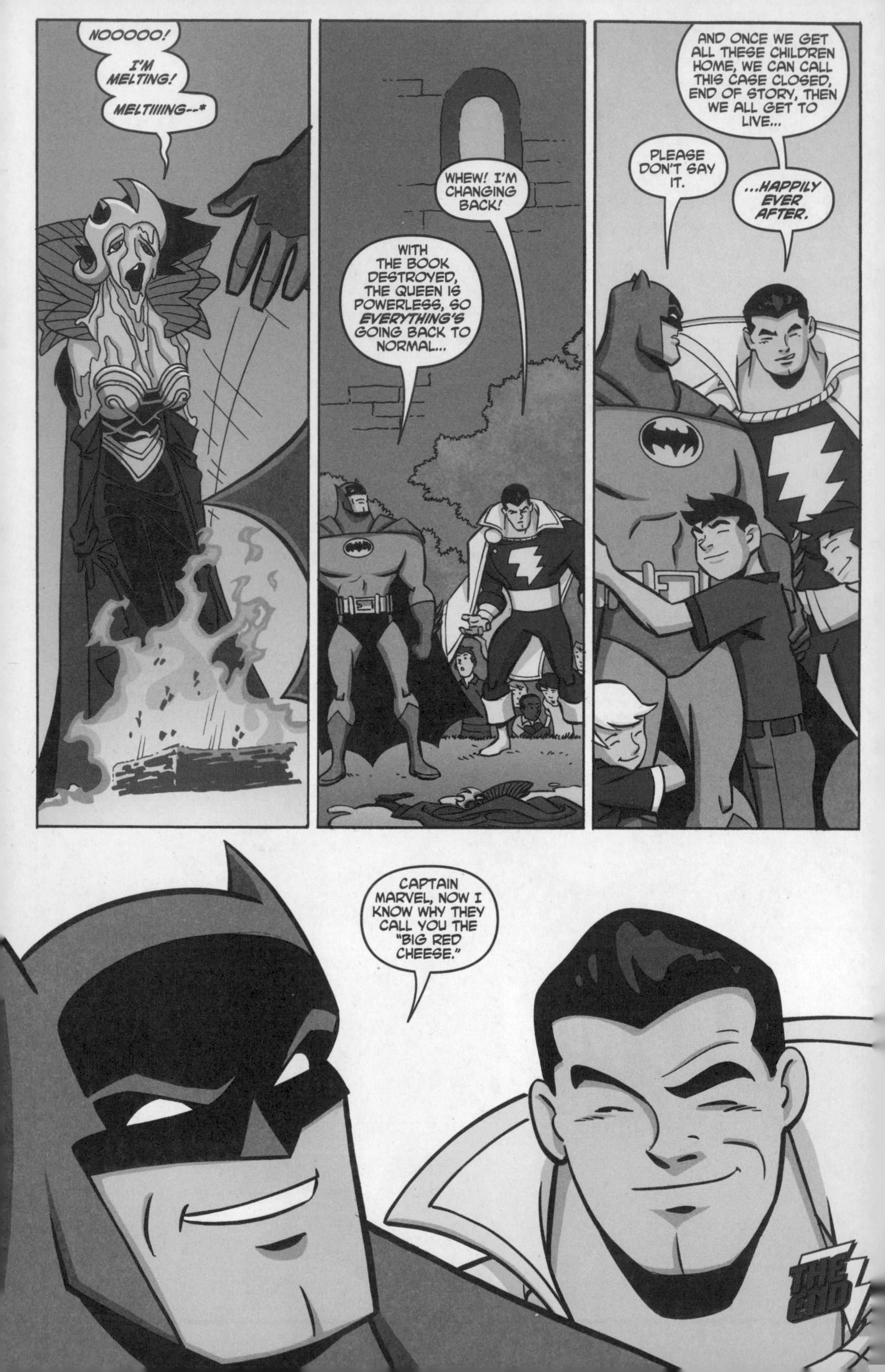
NOOOOO!
I'M MELTING!
MELTIIIING--*
WHEW! I'M CHANGING BACK!
WITH THE BOOK DESTROYED, THE QUEEN IS POWERLESS, SO EVERYTHING'S GOING BACK TO NORMAL...
AND ONCE WE GET ALL THESE CHILDREN HOME, WE CAN CALL THIS CASE CLOSED, END OF STORY, THEN WE ALL GET TO LIVE...
PLEASE DON'T SAY IT.
...HAPPILY EVER AFTER.
CAPTAIN MARVEL, NOW I KNOW WHY THEY CALL YOU THE "BIG RED CHEESE."
THE END

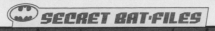

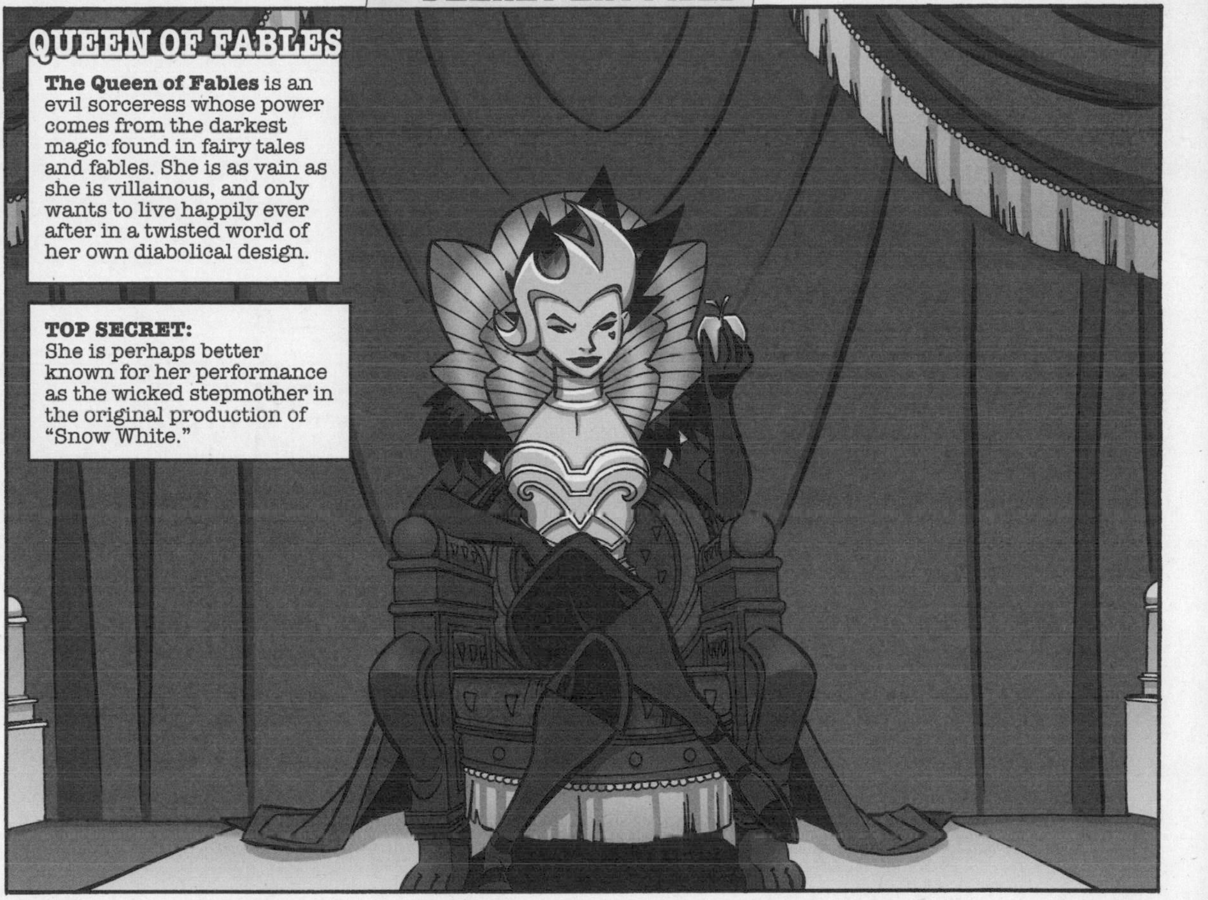
QUEEN OF FABLES
The Queen of Fables is an evil sorceress whose power comes from the darkest magic found in fairy tales and fables. She is as vain as she is villainous, and only wants to live happily ever after in a twisted world of her own diabolical design.
TOP SECRET:
She is perhaps better known for her performance as the wicked stepmother in the original production of "Snow White."

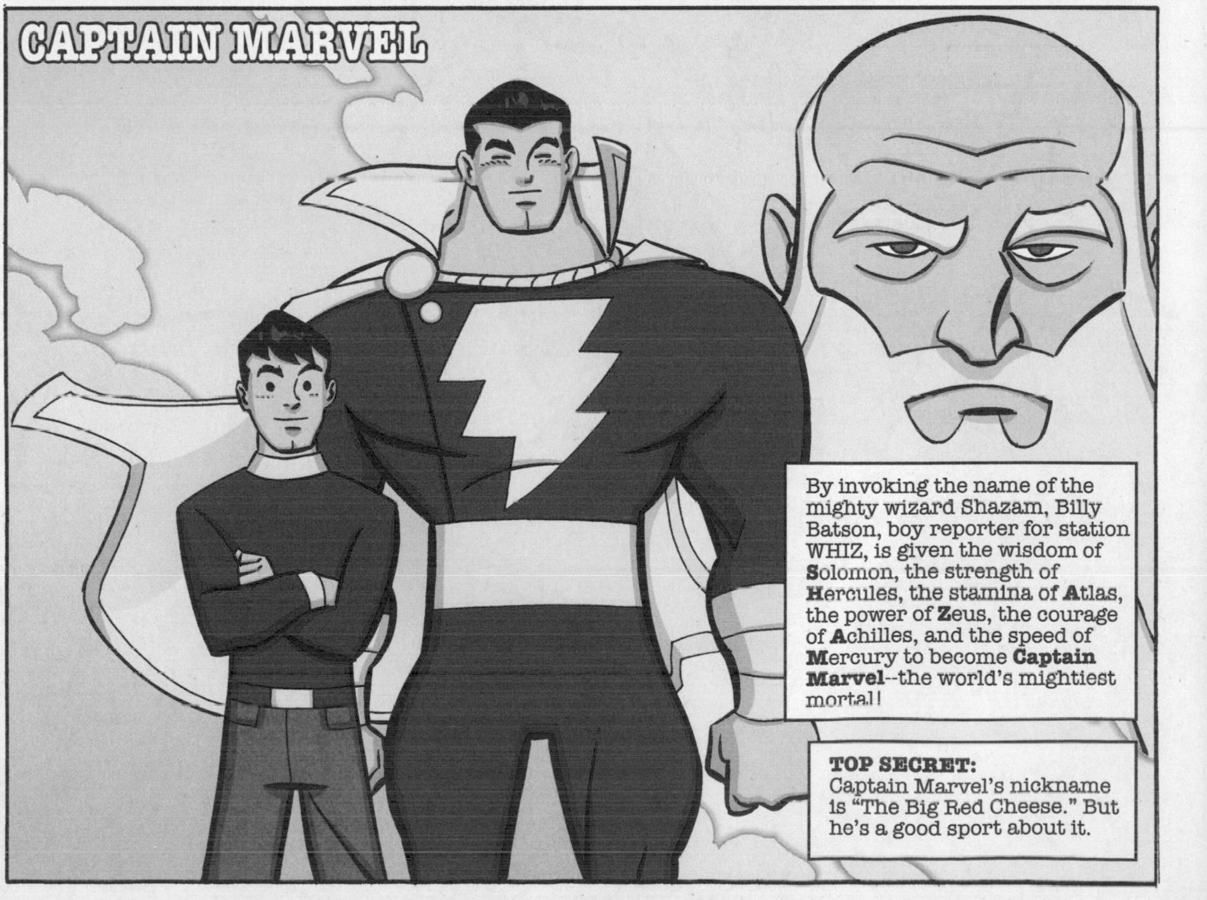
CAPTAIN MARVEL
By invoking the name of the mighty wizard Shazam, Billy Batson, boy reporter for station WHIZ, is given the wisdom of Solomon, the strength of Hercules, the stamina of Atlas, the power of Zeus, the courage of Achilles, and the speed of Mercury to become Captain Marvel--the world's mightiest mortal!
TOP SECRET:
Captain Marvel's nickname is "The Big Red Cheese." But he's a good sport about it.

BATMAN: THE BRAVE AND THE BOLD #6
Cover by Scott Jeralds with Hi-Fi

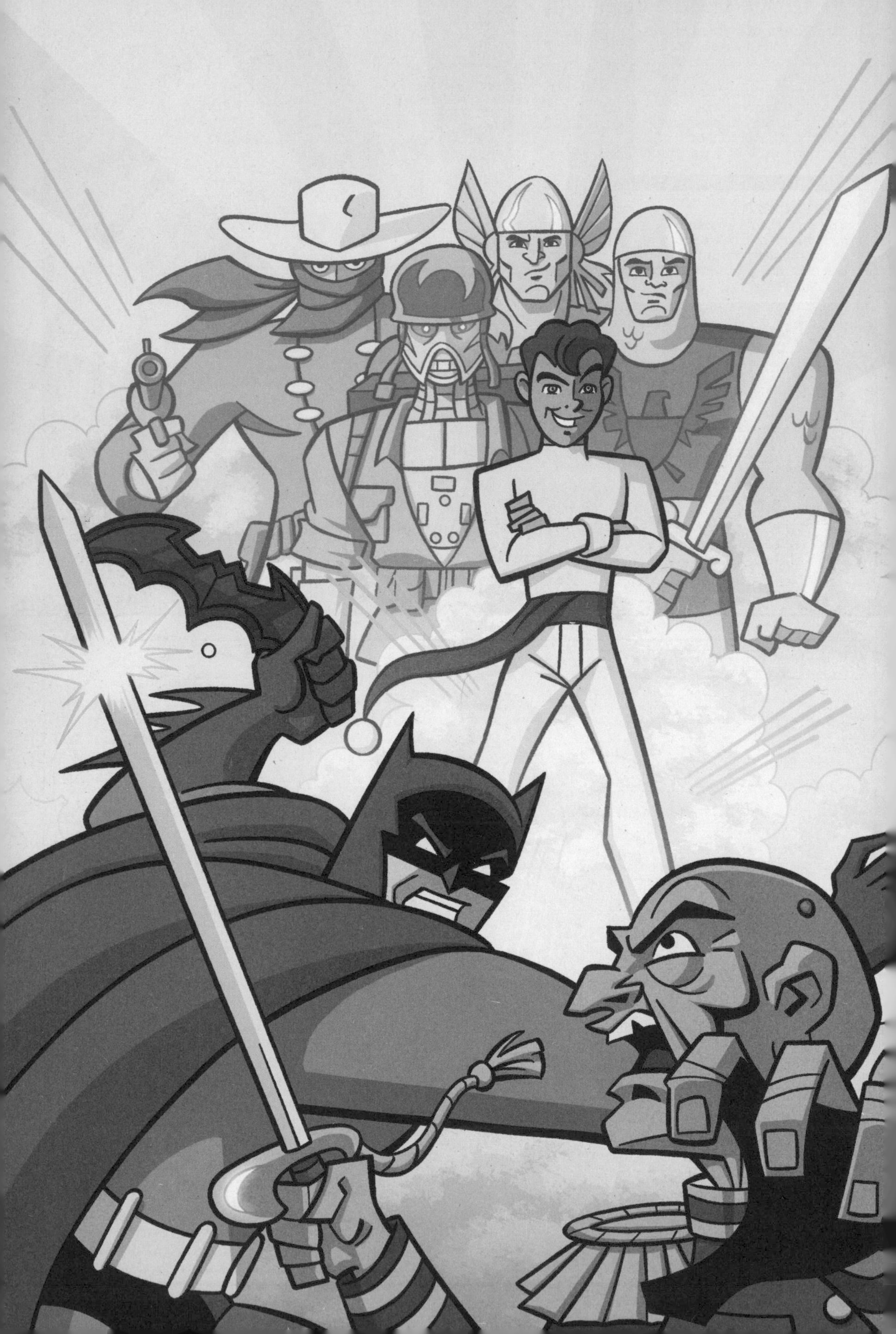

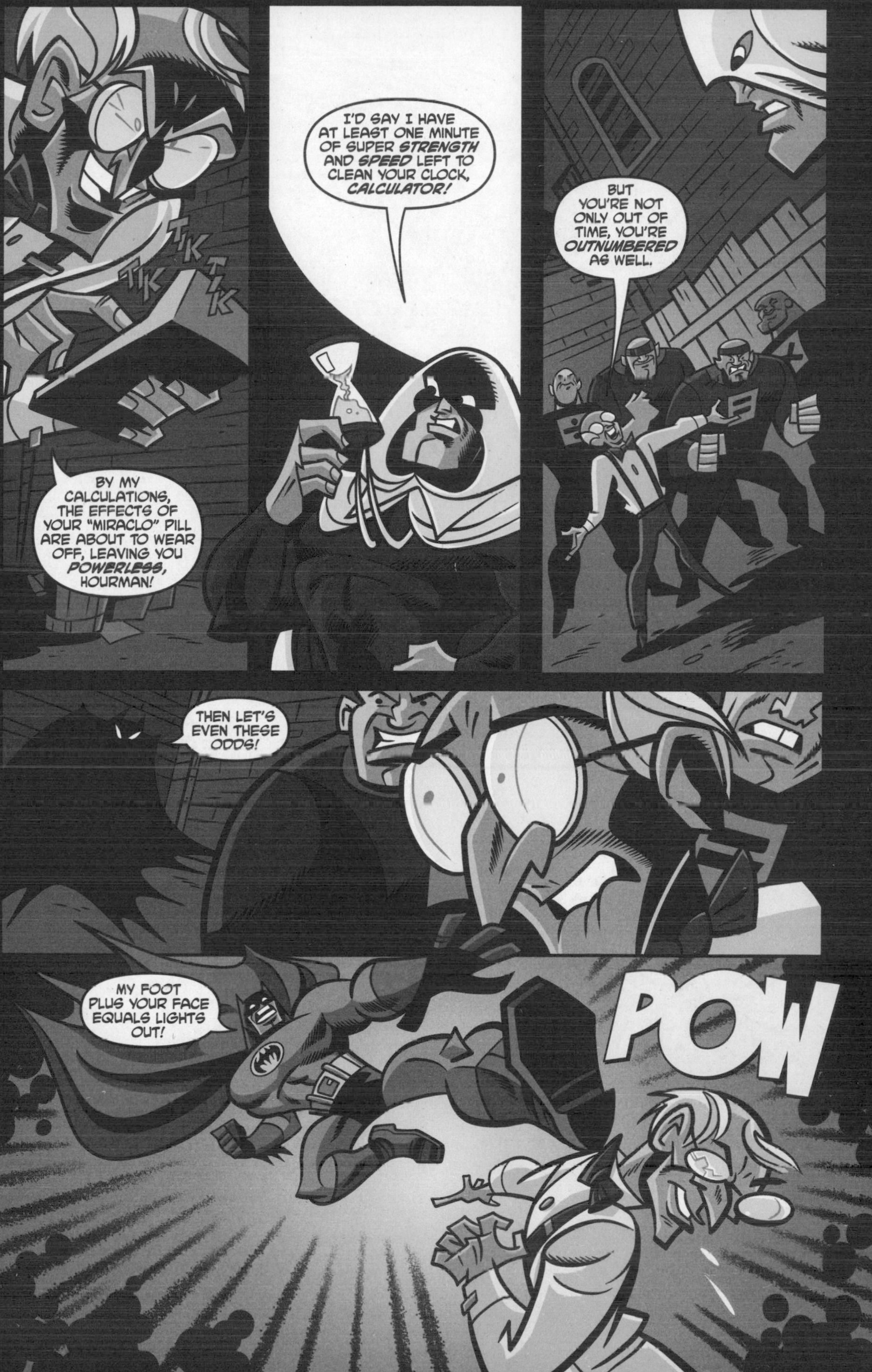
TIK TIK TIK
BY MY CALCULATIONS, THE EFFECTS OF YOUR "MIRACLO" PILL ARE ABOUT TO WEAR OFF, LEAVING YOU POWERLESS, HOURMAN!
I'D SAY I HAVE AT LEAST ONE MINUTE OF SUPER STRENGTH AND SPEED LEFT TO CLEAN YOUR CLOCK, CALCULATOR!
BUT YOU'RE NOT ONLY OUT OF TIME, YOU'RE OUTNUMBERED AS WELL.
THEN LET'S EVEN THESE ODDS!
MY FOOT PLUS YOUR FACE EQUALS LIGHTS OUT!
POW

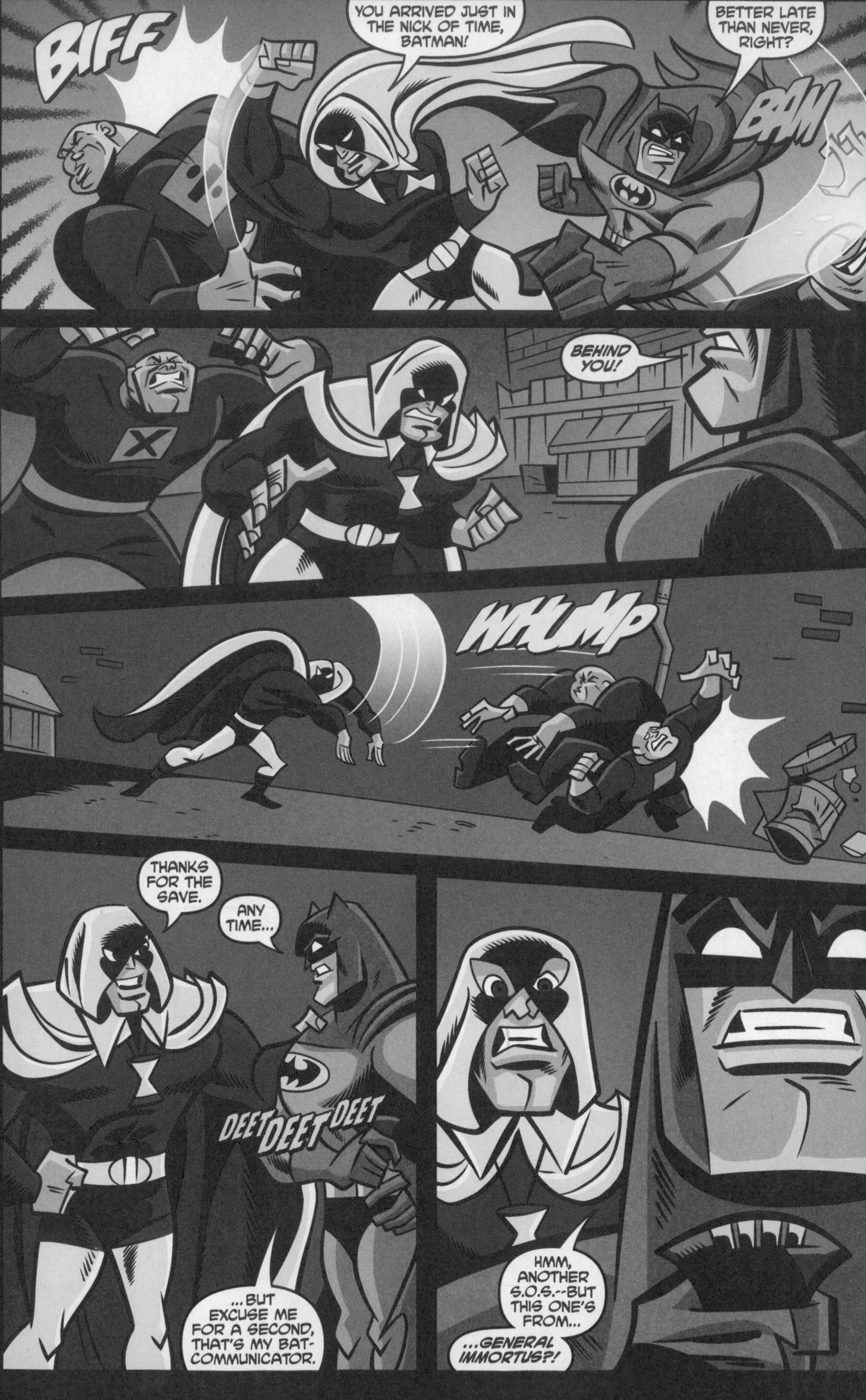
BIFF
YOU ARRIVED JUST IN THE NICK OF TIME, BATMAN!
BETTER LATE THAN NEVER, RIGHT?
BAM
BEHIND YOU!
WHUMP
THANKS FOR THE SAVE.
ANY TIME...
DEET DEET DEET
...BUT EXCUSE ME FOR A SECOND, THAT'S MY BAT-COMMUNICATOR.
HMM, ANOTHER S.O.S.--BUT THIS ONE'S FROM...
...GENERAL IMMORTUS?!

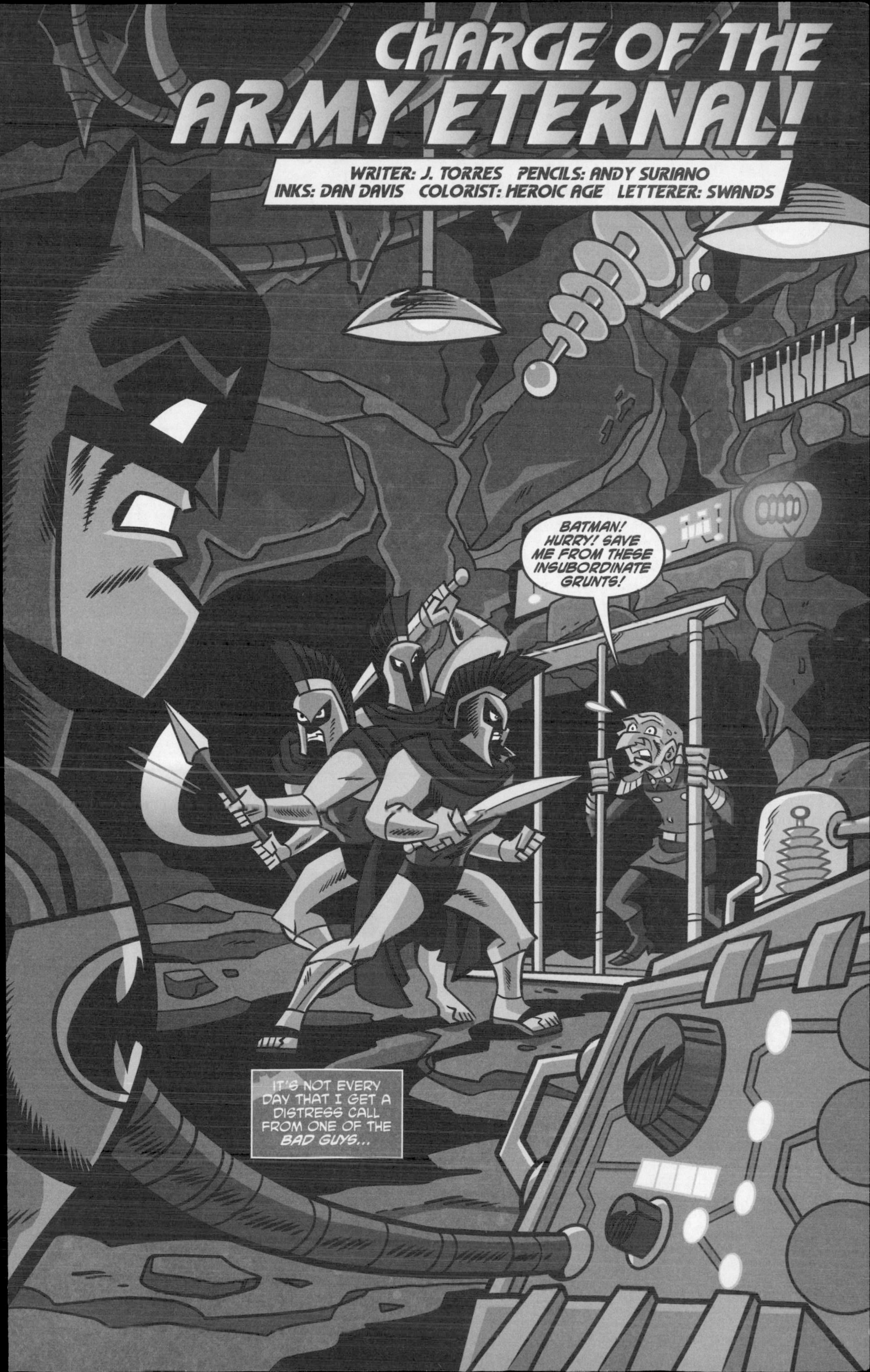
CHARGE OF THE ARMY ETERNAL!
WRITER: J. TORRES PENCILS: ANDY SURIANO
INKS: DAN DAVIS COLORIST: HEROIC AGE LETTERER: SWANDS
BATMAN! HURRY! SAVE ME FROM THESE INSUBORDINATE GRUNTS!
IT'S NOT EVERY DAY THAT I GET A DISTRESS CALL FROM ONE OF THE BAD GUYS...

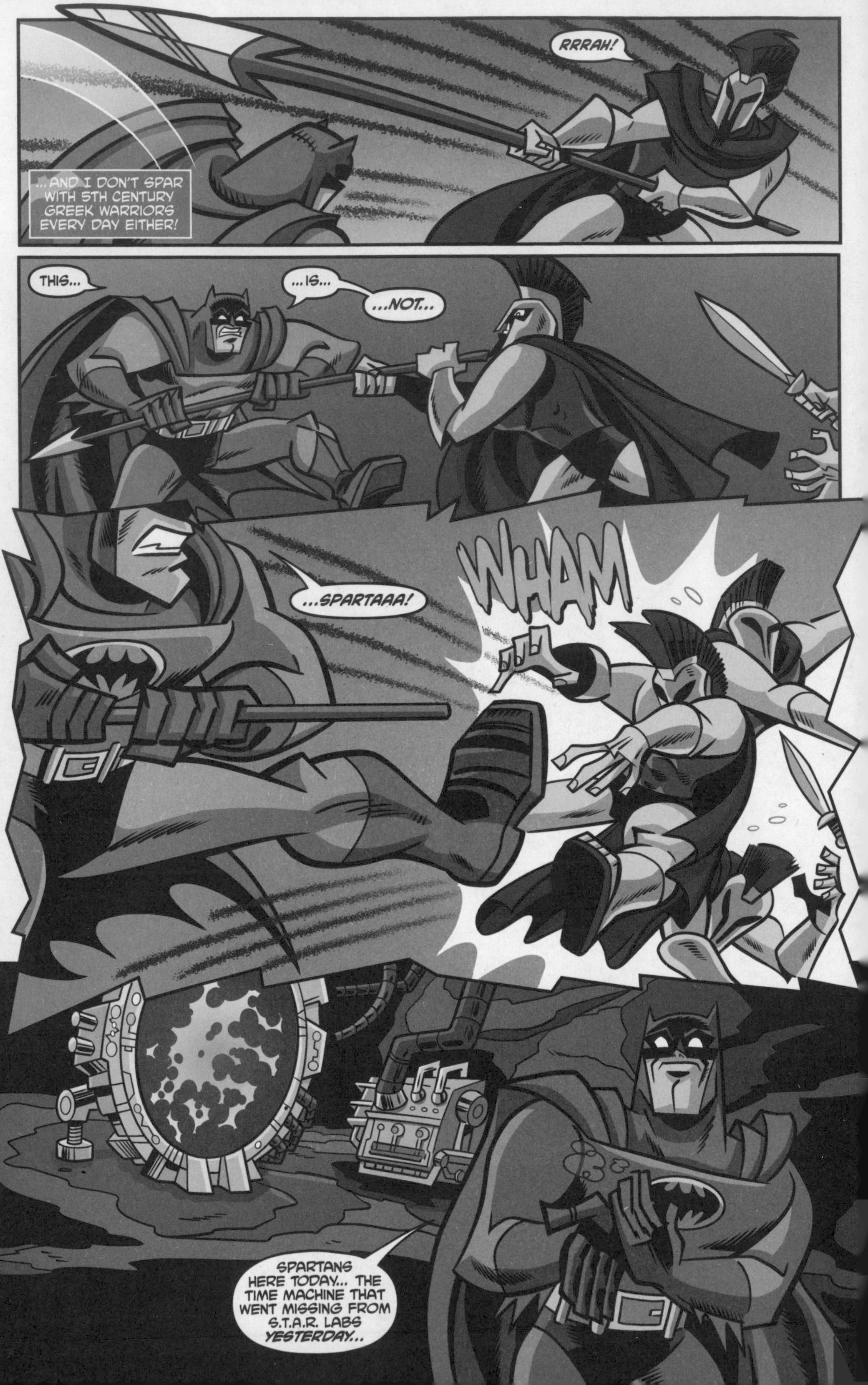
RRRAH!
...AND I DON'T SPAR WITH 5TH CENTURY GREEK WARRIORS EVERY DAY EITHER!
THIS...
...IS...
...NOT...
...SPARTAAA!
WHAM
SPARTANS HERE TODAY... THE TIME MACHINE THAT WENT MISSING FROM S.T.A.R. LABS YESTERDAY...

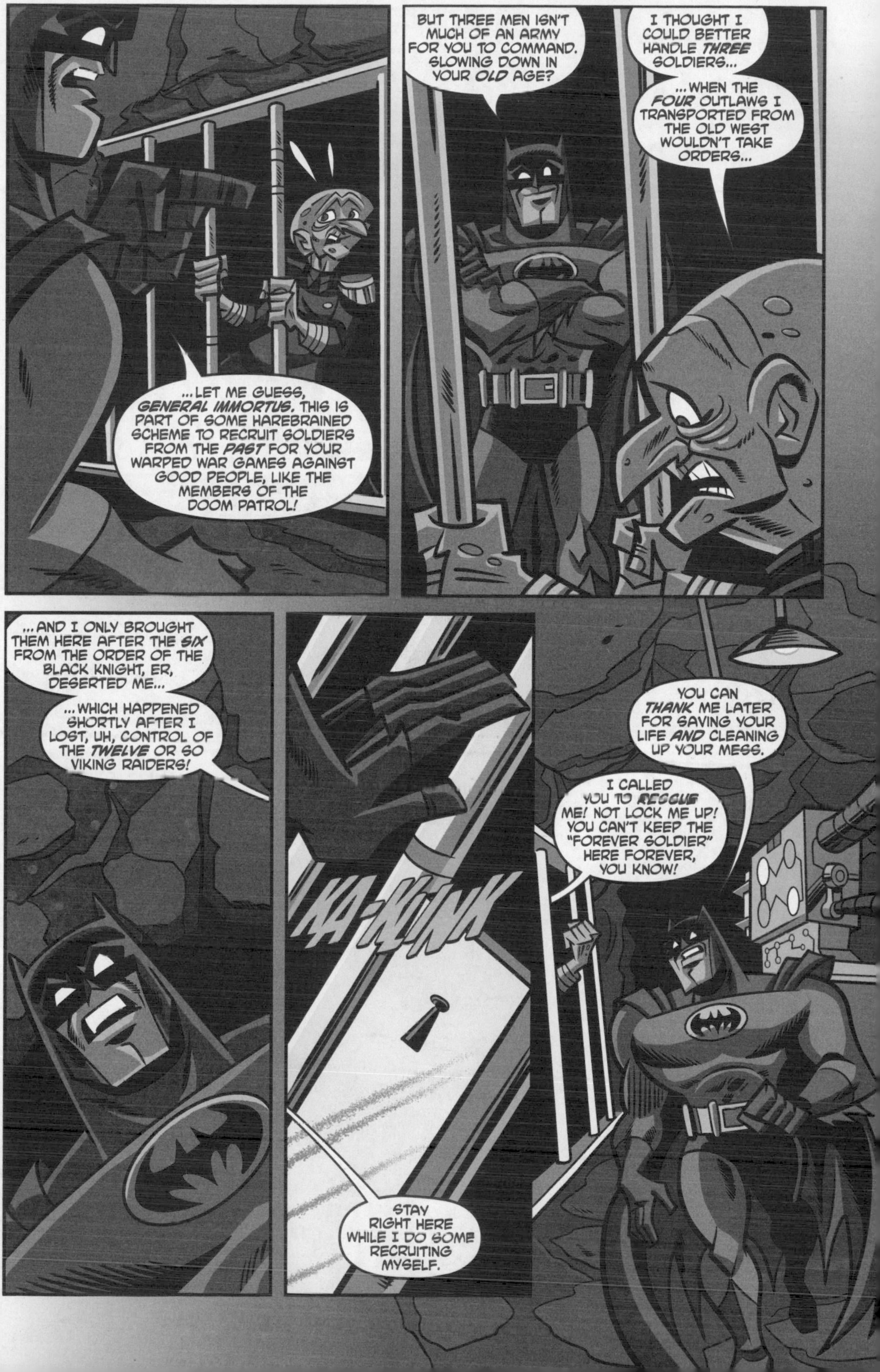
...LET ME GUESS, GENERAL IMMORTUS. THIS IS PART OF SOME HAREBRAINED SCHEME TO RECRUIT SOLDIERS FROM THE PAST FOR YOUR WARPED WAR GAMES AGAINST GOOD PEOPLE, LIKE THE MEMBERS OF THE DOOM PATROL!
BUT THREE MEN ISN'T MUCH OF AN ARMY FOR YOU TO COMMAND. SLOWING DOWN IN YOUR OLD AGE?
I THOUGHT I COULD BETTER HANDLE THREE SOLDIERS...
...WHEN THE FOUR OUTLAWS I TRANSPORTED FROM THE OLD WEST WOULDN'T TAKE ORDERS...
...AND I ONLY BROUGHT THEM HERE AFTER THE SIX FROM THE ORDER OF THE BLACK KNIGHT, ER, DESERTED ME...
...WHICH HAPPENED SHORTLY AFTER I LOST, UH, CONTROL OF THE TWELVE OR SO VIKING RAIDERS!
KA-KLINK
STAY RIGHT HERE WHILE I DO SOME RECRUITING MYSELF.
I CALLED YOU TO RESCUE ME! NOT LOCK ME UP! YOU CAN'T KEEP THE "FOREVER SOLDIER" HERE FOREVER, YOU KNOW!
YOU CAN THANK ME LATER FOR SAVING YOUR LIFE AND CLEANING UP YOUR MESS.

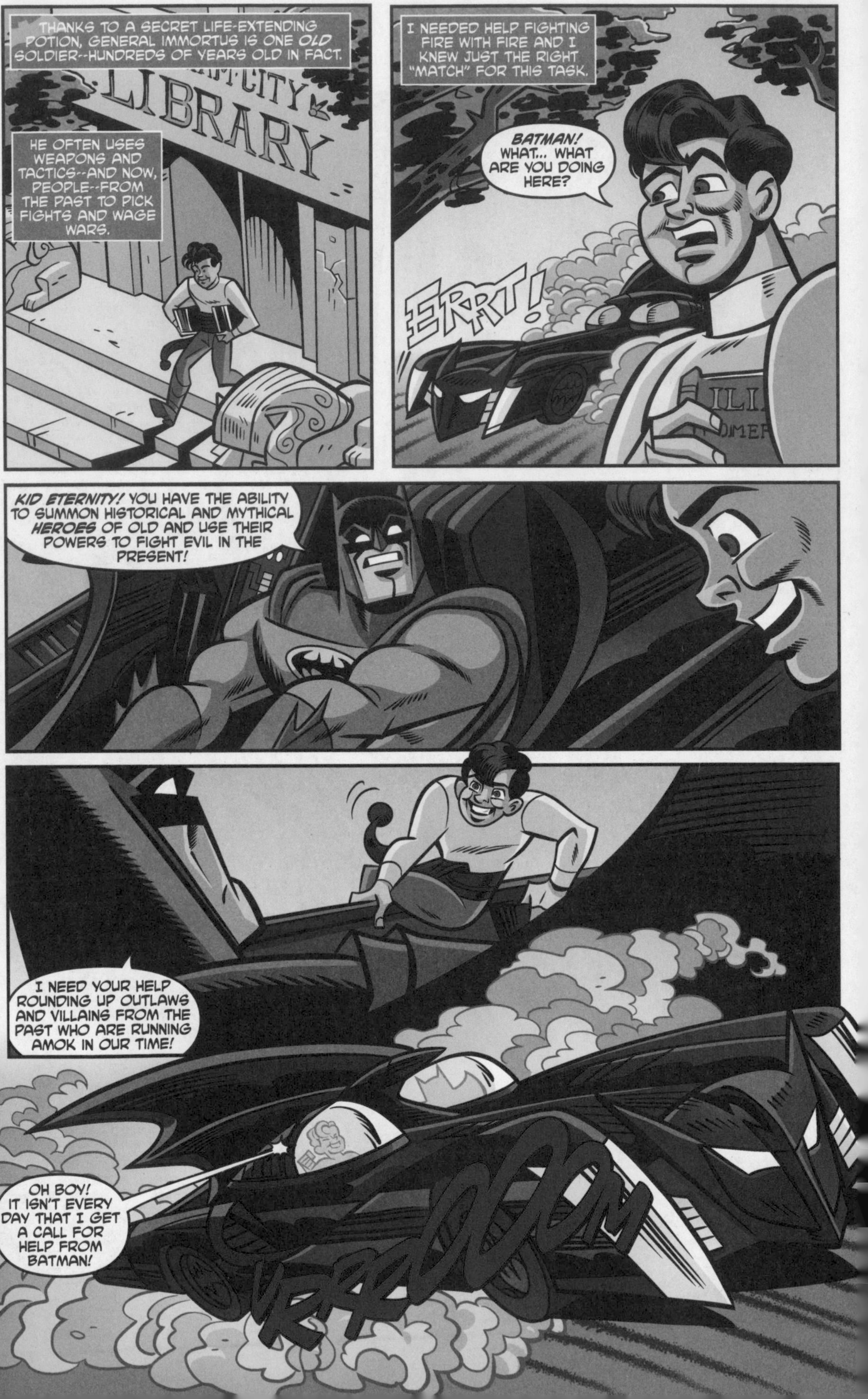
THANKS TO A SECRET LIFE-EXTENDING POTION, GENERAL IMMORTUS IS ONE *OLD* SOLDIER--HUNDREDS OF YEARS OLD IN FACT.
LIBRARY
HE OFTEN USES WEAPONS AND TACTICS--AND NOW, PEOPLE--FROM THE PAST TO PICK FIGHTS AND WAGE WARS.
I NEEDED HELP FIGHTING FIRE WITH FIRE AND I KNEW JUST THE RIGHT "MATCH" FOR THIS TASK.
BATMAN! WHAT... WHAT ARE YOU DOING HERE?
ERRT!
KID ETERNITY! YOU HAVE THE ABILITY TO SUMMON HISTORICAL AND MYTHICAL *HEROES* OF OLD AND USE THEIR POWERS TO FIGHT EVIL IN THE PRESENT!
I NEED YOUR HELP ROUNDING UP OUTLAWS AND VILLAINS FROM THE PAST WHO ARE RUNNING AMOK IN OUR TIME!
OH BOY! IT ISN'T EVERY DAY THAT I GET A CALL FOR HELP FROM BATMAN!
VRRROOOOM

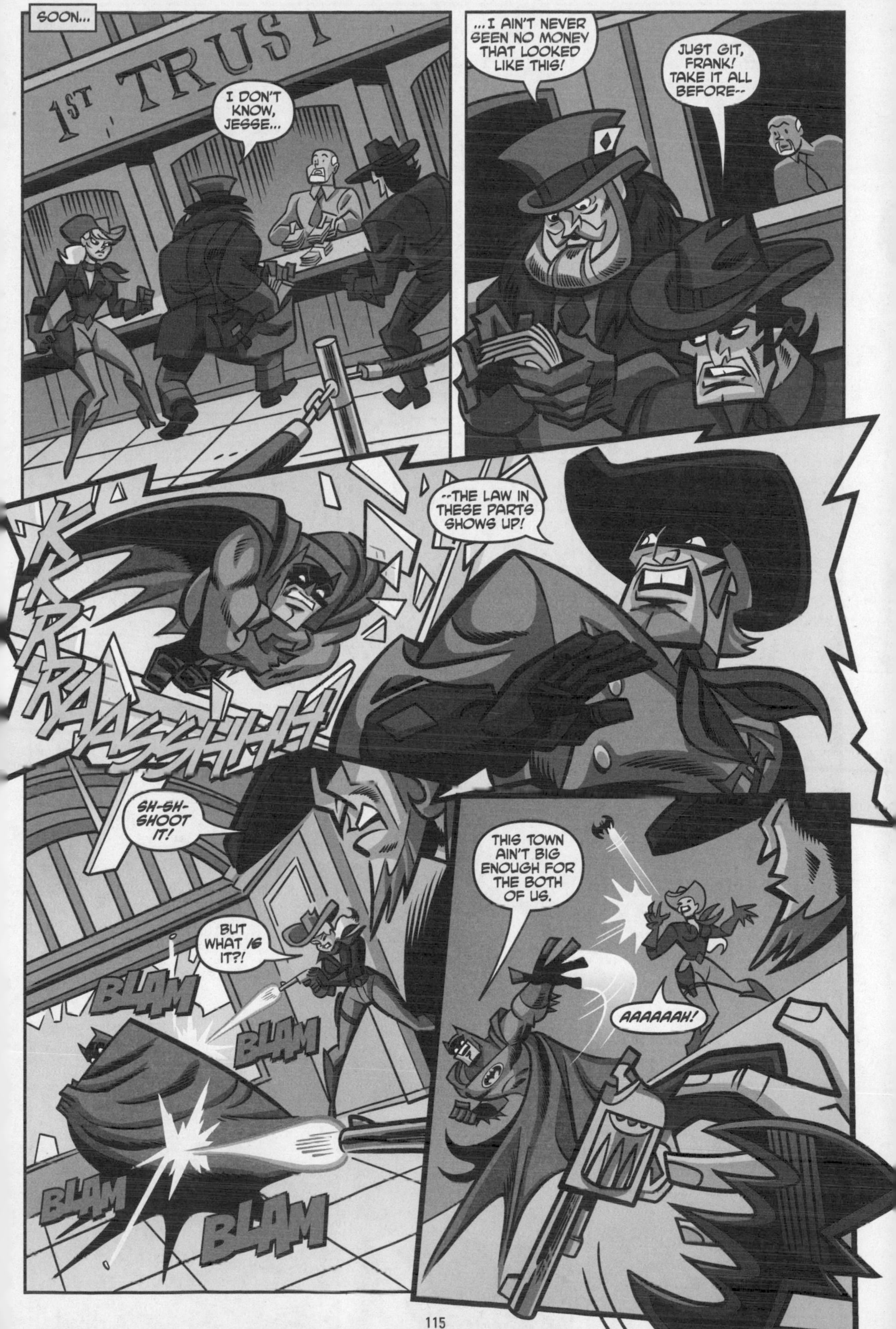
SOON...
1ST TRUST
I DON'T KNOW, JESSE...
...I AIN'T NEVER SEEN NO MONEY THAT LOOKED LIKE THIS!
JUST GIT, FRANK! TAKE IT ALL BEFORE--
KRRAASSHHH
--THE LAW IN THESE PARTS SHOWS UP!
SH-SH-SHOOT IT!
BUT WHAT IS IT?!
BLAM
BLAM
BLAM
BLAM
THIS TOWN AIN'T BIG ENOUGH FOR THE BOTH OF US.
AAAAAAH!

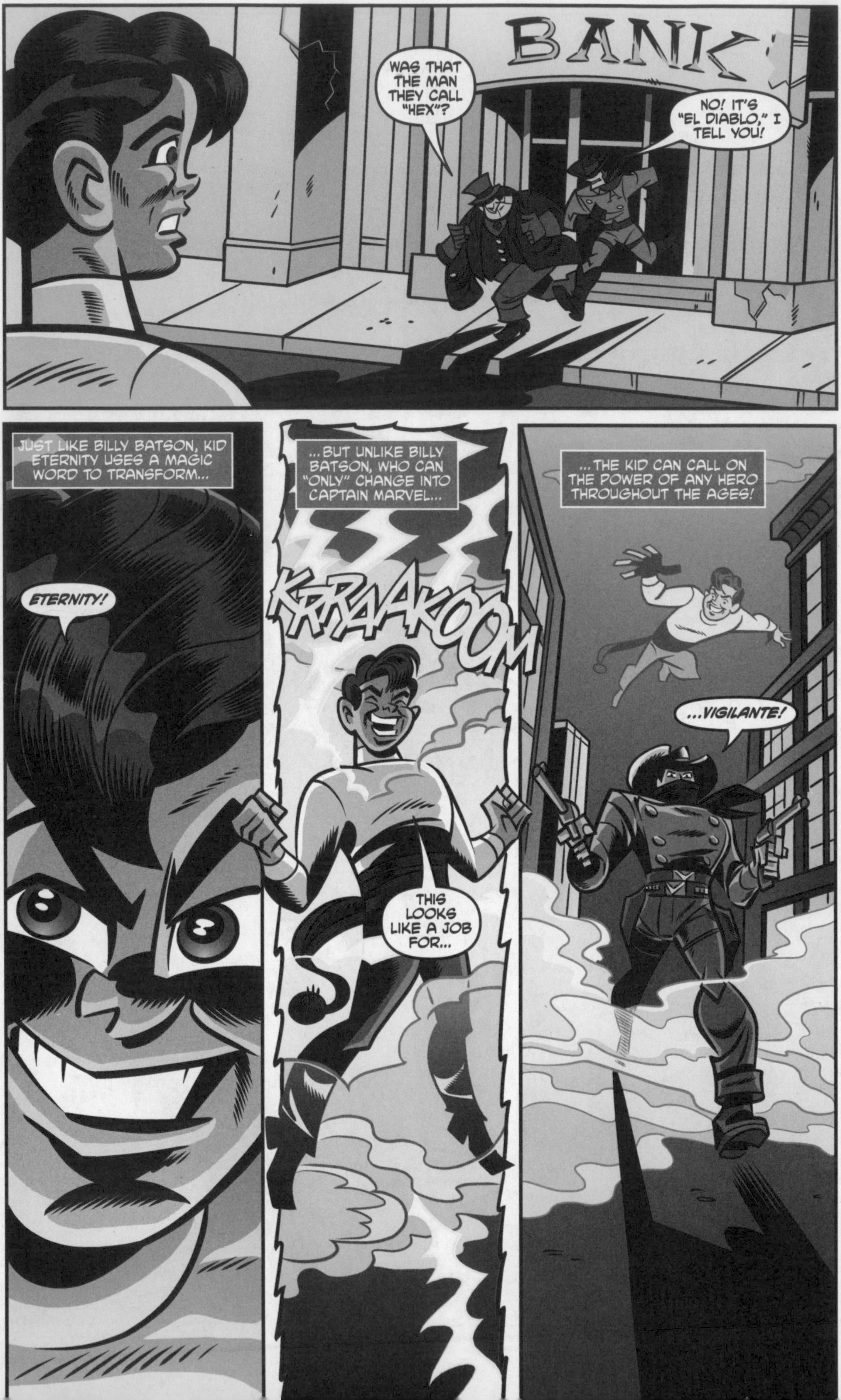
BANK
WAS THAT THE MAN THEY CALL "HEX"?
NO! IT'S "EL DIABLO," I TELL YOU!
JUST LIKE BILLY BATSON, KID ETERNITY USES A MAGIC WORD TO TRANSFORM...
ETERNITY!
...BUT UNLIKE BILLY BATSON, WHO CAN "ONLY" CHANGE INTO CAPTAIN MARVEL...
KRRAAKOOM
THIS LOOKS LIKE A JOB FOR...
...THE KID CAN CALL ON THE POWER OF ANY HERO THROUGHOUT THE AGES!
...VIGILANTE!

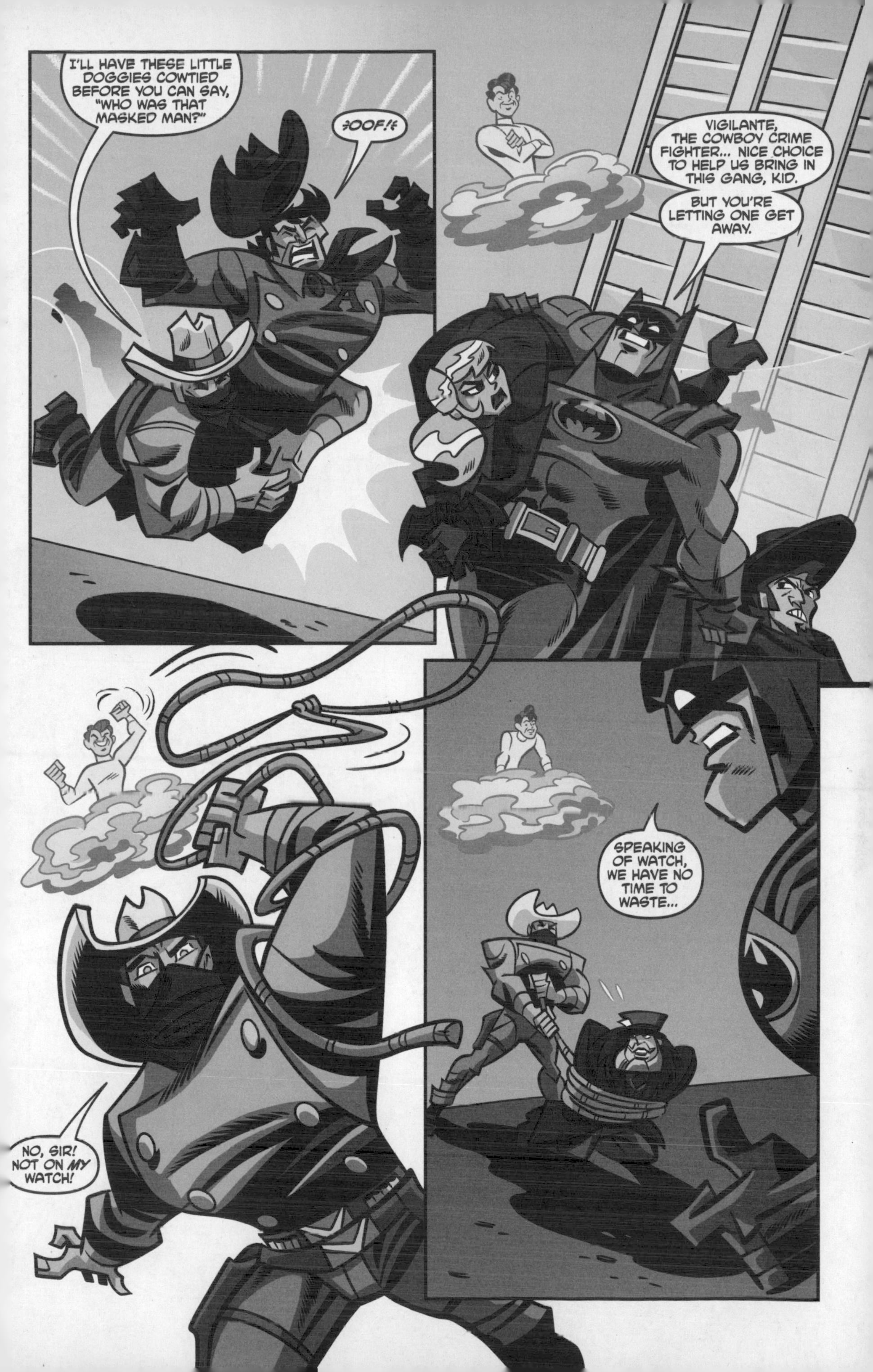

I'LL HAVE THESE LITTLE DOGGIES COWTIED BEFORE YOU CAN SAY, "WHO WAS THAT MASKED MAN?"
OOF!
VIGILANTE, THE COWBOY CRIME FIGHTER... NICE CHOICE TO HELP US BRING IN THIS GANG, KID.
BUT YOU'RE LETTING ONE GET AWAY.
NO, SIR! NOT ON MY WATCH!
SPEAKING OF WATCH, WE HAVE NO TIME TO WASTE...

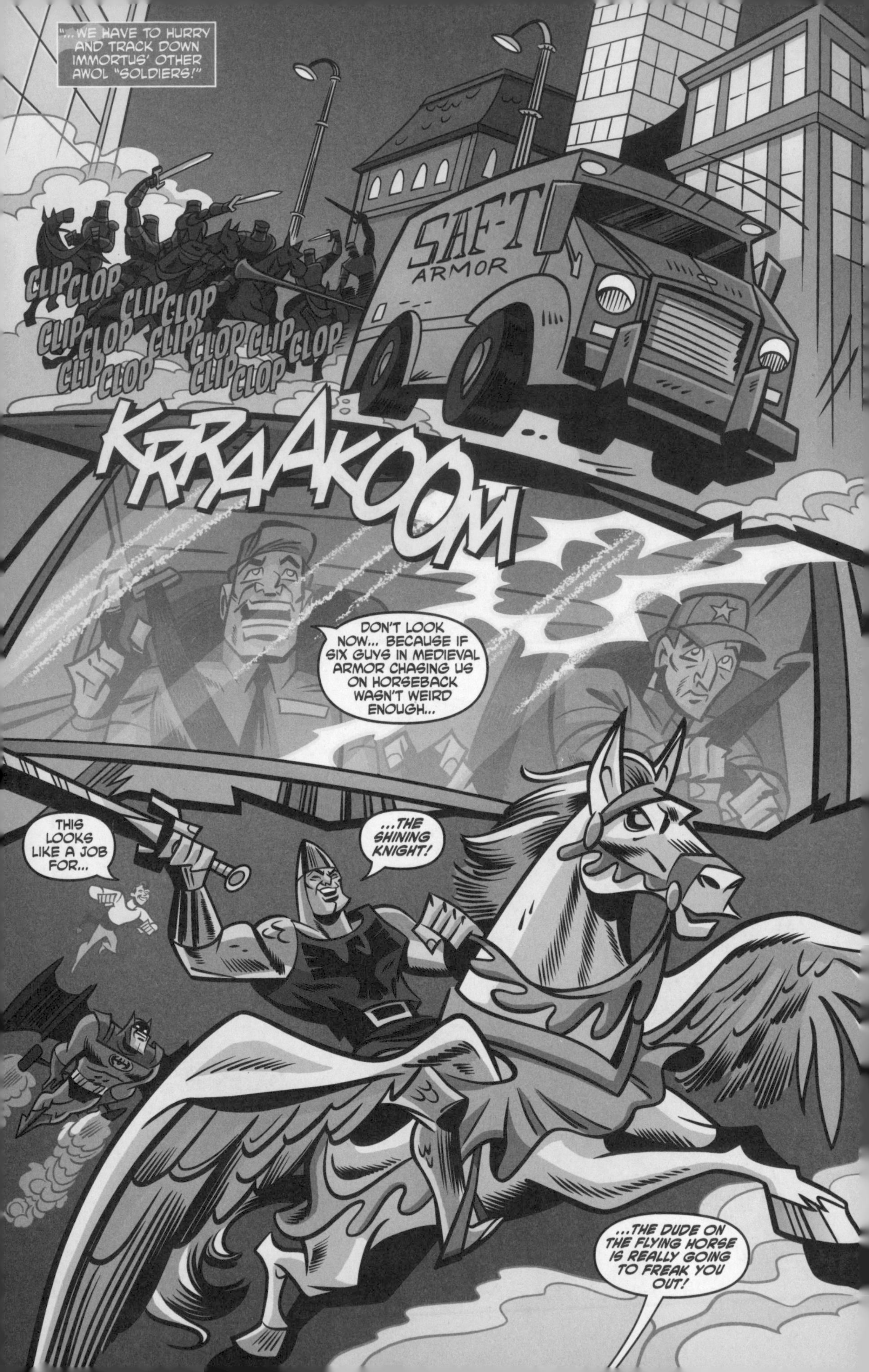
"...WE HAVE TO HURRY AND TRACK DOWN IMMORTUS' OTHER AWOL "SOLDIERS!"
SAF-T ARMOR
CLIP CLOP CLIP CLOP CLIP CLOP CLIP CLOP CLIP CLOP CLIP CLOP CLIP CLOP CLIP CLOP
KRRAAKOOM
DON'T LOOK NOW... BECAUSE IF SIX GUYS IN MEDIEVAL ARMOR CHASING US ON HORSEBACK WASN'T WEIRD ENOUGH...
THIS LOOKS LIKE A JOB FOR...
...THE SHINING KNIGHT!
...THE DUDE ON THE FLYING HORSE IS REALLY GOING TO FREAK YOU OUT!

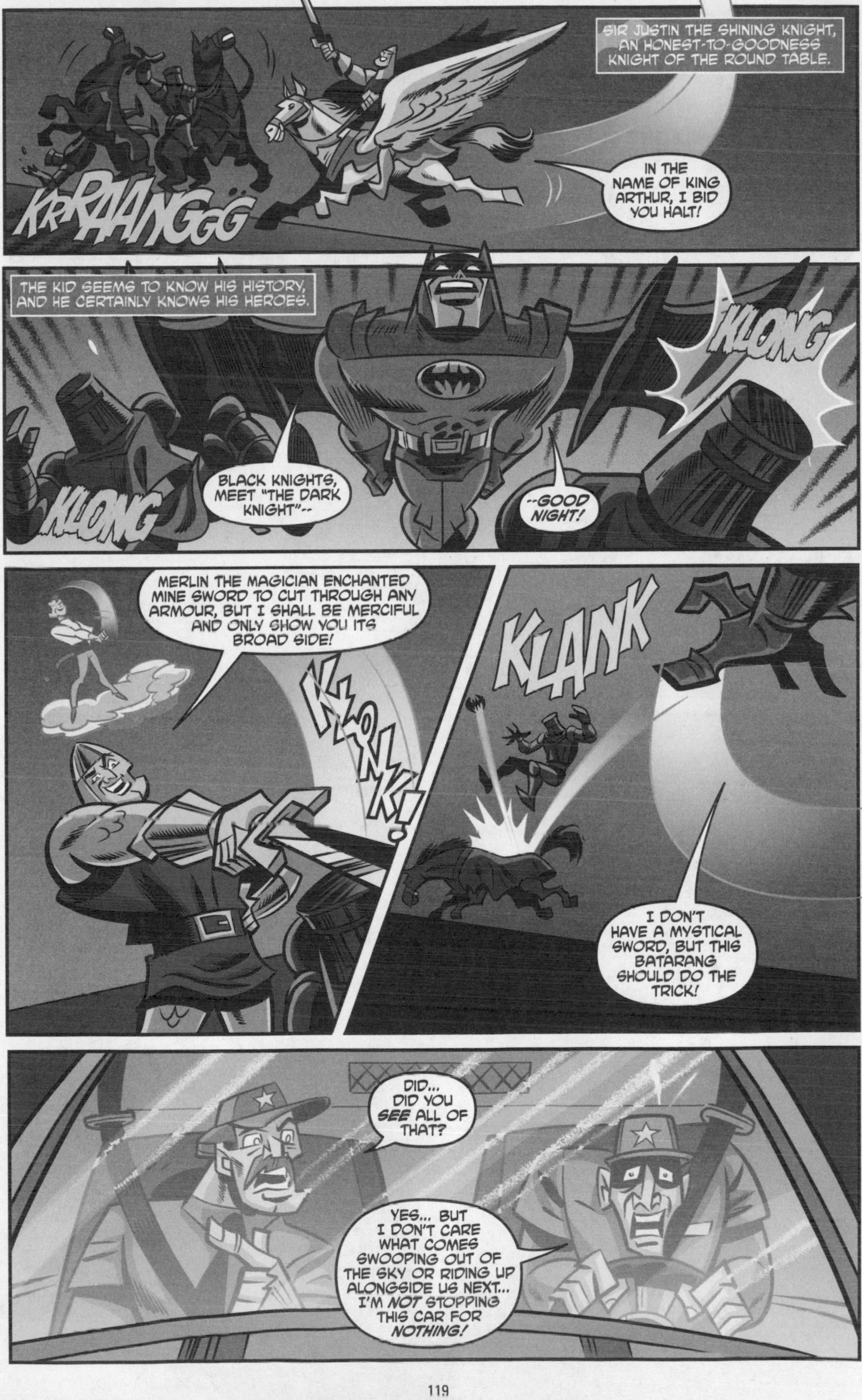
SIR JUSTIN THE SHINING KNIGHT, AN HONEST-TO-GOODNESS KNIGHT OF THE ROUND TABLE.
KRRAANGGG
IN THE NAME OF KING ARTHUR, I BID YOU HALT!
THE KID SEEMS TO KNOW HIS HISTORY, AND HE CERTAINLY KNOWS HIS HEROES.
KLONG
BLACK KNIGHTS, MEET "THE DARK KNIGHT"--
KLONG
--GOOD NIGHT!
MERLIN THE MAGICIAN ENCHANTED MINE SWORD TO CUT THROUGH ANY ARMOUR, BUT I SHALL BE MERCIFUL AND ONLY SHOW YOU ITS BROAD SIDE!
KLONK!
KLANK
I DON'T HAVE A MYSTICAL SWORD, BUT THIS BATARANG SHOULD DO THE TRICK!
DID... DID YOU *SEE* ALL OF THAT?
YES... BUT I DON'T CARE WHAT COMES SWOOPING OUT OF THE SKY OR RIDING UP ALONGSIDE US NEXT... I'M *NOT* STOPPING THIS CAR FOR *NOTHING!*

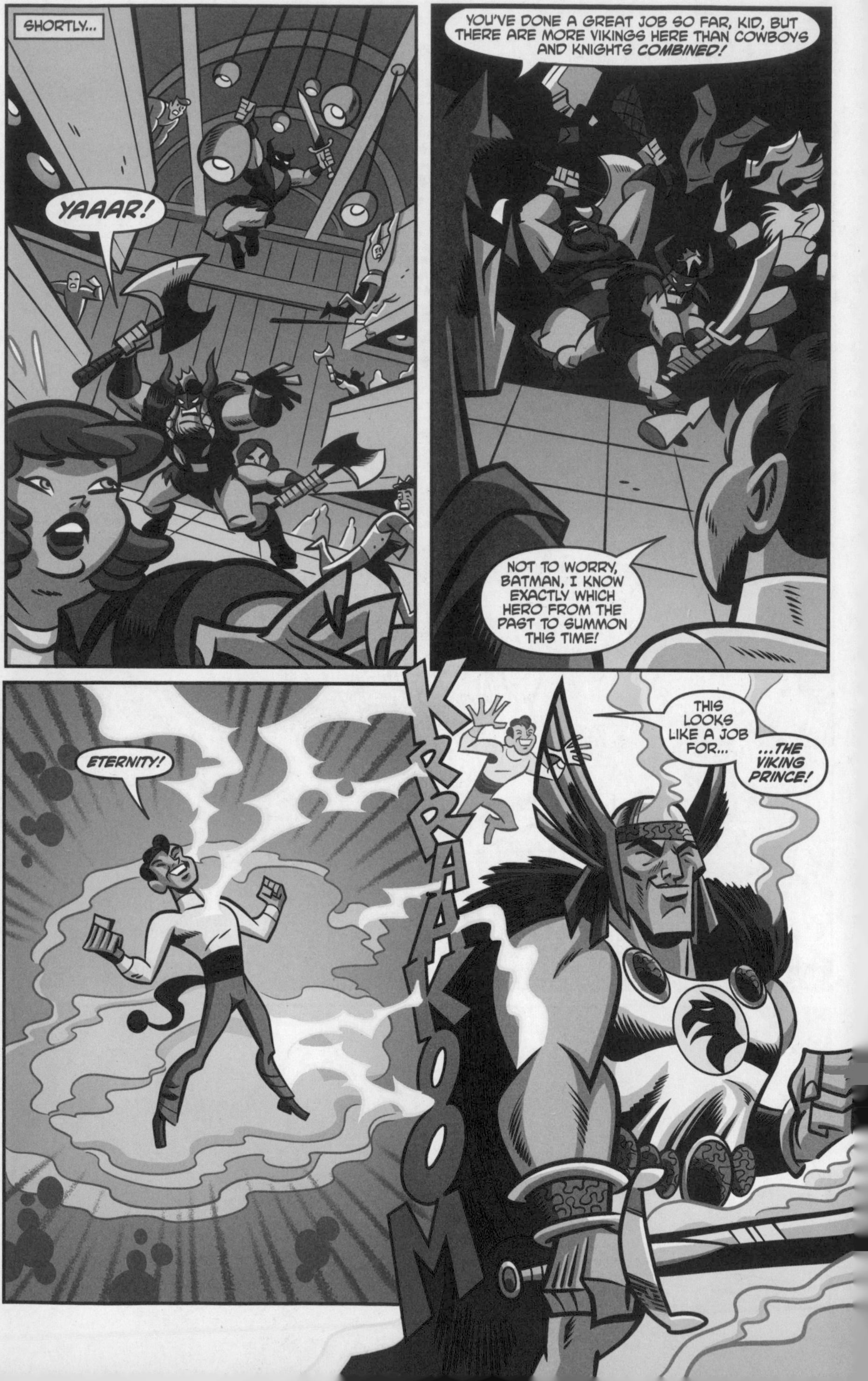
SHORTLY...
YAAAR!
YOU'VE DONE A GREAT JOB SO FAR, KID, BUT THERE ARE MORE VIKINGS HERE THAN COWBOYS AND KNIGHTS COMBINED!
NOT TO WORRY, BATMAN, I KNOW EXACTLY WHICH HERO FROM THE PAST TO SUMMON THIS TIME!
ETERNITY!
KRRAAAKOOOM
THIS LOOKS LIKE A JOB FOR...
...THE VIKING PRINCE!

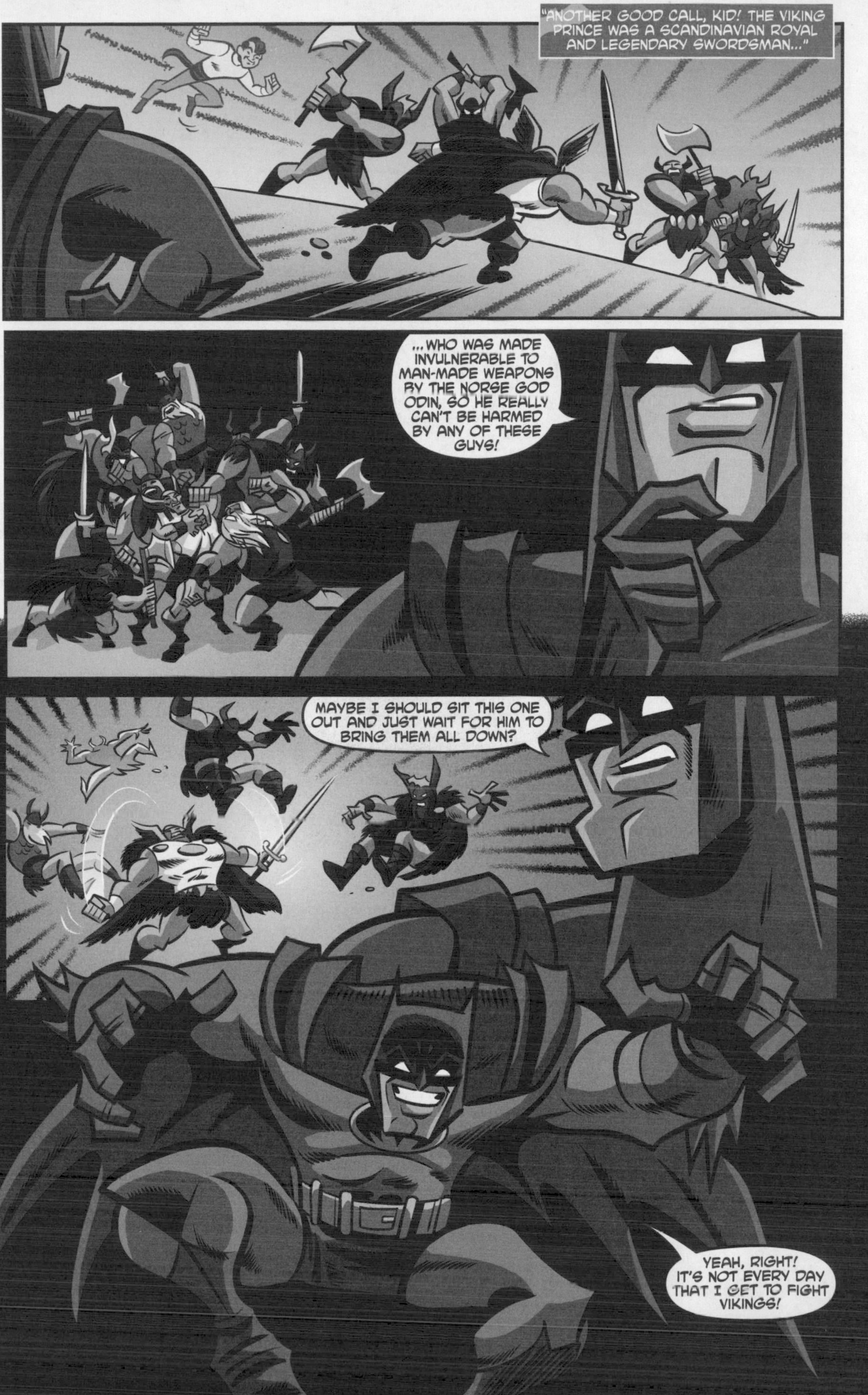
"ANOTHER GOOD CALL, KID! THE VIKING PRINCE WAS A SCANDINAVIAN ROYAL AND LEGENDARY SWORDSMAN..."
...WHO WAS MADE INVULNERABLE TO MAN-MADE WEAPONS BY THE NORSE GOD ODIN, SO HE REALLY CAN'T BE HARMED BY ANY OF THESE GUYS!
MAYBE I SHOULD SIT THIS ONE OUT AND JUST WAIT FOR HIM TO BRING THEM ALL DOWN?
YEAH, RIGHT! IT'S NOT EVERY DAY THAT I GET TO FIGHT VIKINGS!

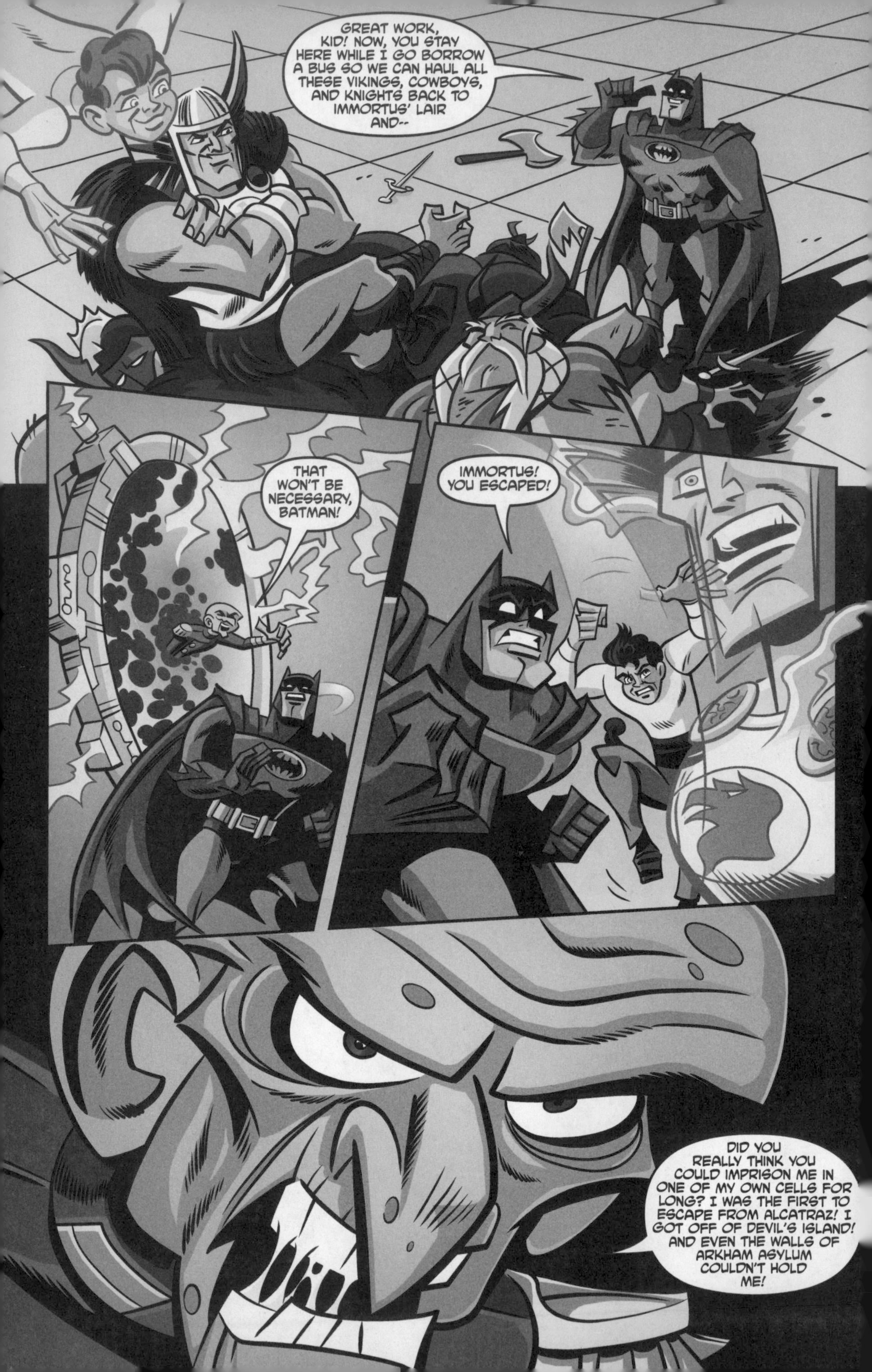
GREAT WORK, KID! NOW, YOU STAY HERE WHILE I GO BORROW A BUS SO WE CAN HAUL ALL THESE VIKINGS, COWBOYS, AND KNIGHTS BACK TO IMMORTUS' LAIR AND--
THAT WON'T BE NECESSARY, BATMAN!
IMMORTUS! YOU ESCAPED!
DID YOU REALLY THINK YOU COULD IMPRISON ME IN ONE OF MY OWN CELLS FOR LONG? I WAS THE FIRST TO ESCAPE FROM ALCATRAZ! I GOT OFF OF DEVIL'S ISLAND! AND EVEN THE WALLS OF ARKHAM ASYLUM COULDN'T HOLD ME!

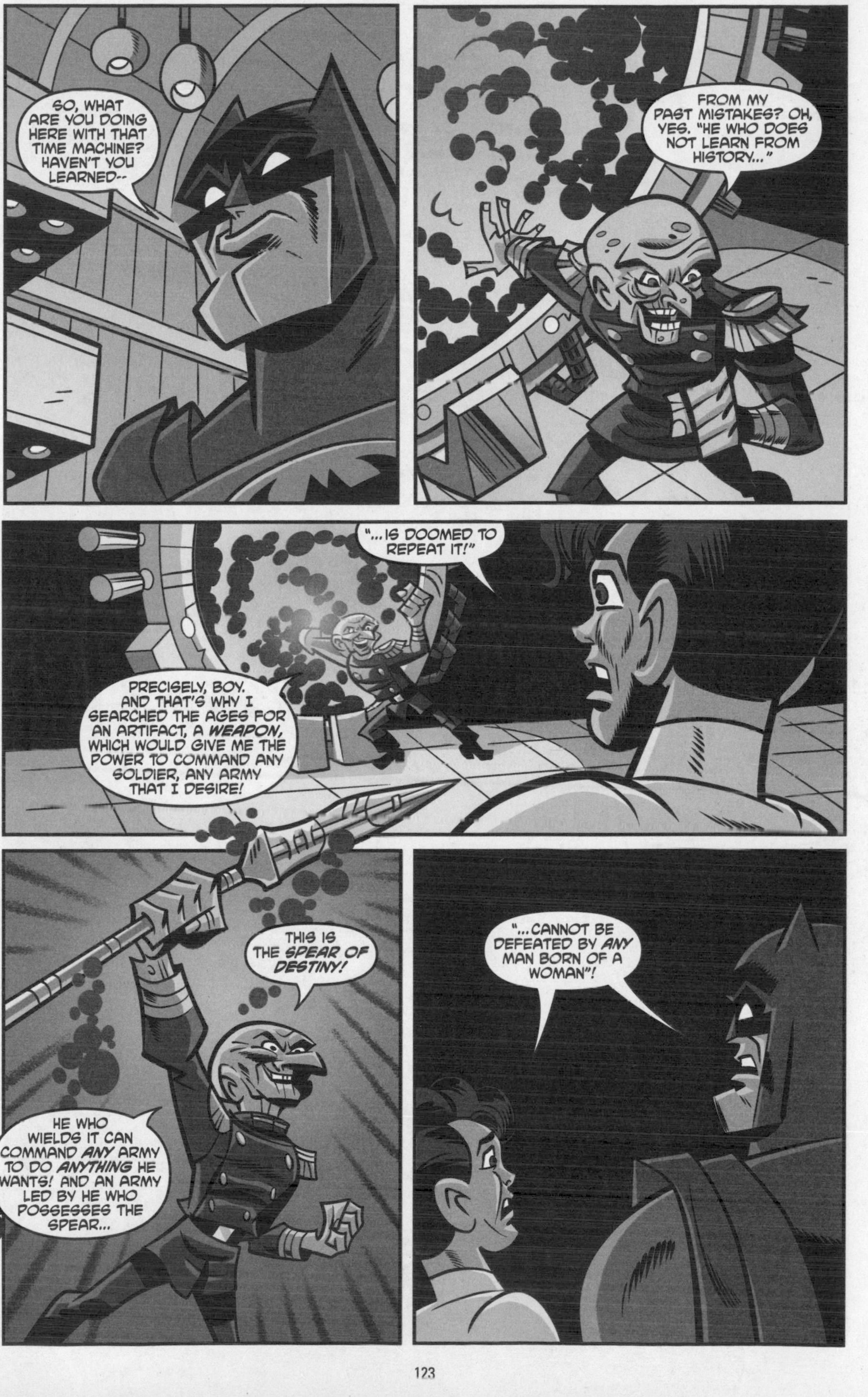
SO, WHAT ARE YOU DOING HERE WITH THAT TIME MACHINE? HAVEN'T YOU LEARNED--
FROM MY PAST MISTAKES? OH, YES. "HE WHO DOES NOT LEARN FROM HISTORY..."
"...IS DOOMED TO REPEAT IT!"
PRECISELY, BOY. AND THAT'S WHY I SEARCHED THE AGES FOR AN ARTIFACT, A *WEAPON*, WHICH WOULD GIVE ME THE POWER TO COMMAND ANY SOLDIER, ANY ARMY THAT I DESIRE!
THIS IS THE *SPEAR OF DESTINY!*
HE WHO WIELDS IT CAN COMMAND *ANY* ARMY TO DO *ANYTHING* HE WANTS! AND AN ARMY LED BY HE WHO POSSESSES THE SPEAR...
"...CANNOT BE DEFEATED BY *ANY* MAN BORN OF A WOMAN"!

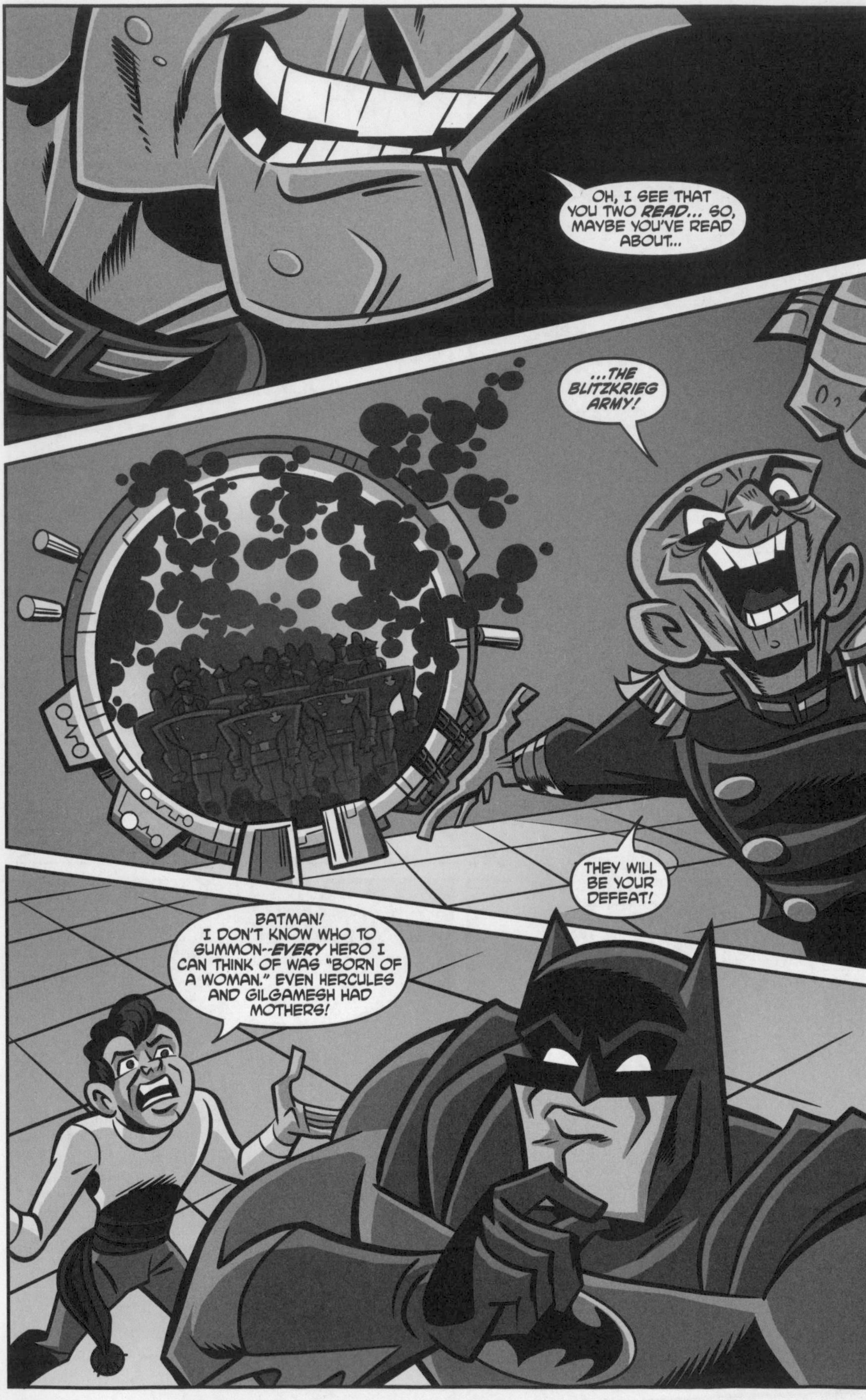
OH, I SEE THAT YOU TWO *READ*... SO, MAYBE YOU'VE READ ABOUT...
...THE BLITZKRIEG ARMY!
THEY WILL BE YOUR DEFEAT!
BATMAN! I DON'T KNOW WHO TO SUMMON--*EVERY* HERO I CAN THINK OF WAS "BORN OF A WOMAN." EVEN HERCULES AND GILGAMESH HAD MOTHERS!

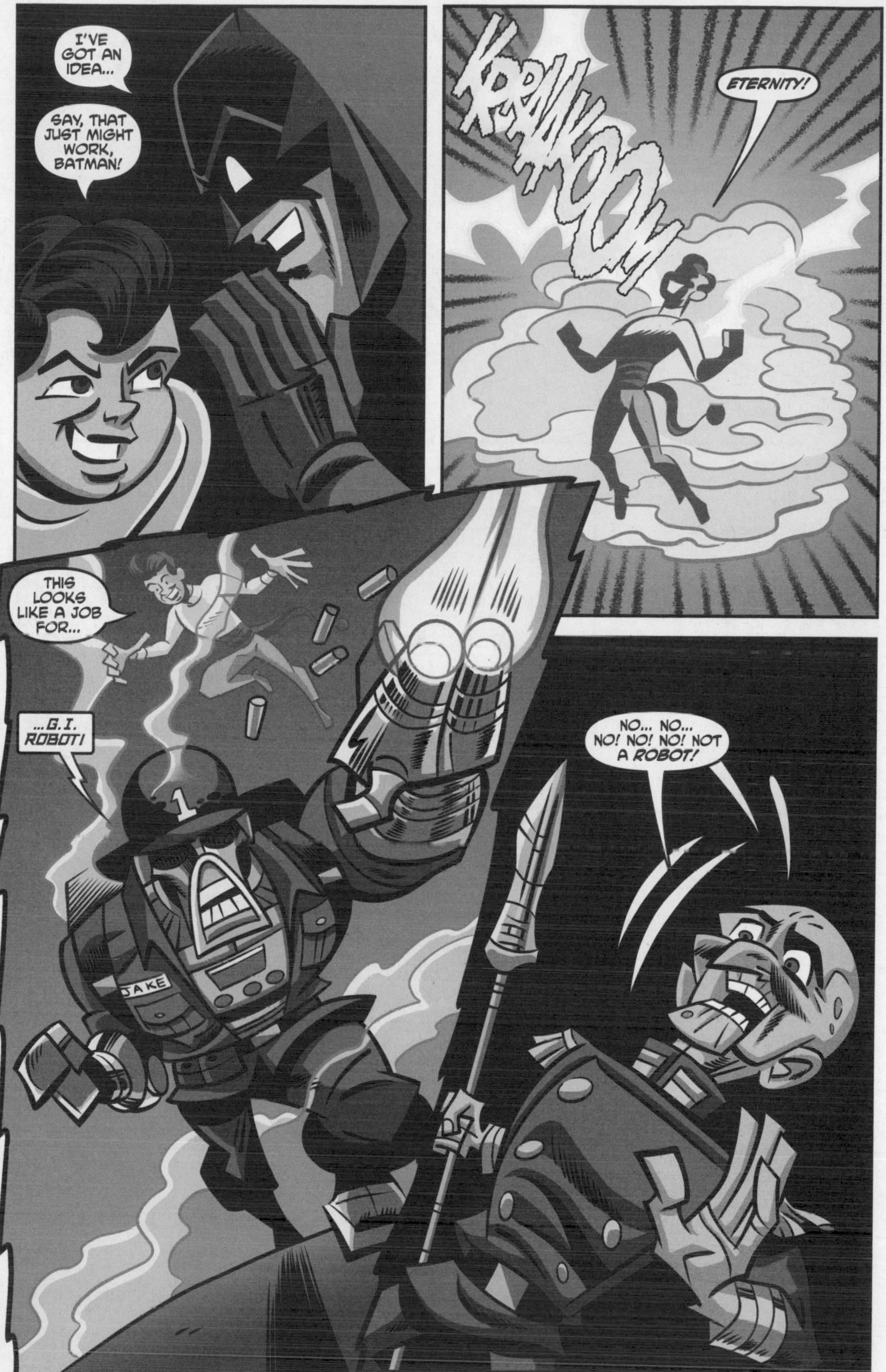
I'VE GOT AN IDEA...
SAY, THAT JUST MIGHT WORK, BATMAN!
KRAKOOM
ETERNITY!
THIS LOOKS LIKE A JOB FOR...
...G.I. ROBOT!
JAKE
NO... NO... NO! NO! NO! NOT A ROBOT!

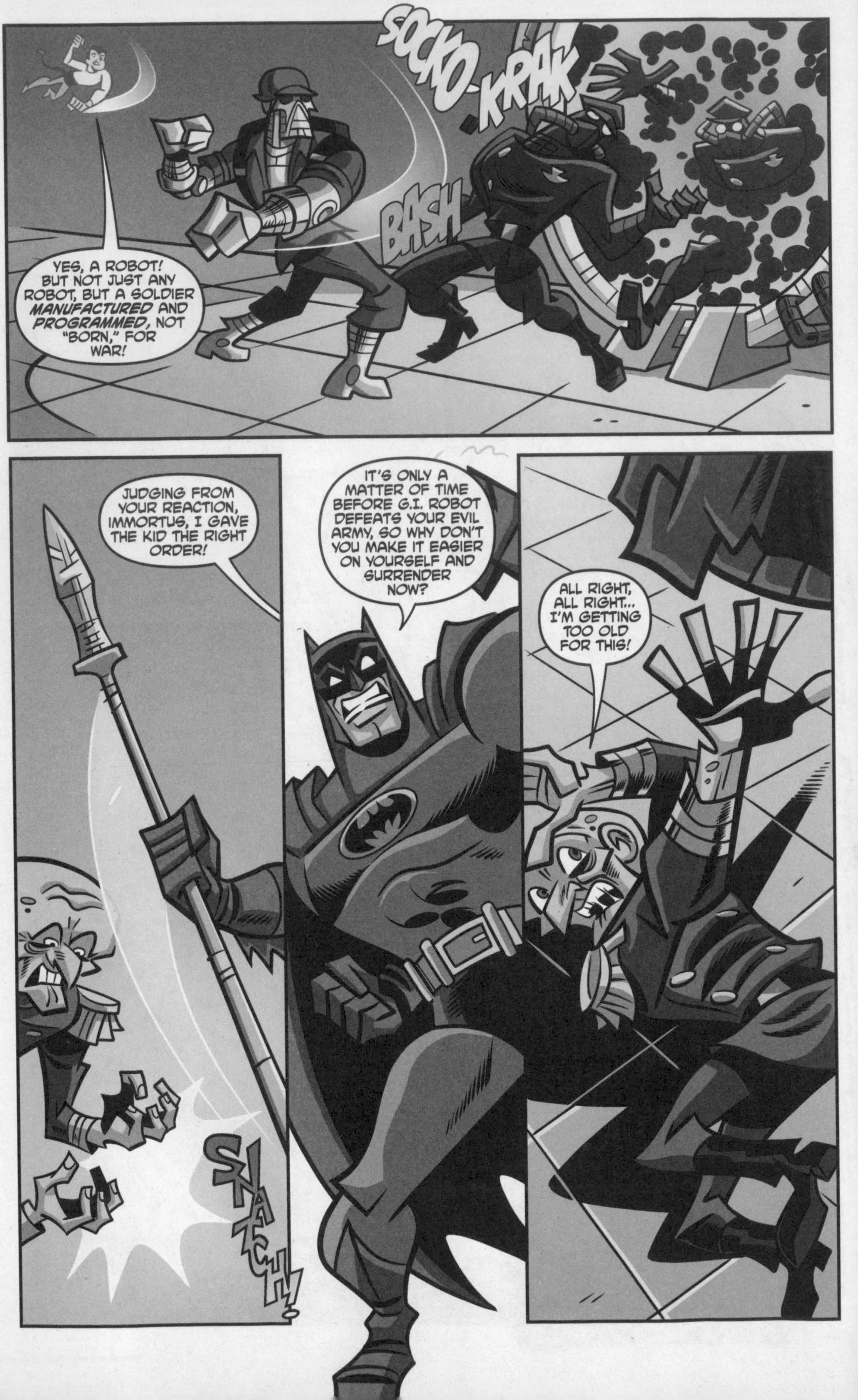
SOCKO
KRAK
BASH
YES, A ROBOT! BUT NOT JUST ANY ROBOT, BUT A SOLDIER *MANUFACTURED* AND *PROGRAMMED*, NOT "BORN," FOR WAR!
JUDGING FROM YOUR REACTION, IMMORTUS, I GAVE THE KID THE RIGHT ORDER!
SNATCH!
IT'S ONLY A MATTER OF TIME BEFORE G.I. ROBOT DEFEATS YOUR EVIL ARMY, SO WHY DON'T YOU MAKE IT EASIER ON YOURSELF AND SURRENDER NOW?
ALL RIGHT, ALL RIGHT... I'M GETTING TOO OLD FOR THIS!

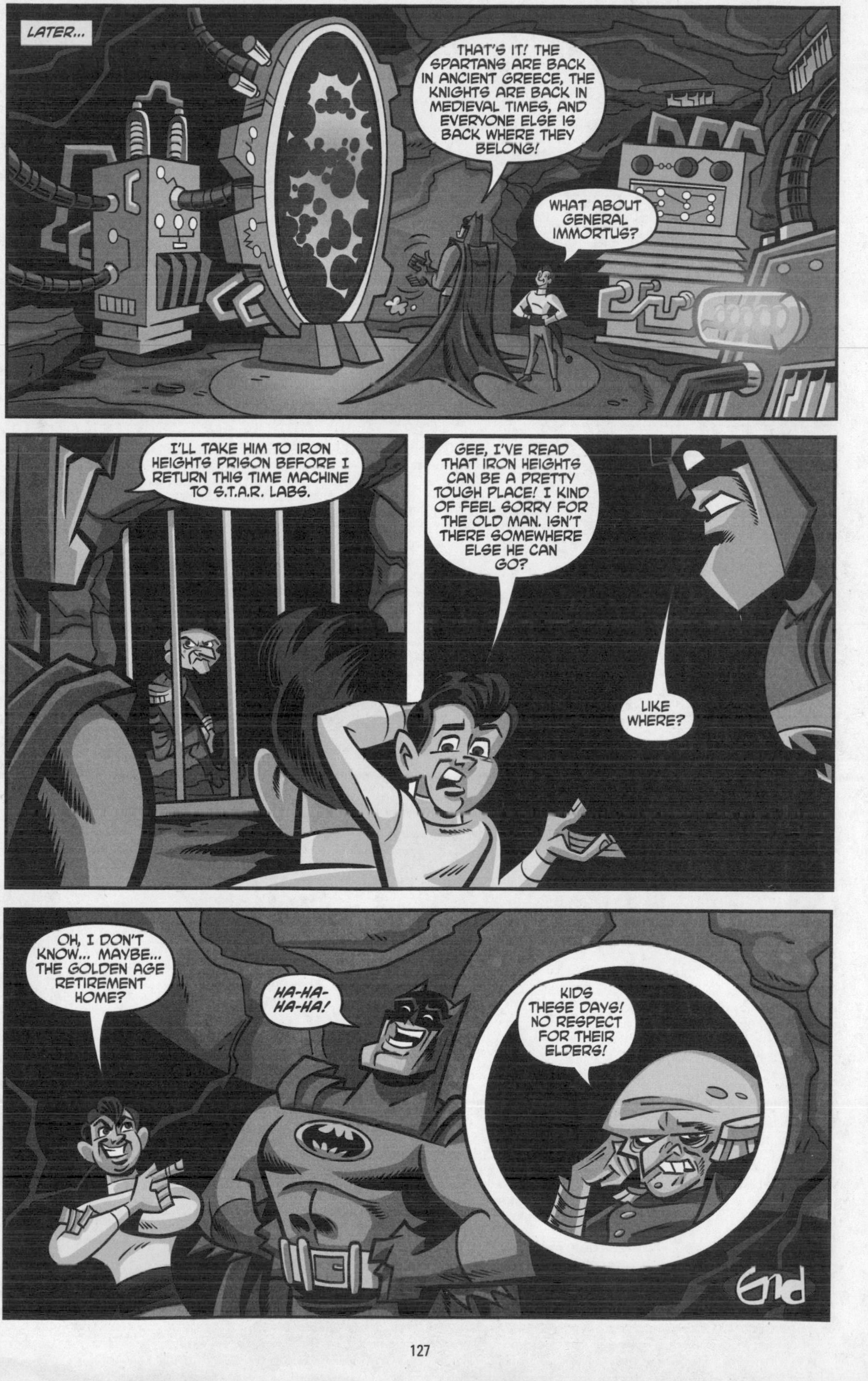
LATER...
THAT'S IT! THE SPARTANS ARE BACK IN ANCIENT GREECE, THE KNIGHTS ARE BACK IN MEDIEVAL TIMES, AND EVERYONE ELSE IS BACK WHERE THEY BELONG!
WHAT ABOUT GENERAL IMMORTUS?
I'LL TAKE HIM TO IRON HEIGHTS PRISON BEFORE I RETURN THIS TIME MACHINE TO S.T.A.R. LABS.
GEE, I'VE READ THAT IRON HEIGHTS CAN BE A PRETTY TOUGH PLACE! I KIND OF FEEL SORRY FOR THE OLD MAN. ISN'T THERE SOMEWHERE ELSE HE CAN GO?
LIKE WHERE?
OH, I DON'T KNOW... MAYBE... THE GOLDEN AGE RETIREMENT HOME?
HA-HA-HA-HA!
KIDS THESE DAYS! NO RESPECT FOR THEIR ELDERS!
End

GENERAL IMMORTUS:

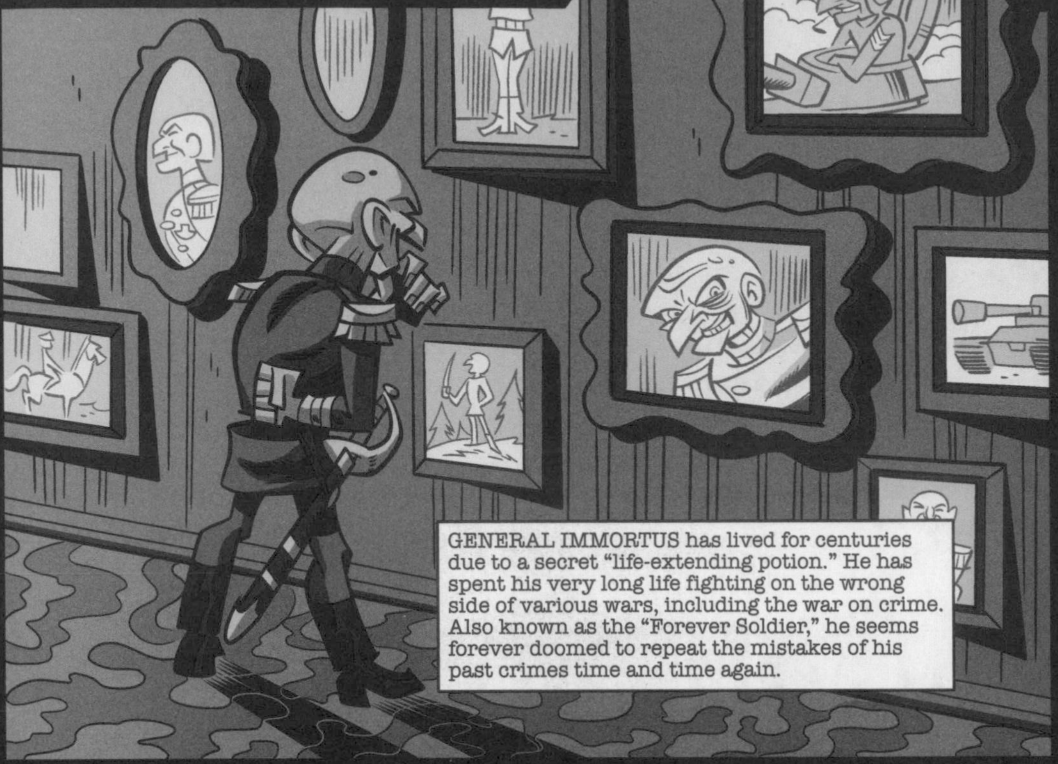
GENERAL IMMORTUS has lived for centuries due to a secret "life-extending potion." He has spent his very long life fighting on the wrong side of various wars, including the war on crime. Also known as the "Forever Soldier," he seems forever doomed to repeat the mistakes of his past crimes time and time again.

KID ETERNITY:

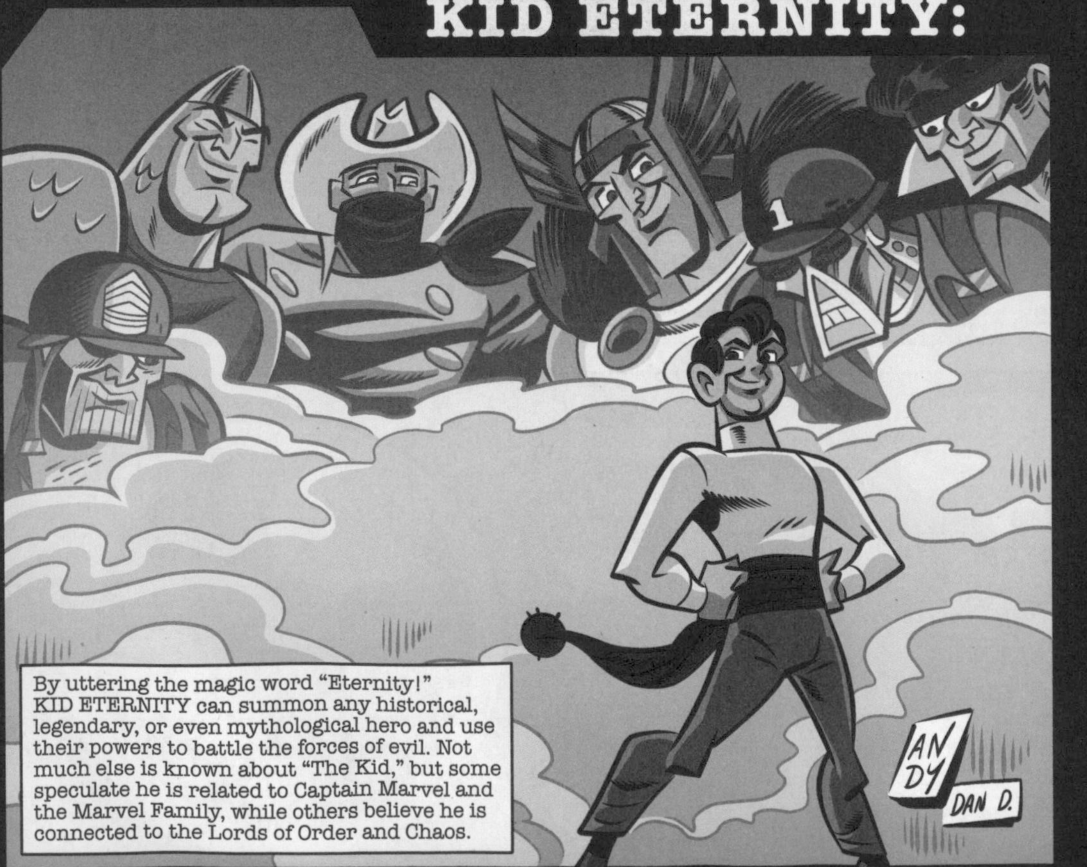
By uttering the magic word "Eternity!" KID ETERNITY can summon any historical, legendary, or even mythological hero and use their powers to battle the forces of evil. Not much else is known about "The Kid," but some speculate he is related to Captain Marvel and the Marvel Family, while others believe he is connected to the Lords of Order and Chaos.
ANDY
DAN D.